Rebuilding Ukraine
A Blueprint for Sustainable Post-War Urban Reconstruction

Thomas A.Q.T. Truong

Contents

Chapter 1: Immediate Stabilization and Recovery — 3
    Section 1.1: Damage Assessment and Prioritization — 3
    Section 1.2: Emergency Infrastructure Restoration — 5
    Section 1.3: Temporary Housing Solutions — 8

Chapter 2: Short-Term Reconstruction and Upgrade — 10
    Section 2.1: Energy Infrastructure Overhaul — 10
    Section 2.2: Water and Sanitation Systems — 13
    Section 2.3: Transportation Network Restoration — 15

Chapter 3: Medium-Term Urban Transformation (2-5 years) — 18
    Section 3.1: Sustainable Housing Development — 18
    Section 3.2: Green Space and Biodiversity Integration — 20
    Section 3.3: Circular Economy Implementation — 23

Chapter 4: Long-Term Visionary Development (5-20 years) — 27
    Section 4.1: Advanced Transportation Systems — 27
    Section 4.2: Next-Generation Energy Solutions — 30
    Section 4.3: Climate Resilience and Environmental Restoration — 33

Chapter 5: Sector-Specific Reconstruction Strategies — 36
    Section 5.1: Industrial Revitalization — 36
    Section 5.2: Agricultural Modernization — 39
    Section 5.3: Cultural Heritage Preservation and Tourism — 42

Chapter 6: Financing and Resource Allocation — 46
    Section 6.1: Innovative Funding Mechanisms — 46
    Section 6.2: Resource Optimization Strategies — 50
    Section 6.3: International Cooperation Frameworks — 53

Chapter 7: Implementation and Governance — 56
    Section 7.1: Project Management and Coordination — 56
    Section 7.2: Capacity Building and Skill Development — 59

Section 7.3: Monitoring and Evaluation Systems 62

Chapter 8: Resilience and Future-Proofing   65
Section 8.1: Multi-Hazard Resilience Strategies 65
Section 8.2: Cybersecurity and Digital Resilience 68
Section 8.3: Social Cohesion and Community Resilience 71

Chapter 9: Technology Integration   74
Section 9.1: Smart City Technologies 74
Section 9.2: Digital Public Services 78
Section 9.3: Data Analytics for Urban Planning 81

Chapter 10: Housing Reconstruction   84
Section 10.1: Temporary Housing 84
Section 10.2: Permanent Housing 87
Section 10.3: Sustainable Neighborhoods 91

Chapter 11: Public Services   94
Section 11.1: Healthcare Systems 94
Section 11.2: Educational Institutions 98
Section 11.3: Government Buildings and Public Transport 101

Chapter 12: Economic Revitalization   104
Section 12.1: Business Support and Incentives 104
Section 12.2: Industrial Parks and Technology Hubs 107
Section 12.3: Job Training Programs 111

Chapter 13: Environmental Remediation   114
Section 13.1: Contaminated Sites Cleanup 114
Section 13.2: Reforestation and Urban Greening 117
Section 13.3: Sustainable Waste Management 120

Chapter 14: Funding and Resource Allocation   123
Section 14.1: Donor Coordination 123
Section 14.2: Transparent Fund Distribution 127
Section 14.3: Anti-Corruption Measures 129

Chapter 15: Community Engagement   132
Section 15.1: Participatory Planning 132
Section 15.2: Social Cohesion Programs 135
Section 15.3: Citizen Feedback and Participation 139

Chapter 16: Sustainability and Climate Resilience   142
Section 16.1: Renewable Energy Integration 142
Section 16.2: Green Building Standards 146
Section 16.3: Climate Adaptation Measures 150

Chapter 17: Innovative Educational Ecosystems   **154**
    Section 17.1: AR and VR Learning Environments 154
    Section 17.2: AI-Powered Personalized Education 157
    Section 17.3: Virtual Reality Historical Reconstructions 161

Chapter 18: Healthcare Transformation   **164**
    Section 18.1: Autonomous Mobile Clinics 164
    Section 18.2: Nanomedicine and Personalized Treatments 166
    Section 18.3: Bioprinting Centers for Organ Engineering 169

Chapter 19: Governance and Adaptive Structures   **173**
    Section 19.1: AI-Assisted Policy-Making Platforms 173
    Section 19.2: Blockchain-Based Voting Systems 177
    Section 19.3: Gamified Citizen Engagement Platforms 180

Chapter 20: Resilient Food Systems   **183**
    Section 20.1: Rooftop and Vertical Hydroponic Farms 183
    Section 20.2: Underground Mushroom Farms 186
    Section 20.3: Aquaponic Systems in Public Spaces 189

Chapter 21: Innovative Governance Systems   **191**
    Section 21.1: AI-Ethics Boards for Smart City Implementation 191
    Section 21.2: Decentralized Autonomous Organizations (DAOs) for
        Urban Governance 194
    Section 21.3: Dynamic Regulatory Frameworks 197

Chapter 22: Monitoring, Evaluation, and Adaptation   **201**
    Section 22.1: IoT Sensor Networks for Progress Monitoring 201
    Section 22.2: AI-Driven Impact Assessment Tools 205
    Section 22.3: Citizen Feedback Platforms and Continuous Improvement 208

Chapter 1: Immediate Stabilization and Recovery

Section 1.1: Damage Assessment and Prioritization

In the early days of peace, Ukraine must take proactive measures to assess and prioritize the extensive damage inflicted by war. A methodical and comprehensive approach will be essential to facilitate an effective and sustainable reconstruction process.

Damage Surveys: Harnessing Modern Technologies

The cornerstone of an effective damage assessment involves leveraging cutting-edge technologies to conduct thorough surveys. Drones and satellites will play a critical role in providing rapid, high-resolution assessments of the areas affected by conflict. A swift deployment of AI-powered drones can gather real-time data, creating detailed topographical maps that highlight damaged structures, roads, utilities, and landscapes.

To complement aerial surveys, ground teams equipped with advanced monitoring devices will conduct on-site inspections. These teams will verify and augment drone-collected data, providing a comprehensive understanding of the destruction. Blockchain-based damage reporting systems will ensure transparent and tamper-proof documentation of findings, fostering trust and accountability among stakeholders.

Infrastructure Evaluation: A Critical Systems Analysis

Key infrastructure systems, including power, water, transportation, and communication networks, need a thorough evaluation to determine their current condition and functionality. Each system's strategic importance dictates its prioritization for repair and restoration.

1. **Power Infrastructure**: Assessing the damage to power plants, transmission lines, and substations is crucial. This evaluation will inform the development of immediate stabilization measures such as the deployment of temporary power solutions and the creation of alternative energy sources.

2. **Water and Sanitation Systems**: Surveys will identify breaches in water treatment plants, sewage systems, and pipelines. Temporary water purification units and mobile sanitation facilities will be crucial to mitigate immediate health risks and ensure basic hygiene.

3. **Transportation Networks**: Evaluating roads, railways, airports, and seaports will establish a roadmap for restoring connectivity. Autonomous sensing technologies on drones and vehicles can provide detailed assessments of structural integrity and usability.

4. **Communication Networks**: Telecommunications infrastructure, including internet connectivity and broadcast towers, requires immediate attention to reestablish communication lines critical for coordination and information dissemination.

Area Prioritization: Strategic and Systematic Reconstruction

Following the damage assessment and infrastructure evaluation, it is imperative to prioritize areas for reconstruction based on a triage-like system, assessing both the severity of damage and strategic importance.

1. **Critical Urban Centers**: Major urban areas such as Kyiv, Kharkiv, and Mariupol will be the primary focus due to their significant population density and economic impact. Restoring these cities will have a broad ripple effect, enhancing national stability and growth.

2. **Key Transportation Nodes**: Strategic transportation hubs connecting various parts of the country should be prioritized to ensure the efficient movement of goods, services, and people, essential for economic recovery and humanitarian aid distribution.
3. **Vital Utilities**: Areas with extensive damage to utilities impacting large populations must be targeted for the swift restoration of essential services like electricity, water, and sanitation.
4. **Cultural and Historical Sites**: Sites of cultural and historical significance must be assessed and prioritized not only for preservation but also to restore a sense of normalcy and identity among the populace.

Data Collection and Real-Time Monitoring

Continuous data collection using IoT sensors and satellite imagery will be integral to monitor progress, uncover hidden damages, and adapt strategies in real-time. Establishing a national command center with a digital twin of affected areas—an interactive and real-time virtual replica—will allow decision-makers to simulate, analyze, and predict outcomes of reconstruction efforts effectively.

The combination of real-time data analytics and AI-driven insights will enhance decision-making, ensuring resources are allocated efficiently and any emerging issues are promptly addressed.

Conclusion

By implementing a systematic and technologically advanced approach to damage assessment and prioritization, Ukraine can lay a strong foundation for its reconstruction efforts. These initial steps will set the stage for sustainable rebuilding, fostering resilience, and ultimately leading the nation towards a prosperous post-war future.

This section emphasizes a structured, data-driven methodology to damage assessment and area prioritization, ensuring a coherent and transparent approach to rebuilding Ukraine's urban and infrastructure landscape.

Section 1.2: Emergency Infrastructure Restoration

As the immediate wave of stabilization efforts lays down the foundation, the next critical step is the rapid restoration of essential infrastructure. This section delves into strategic approaches to re-establishing power, water, transportation, and communication systems, ensuring Ukraine's cities can support their populations and foster economic revival.

Power Grid: Rebuilding the Lifeline

The restoration of Ukraine's power grid stands as a top priority, essential for enabling all subsequent reconstruction efforts. Key actions include:

- **Repair and Rebuild**: Begin with the repair of existing power plants, transmission lines, and substations. Deploy rapid-response teams equipped with advanced tools and materials. Leverage partnerships with international energy companies to secure the necessary expertise and resources.
- **Smart Grids and Microgrids**: Implement smart grid technologies to optimize energy distribution and consumption. Use decentralized microgrids powered by renewable energy sources like solar and wind, especially in rural and semi-urban areas. These resilient systems will ensure a continuous supply, even if the central grid faces disruptions 12:0†source .
- **Energy Storage Solutions**: Develop large-scale energy storage systems using technologies such as lithium-ion batteries and pumped hydro storage. These systems can store excess energy during low usage periods and release it when demand spikes, stabilizing the grid and preventing blackouts.

Water and Sanitation Systems: Ensuring Health and Hygiene

The next pillar of infrastructure restoration focuses on water and sanitation:

- **Restoration of Treatment Plants and Pipelines**: Repair water treatment plants, sewage systems, and main pipelines swiftly. Utilize modular, mobile water treatment units to provide immediate solutions while permanent facilities are restored.
- **Smart Water Networks**: Install IoT-enabled sensors across water distribution networks to monitor usage, detect leaks in real-time, and automate resource management. Adopt AI-driven data analytics to optimize the distribution and usage of water resources efficiently.
- **Rainwater Harvesting and Decentralized Systems**: Encourage the installation of rainwater harvesting systems in both urban and rural settings. Establish decentralized wastewater treatment facilities to handle local capacity and reduce the load on central systems 12:0†source .

Transportation Networks: The Arteries of a Reviving Economy

An efficient and resilient transportation network is crucial for economic recovery and mobility:

- **Reconstruction of Major Routes**: Focus on repairing and upgrading primary roads, railways, airports, and seaports. Utilize self-healing materials for road construction that can repair micro-damages autonomously, extending the life of infrastructure and reducing maintenance costs.
- **Autonomous and Smart Transport Systems**: Develop autonomous public transportation networks, including electric buses and driverless trains, integrated with AI-driven traffic management systems to enhance efficiency and safety.

- **Multipurpose Transport Hubs**: Establish transport hubs that combine road, rail, and air connectivity, supported by smart logistics centers to optimize the movement of goods and people 12:0†source .

Communications: Reconnecting the Nation

Restoring and enhancing communication networks is vital for governance, commerce, and daily life:

- **Telecommunications Networks**: Prioritize the repair and upgrade of telecommunications infrastructure, including mobile towers, fiber optic cables, and internet nodes. Establish emergency communication networks using satellite-based systems to ensure connectivity during transitional periods.

- **Next-Generation Digital Infrastructure**: Deploy 5G and prepare for 6G network rollouts to support more robust, faster, and more reliable communication channels. Integrate edge computing capabilities to increase data processing efficiency and reduce latency.

- **Cybersecurity Measures**: Implement rigorous cybersecurity measures to protect restored communication infrastructure from potential threats. Use blockchain technology for secure data transmissions and to ensure the integrity of communication systems 12:0†source .

Implementation Framework

1. **Coordination with International Partners**: Work closely with international bodies and governments to secure funding, technology, and expertise. Establish frameworks for continuous support and collaboration.

2. **Community and Stakeholder Engagement**: Ensure that local communities and key stakeholders are involved in the planning and implementation processes. Create platforms for feedback and incorporate community needs and preferences into reconstruction plans.

3. **Monitoring and Evaluation**: Implement robust monitoring and evaluation systems using IoT sensors and data analytics to track progress, identify issues, and adapt strategies in real-time. Regularly review and adjust plans based on feedback and evolving circumstances.

Conclusion

By rebuilding the power grid, water systems, transportation networks, and communication infrastructure, Ukraine can restore essential services, support economic activities, and enhance the quality of life for its citizens. These efforts will create a more resilient, efficient, and sustainable foundation for future growth and development.

Section 1.3: Temporary Housing Solutions

In the aftermath of conflict, providing immediate shelter to displaced residents is paramount to stabilizing communities and fostering a sense of security. This section outlines a strategic approach to developing temporary housing solutions that are not only swift to deploy but also adaptable and sustainable, ensuring that affected populations have access to dignified living conditions while permanent reconstruction efforts are underway.

Rapid Deployment of Temporary Shelters

The immediate goal is to establish temporary housing using innovative and rapid-deployment methods:

- **3D-Printed Shelters**: Utilize advanced 3D printing technology to construct emergency shelters quickly using locally sourced materials. These structures can be erected within hours to days, providing immediate relief to displaced families.
- **Modular Housing Units**: Deploy modular housing units that can be transported and assembled on-site. These units are designed to be scalable, allowing for the expansion as needed. Integrate renewable energy solutions like solar panels and wind turbines to ensure an independent power supply.
- **Smart Refugee Camps**: Develop smart refugee camps equipped with IoT-enabled resource management systems. These systems monitor water, electricity, and waste management in real-time, optimizing resource allocation and improving living conditions.

Seamless Integration with Existing Infrastructure

Ensuring the integration of temporary housing with existing urban infrastructure is crucial for sustainability and functionality:

- **Conversion of Vacant Buildings**: Identify and convert vacant buildings, such as hotels, schools, and office spaces, into temporary housing. Implement IoT technology for efficient management of these transformed spaces, including smart access control and environmental monitoring.
- **Public-Private Partnerships**: Foster collaborations between government bodies, non-profit organizations, and private sector partners to leverage resources and expertise. Public-private partnerships can facilitate the provision of essential services such as healthcare, education, and security within temporary housing communities.
- **Community Involvement**: Engage local communities in the planning and execution of temporary housing projects. Involving residents in decision-making processes ensures that solutions are tailored to their specific needs and enhances social cohesion.

Sustainable and Adaptable Solutions

The focus on sustainability ensures that temporary housing solutions do not exacerbate environmental issues and can adapt to the needs of the population:

- **Eco-Friendly Materials**: Use eco-friendly and recyclable materials in the construction of temporary housing. This approach reduces environmental impact and sets a precedent for sustainable reconstruction practices.
- **Energy Self-Sufficiency**: Incorporate renewable energy sources such as solar panels and wind turbines to provide power for temporary housing units. Solar-powered water heaters and energy-efficient lighting systems contribute to self-sufficiency and reduce dependency on external power grids.
- **Adaptability for Future Use**: Design temporary housing solutions with future adaptability in mind. These structures should be easily convertible into permanent housing or other community facilities once the immediate crisis has passed.

Health and Safety Considerations

Integrating health and safety measures into temporary housing solutions is critical to protecting vulnerable populations:

- **Healthcare Facilities**: Establish temporary healthcare facilities within housing units, equipped with telemedicine capabilities and staffed by healthcare professionals. These facilities ensure that residents have access to medical care and mental health support.
- **Sanitation and Hygiene**: Implement proper sanitation facilities, including portable toilets, handwashing stations, and waste management systems, to prevent the outbreak of diseases and maintain hygienic conditions.
- **Safety Protocols**: Develop and enforce safety protocols to protect residents from potential hazards, including fire safety measures, secure access points, and emergency response plans.

Funding and Resource Allocation

Securing and efficiently utilizing funding is essential for the successful implementation of temporary housing solutions:

- **International Donor Support**: Engage with international donors and financial institutions to secure funding for temporary housing projects. Transparent fund distribution mechanisms and anti-corruption measures ensure that resources are used effectively and reach those in need .
- **Resource Optimization**: Utilize advanced project management tools and data analytics to optimize the allocation of resources. Ensure that

funding is directed towards high-impact areas and that projects are completed on time and within budget .

Case Studies and Best Practices

Drawing from global examples of successful post-conflict housing initiatives can provide valuable insights:

- **"Safe Homes" Initiative**: The EU's "Safe Homes" initiative supports the provision of housing by mobilizing resources from the Asylum, Migration, and Integration Fund. This initiative strengthens public reception systems and ensures the integration of temporary housing with community-based services, especially for those with special needs .
- **Public Sector and Charitable Organization Collaboration**: Collaboration between public authorities and charitable organizations has been instrumental in providing immediate accommodation while developing sustainable medium-term solutions .

Conclusion

Temporary housing solutions are a critical component of the immediate stabilization and recovery phase. By using innovative technologies, sustainable practices, and community collaboration, Ukraine can provide dignified, safe, and adaptable housing for displaced residents. These efforts not only address the urgent needs of affected populations but also pave the way for a resilient and inclusive reconstruction process.

This comprehensive approach to temporary housing ensures that the rebuilding of Ukrainian cities and infrastructure begins on a solid and sustainable foundation, ultimately contributing to a brighter, more resilient future for the nation.

Chapter 2: Short-Term Reconstruction and Upgrade

Section 2.1: Energy Infrastructure Overhaul

The path to a rejuvenated Ukraine, resilient and sustainable, begins with a robust overhaul of its energy infrastructure. This section brings into focus the urgent need to transform Ukraine's power grid to meet both immediate needs and long-term sustainability goals, capitalizing on advanced technologies and international cooperation.

1. Immediate Rehabilitation and Resilience Measures

Rapid Repairs and Stabilization Efforts: The initial phase targets the repairs of war-damaged power plants, transmission lines, and substations to stabilize the energy supply. Teams equipped with advanced repair tools and materials must be deployed to critical points in the network. Priority should be given to strategic locations, ensuring minimal disruption to essential services such as hospitals, emergency response units, and water treatment facilities.

Deployment of Modular Power Systems: To address immediate power needs, deploy rapidly assembled, modular power units that utilize renewable energy sources such as solar and wind. These units should be mobile and scalable, allowing for flexible deployment in areas where the traditional grid is compromised. Integrating battery storage solutions will enable these units to provide uninterrupted power .

2. Integration of Smart Grid Technologies

Smart Grid Design and Implementation: Revamping Ukraine's power grid involves designing and implementing smart grid technologies that optimize the generation, distribution, and consumption of electricity. Smart grids incorporate real-time monitoring and adaptive control mechanisms, reducing energy waste and enhancing grid reliability. Implement AI-driven load balancing to manage energy flow efficiently and mitigate blackouts during peak demand periods .

Decentralized Microgrids: Develop decentralized microgrids for urban and rural communities, each designed to operate both independently and in conjunction with the main grid. Microgrids, leveraging local renewable energy sources, enhance resilience by isolating outages and ensuring continuous power supply during grid failures. These systems should incorporate energy storage solutions like second-life EV batteries, providing a robust backup during supply fluctuations .

3. Expansion of Renewable Energy Infrastructure

Nationwide Solar and Wind Projects: Launch extensive solar and wind energy projects across the nation. Collaborate with international partners to install large-scale solar farms and wind turbines, particularly in regions with optimal climatic conditions. Encourage the adoption of rooftop solar installations in urban areas through incentives and subsidies, promoting energy self-sufficiency at the household level .

Hydropower and Biogas Utilization: Incorporate hydropower projects on Ukraine's rivers to harness clean energy while facilitating water management and flood control. Develop biogas plants utilizing agricultural and organic waste, converting biomass into renewable energy and contributing to waste management. These initiatives will diversify Ukraine's energy portfolio, reducing dependency on fossil fuels and enhancing sustainability .

4. Innovation in Energy Storage and Distribution

Advanced Energy Storage Systems: Develop and implement large-scale energy storage systems, such as lithium-ion batteries, pumped hydro storage, and emerging technologies like flow batteries. These systems will store excess energy generated during low consumption periods and release it when demand peaks, ensuring a stable and reliable energy supply.

Smart Energy Distribution Networks: Create smart energy distribution networks equipped with IoT-enabled sensors and automated management systems. These networks will facilitate real-time monitoring of energy flow, swiftly detect and address disruptions, and optimize energy distribution based on consumption patterns. Blockchain technology can ensure secure and transparent energy transactions, fostering trust and efficiency in energy management .

5. Collaborative International Efforts and Financial Strategies

International Partnerships and Cooperation: Forge strategic partnerships with international energy corporations, non-governmental organizations, and financial institutions to garner the expertise, technology, and funding essential for Ukraine's energy transformation. These collaborations should focus on knowledge transfer, capacity building, and the joint development of innovative solutions tailored to Ukraine's specific needs .

Leveraging Green Bonds and Climate Funds: Access global climate finance mechanisms, including green bonds and climate funds, to secure the capital needed for large-scale energy projects. Developing a transparent and accountable framework for fund distribution will attract investment and instill confidence among international donors. Initiate public-private partnerships to pool resources and share risks, ensuring sustainable financial support for energy infrastructure projects .

6. Educational and Community Engagement Initiatives

Community Educational Programs: Implement educational programs aimed at raising awareness about renewable energy and energy conservation practices. These programs should be integrated into school curricula and community workshops, highlighting the importance of sustainable energy and encouraging active participation in the nation's energy transition .

Stakeholder Engagement and Participatory Planning: Involve local communities, stakeholders, and energy consumers in the planning and implementation of energy projects. Establish platforms for community input and feedback, ensuring that the reconstruction efforts align with the needs and aspirations of the population. This participatory approach will foster a sense of ownership and responsibility, enhancing the sustainability of the initiatives .

Conclusion

By embracing cutting-edge technologies, fostering international cooperation, and actively involving communities, Ukraine can transform its energy infrastructure into a resilient, efficient, and sustainable system. The strategic overhaul of the energy sector will not only address immediate power needs but also lay the foundation for long-term economic growth and environmental stewardship, paving the way for a brighter future.

This section integrates extensive research and best practices in energy infrastructure restoration, aligning with the overarching goals of sustainability and resilience in the post-war reconstruction of Ukraine.

Section 2.2: Water and Sanitation Systems

The integrity of water and sanitation systems is not only crucial for human survival but also for ensuring public health and safety during the reconstruction phase. In Ukraine's ambitious journey of rebuilding, ensuring the swift rehabilitation and sustainable development of water and sanitation infrastructure is imperative.

Immediate Restoration of Water Supply and Sanitation Systems

Emergency Water Provision and Treatment: In the watery chaos left behind by conflict, immediate access to clean water is critical. Deploying modular, mobile water treatment units can provide immediate solutions while permanent facilities are established. These units, powered by renewable energy sources, will ensure a continuous supply of potable water, mitigating the risk of waterborne diseases.

Repairing and Rehabilitating Infrastructure: Priority must be given to repairing essential water treatment plants, sewage systems, and main pipelines. Rapid assessment teams should employ AI-powered diagnostics to swiftly identify and categorize damage. Real-time data collection and analysis will guide repair crews, ensuring that resources are efficiently allocated to the most critical needs first.

Strategic Long-Term Solutions

Decentralized Water Treatment: One of the hallmarks of resilient urban planning is the decentralization of essential services. Developing decentralized, modular wastewater treatment plants across urban and rural areas will enhance redundancy and independence from centralized systems. These plants should be capable of treating local wastewater, thereby reducing the strain on central facilities and ensuring continuous operation even in times of crisis.

Smart Water Networks: Integrating smart technologies into water distribution systems can significantly enhance operational efficiency and service reliability. IoT-enabled sensors across distribution networks will provide real-time monitoring of water flow, pressure, and quality. These sensors can detect leaks, breakages, and contamination instantly, allowing for prompt intervention.

Rainwater Harvesting Systems: Given the increasing strain on freshwater resources, implementing rainwater harvesting systems is a sustainable practice. Collecting and storing rainwater for non-potable uses, such as irrigation and landscaping, can reduce the demand on treated water supplies. Integrating these systems into building designs and urban planning can be both an immediate and long-term solution to water scarcity.

Advanced Technologies in Water Management

AI and Data Analytics: Leveraging AI and data analytics will revolutionize water management practices in reconstructed urban areas. AI algorithms can predict demand patterns, identify inefficiencies, and suggest optimal management strategies. Geographic Information System (GIS) mappings can plan and manage water resources efficiently, anticipating future urban growth and environmental changes.

Blockchain for Transparency: Utilizing blockchain technology to manage and document water usage and transactions ensures transparency and trust. Blockchain can track water consumption, billing, and quality data, making it accessible to stakeholders and ensuring accountability in water management practices.

Green Infrastructure Integration: Incorporating green infrastructure, such as constructed wetlands and green roofs, will aid in natural water purification and stormwater management. These systems mimic natural processes, reducing runoff, filtering pollutants, and enhancing urban resilience to extreme weather events.

Community Involvement and International Cooperation

Community-based Water Management: Active community involvement in water management fosters ownership and sustainability. Local communities should be trained and equipped to manage and maintain water infrastructure. Establishing community water councils can ensure that local needs and priorities are addressed, promoting sustainable usage practices.

International Support and Partnerships: Collaboration with international organizations and donor agencies will be essential in the rehabilitation of Ukraine's water and sanitation infrastructure. Strategic partnerships can provide the necessary funding, technology, and expertise to implement advanced solutions. Programs such as the EU's Solidarity with Ukraine initiative can mobilize resources, ensuring immediate and long-term support for water management projects 21:0†source 21:4†source .

Health and Environmental Considerations

Ensuring Sanitary Excellence: Rebuilding efforts must prioritize sanitary improvements to safeguard public health. Temporary sanitation facilities, such as portable toilets and handwashing stations, should be installed promptly in areas awaiting permanent infrastructure. Sustainable sanitation solutions, including composting toilets and biogas systems, can provide long-term benefits by converting waste into energy and fertilizer.

Environmental Impacts: Addressing contamination and pollution is critical for environmental health. Cleaning up contaminated sites and restoring natural water bodies should be integral to the reconstruction efforts. Implementing environmentally sensitive practices, such as using biodegradable materials and eco-friendly chemicals, will minimize the ecological footprint of water management activities.

Conclusion

Transforming Ukraine's water and sanitation systems in the post-war context demands a multifaceted strategy that combines immediate restoration with long-term resilience and sustainability. By harnessing advanced technologies, fostering community involvement, and ensuring international cooperation, Ukraine can rebuild these systems to be more robust, efficient, and ecologically responsible than ever before. This comprehensive approach will not only meet the immediate needs of the population but also create a foundation for enduring prosperity and health.

Section 2.3: Transportation Network Restoration

A country's recovery and future prosperity hinge significantly on its mobility infrastructure. For Ukraine, the restoration and modernization of its transportation networks are not just necessary for economic revival but also for social cohesion and access to essential services. This section presents a bold vision for overhauling Ukraine's transportation systems, integrating advanced technologies for a resilient and sustainable future.

Immediate Infrastructure Repair and Reinforcement

Swift Restoration of Major Routes: The initial phase emphasizes the urgent reconstruction of key transport routes - roads, railways, airports, and seaports, which are critical for ensuring connectivity and facilitating the movement of people and goods. Repair teams will use autonomous drones for detailed damage assessments, allowing for precise planning and resource allocation. Teams equipped with advanced materials and tools will undertake rapid repairs, ensuring these vital corridors are operational at the earliest.

Self-Healing Roadways: Incorporate nanotechnology-enhanced, self-healing materials for road construction and repair. These materials autonomously seal minor cracks and damages, extending the lifespan of roadways and reducing maintenance costs. Such technologies will ensure the durability and reliability of reconstructed road networks, minimizing disruptions and promoting consistent mobility.

Development of Modernized and Resilient Rail Networks

High-Speed Rail Corridors: Establish high-speed rail corridors interlinking key cities like Kyiv, Lviv, and Odessa. These corridors will bolster economic activities, reduce travel times, and promote regional development. High-efficiency trains powered by renewable energy sources such as solar and wind will be prioritized, reducing the carbon footprint and aligning with sustainability goals.

Autonomous and Smart Rail Systems: Introduce autonomous trains and AI-driven rail management systems. These systems will optimize scheduling, enhance safety, and ensure efficient utilization of rail infrastructure. Real-time data analytics, facilitated by IoT sensors deployed across the rail network, will monitor conditions and predict maintenance needs, preventing delays and minimizing the risk of accidents.

Sustainable Urban Mobility Solutions

Electric Public Transport Networks: Deploy fleets of electric buses and trams across urban areas to reduce greenhouse gas emissions and enhance air quality. These fleets will be integrated with smart traffic management systems, leveraging AI to optimize routes and minimize wait times. Charging infrastructure powered by renewable energy will be established at strategic locations to ensure seamless operations.

Autonomous Vehicles and Ride-Sharing Platforms: Implement autonomous vehicle (AV) technology in public and shared transportation services. AVs will offer efficient, safe, and flexible transportation options, particularly beneficial for underserved regions and for enhancing mobility for the elderly and disabled. Ride-sharing platforms, integrated with these autonomous services, will optimize vehicle usage, reduce congestion, and promote sustainable urban mobility.

Advanced Airport and Seaport Infrastructure

Smart Airports: Revamp airports with cutting-edge technologies such as automated check-in, biometric security systems, and AI-driven baggage handling. These enhancements will streamline operations, reduce wait times, and improve passenger experiences. Energy-efficient designs and renewable energy sources will be integral to airport infrastructure, minimizing environmental impact.

Resilient and Efficient Seaports: Modernize seaports with smart cargo handling and logistics management systems. Automated cranes and AI-powered logistics platforms will enhance operational efficiency and reduce turnaround times. Ports will also incorporate green energy solutions, like solar power and wind turbines, to support sustainable operations.

Collaboration and International Partnerships

Trans-European Transport Network (TEN-T) Integration: Integrate Ukraine into the Trans-European Transport Network (TEN-T) to enhance connectivity with neighboring European nations. This collaboration will facilitate the seamless movement of goods and people across borders, boosting trade and commerce. Strengthening this network will ensure that Ukraine remains a pivotal link between Europe and Asia 24:10†source 24:12†source .

Global Best Practices and Partnerships: Engage in partnerships with global leaders in transportation technology and infrastructure. By adopting best practices from countries with advanced transport systems, such as Japan's high-speed rail or Germany's autobahn, Ukraine can leapfrog existing limitations. Collaborative research and development initiatives will drive innovation and ensure that transportation solutions are tailored to local needs.

Funding and Resource Mobilization

Smart Finance Mechanisms: Utilize innovative finance mechanisms such as green bonds and public-private partnerships to fund transportation projects. Leveraging international climate funds will align financial investments with sustainability goals, attracting global support and ensuring financial stability for long-term projects 24:0†source 24:7†source .

Transparent Resource Allocation: Implement blockchain-based systems for transparent management of funds and resources. These systems will enhance accountability, prevent corruption, and ensure that investments are efficiently directed towards high-impact projects. Regular audits and public disclosure of financial activities will build trust and confidence among stakeholders.

Community Engagement and Capacity Building

Participatory Planning Processes: Actively engage local communities in transportation planning processes. Establish platforms for public consultations, ensuring that the needs and preferences of residents are incorporated into project designs. This participatory approach will foster community support and ensure that transportation solutions are inclusive and equitable.

Training and Education: Invest in capacity building and training programs for local workforce development. Equip engineers, urban planners, and construction professionals with advanced skills in new technologies and sustainable practices. Partnerships with academic institutions will promote continuous learning and innovation in transportation fields 24:12†source 24:2†source .

Conclusion

Revamping Ukraine's transportation network is a cornerstone of its reconstruction efforts. By integrating advanced technologies, fostering international collaborations, and emphasizing sustainability and community engagement, Ukraine can build a resilient, efficient, and modern transportation system. This transformation will not only facilitate economic recovery but also set the stage for long-term growth and prosperity, ensuring that Ukraine's transport infrastructure stands as a testament to innovation, resilience, and sustainable development.

Chapter 3: Medium-Term Urban Transformation (2-5 years)

Section 3.1: Sustainable Housing Development

Introduction

As Ukraine embarks on the journey of rebuilding its war-torn cities, housing development stands as the cornerstone of urban transformation. Sustainable housing development is not merely about erecting structures but about fostering communities, ensuring environmental stewardship, and integrating cutting-edge technology. This section outlines a comprehensive approach to constructing energy-positive, resilient, and community-centric housing that can serve as a model for sustainable living for years to come.

Energy-Positive Residential Complexes

Innovative Design and Construction: Creating energy-positive residential complexes involves harnessing innovative design principles and construction methods. Incorporate passive solar design, building orientation, and high-performance building envelopes to maximize energy efficiency. Utilize prefabricated and modular construction techniques to reduce waste, lower costs, and accelerate construction timelines.

- **Renewable Energy Integration**: Embed renewable energy systems such as photovoltaic panels, wind turbines, and geothermal heat pumps within housing developments. Implement building-integrated photovoltaics (BIPV) where solar panels are a fundamental part of the building's structure – including façades and roofs.

- **Energy Storage Solutions**: Pair renewable energy systems with advanced energy storage solutions like lithium-ion batteries and thermal storage systems. These storage systems will ensure that excess energy can be stored and used during periods of high demand, achieving a stable and self-sufficient power supply.

Modular and Adaptable Housing Units

Scalability and Flexibility: Develop modular housing units that are scalable and adaptable to different family sizes and community needs. These units can be easily expanded or reduced in size to accommodate fluctuating demographics, ensuring long-term utility and relevance.

- **Circular Material Flows**: Incorporate principles of the circular economy in housing construction and design. Use recycled and recyclable materials to minimize waste and environmental impact. Establish local material banks to facilitate the exchange and reuse of construction materials, fostering a sustainable and resource-efficient construction ecosystem.
- **Smart Home Technologies**: Integrate IoT-enabled smart home technologies that optimize energy usage, enhance security, and improve the quality of life for residents. These systems can include smart thermostats, automated lighting, and security systems that can be controlled remotely, enhancing convenience and efficiency.

Community-Based Living Systems

Shared Resources and Services: Promote community-based living systems that encourage resource sharing and social interaction. Develop communal spaces such as community gardens, co-working spaces, and recreational areas that serve as the heart of the community, fostering a sense of belonging and cooperation among residents.

- **Green Building Standards**: Adhere to stringent green building standards and certifications such as LEED (Leadership in Energy and Environmental Design) and BREEAM (Building Research Establishment Environmental Assessment Method). These standards ensure that buildings meet high environmental performance metrics, contributing to sustainability and health.
- **Participatory Planning and Design**: Facilitate community engagement in the planning and design processes to ensure that housing developments meet the actual needs and preferences of residents. Establish local planning committees and conduct regular consultations, allowing residents to voice their opinions and be an integral part of the decision-making process 20:14†source .

Integrative Green Spaces and Biodiversity

Urban Green Corridors: Create interconnected green corridors within urban areas that provide pathways for wildlife and recreational spaces for residents. These green corridors will enhance urban biodiversity, improve air quality, and offer aesthetic and health benefits .

- **Vertical Gardens and Green Roofs**: Utilize vertical gardens and green roofs to enhance building insulation and reduce urban heat island effect. These features not only improve energy efficiency but also offer residents easy access to nature, promoting mental well-being and social cohesion.
- **Water Management Solutions**: Implement sustainable urban drainage systems (SUDS) to manage stormwater, reduce flooding risks, and pro-

mote water reuse. Integrate rainwater harvesting systems and green infrastructure to create resilient and water-efficient urban environments .

Social and Economic Initiatives

Affordable Housing Programs: Develop affordable housing programs that ensure equitable access to quality housing for all segments of the population. Collaborate with government agencies, non-profit organizations, and private sector partners to provide financial assistance, subsidies, and supportive services to those in need.

- **Job Creation and Training**: Establish job training programs and employment opportunities within housing projects to equip residents with the skills required for construction, maintenance, and management roles. These initiatives will not only aid in the immediate reconstruction efforts but also contribute to long-term economic stability and growth .
- **Health and Well-being Initiatives**: Incorporate health and well-being initiatives within housing developments, such as fitness centers, walking trails, and wellness programs. Ensure that housing environments promote physical activity, mental health, and social interaction, contributing to the overall quality of life of residents .

Conclusion

Sustainable housing development is fundamental to Ukraine's medium-term urban transformation, providing a blueprint for creating resilient, energy-efficient, and vibrant communities. By integrating renewable energy, innovative construction techniques, and community-centric approaches, Ukraine can set a benchmark in post-war urban reconstruction, paving the way for a sustainable and prosperous future 20:14†source .

By incorporating these innovative and sustainable practices, Ukraine can transform its housing infrastructure, ensuring that it meets the present needs while being resilient against future challenges. This section serves as a comprehensive guide for stakeholders to develop housing solutions that are inclusive, environmentally friendly, and economically viable.

Section 3.2: Green Space and Biodiversity Integration

Introduction

In the pursuit of rebuilding Ukraine post-war, the integration of green spaces and biodiversity stands as a fundamental pillar for fostering resilient and healthy urban environments. This section outlines a visionary approach to embedding nature within urban landscapes, ensuring ecological balance, enhancing community well-being, and promoting economic vitality through strategic development of green spaces and biodiversity corridors.

Urban Green Corridors: The Veins of Ecological Resilience

Creation of Interconnected Green Networks: Green corridors will serve as vital connectors between urban green spaces, wildlife habitats, and water bodies. These corridors are designed to provide seamless pathways for flora and fauna, enhancing urban biodiversity. By integrating parks, urban forests, community gardens, and natural reserves, these networks will form the backbone of Ukraine's green urban infrastructure.

- **Flora and Fauna Diversity**: Plant a diverse array of native vegetation along these corridors to support local wildlife populations. Establish zones with varying vegetation densities to cater to different species' needs, promoting a rich and balanced ecosystem.

- **Ecological Bridges**: Construct ecological bridges and underpasses across roads and railways to facilitate safe wildlife crossings, reducing habitat fragmentation and vehicle-wildlife collisions.

Multifunctional Green Spaces: Design green spaces to serve multiple purposes – recreational, educational, and ecological. These spaces will not only provide respite from urban hustle but also offer educational opportunities about local ecosystems and sustainability practices.

- **Community Parks**: Develop community parks with playgrounds, sports facilities, and picnic areas to encourage active lifestyles and social interaction among residents.

- **Educational Natural Reserves**: Establish urban natural reserves with educational trails, information boards, and guided tours. These reserves will foster environmental awareness and stewardship among residents, particularly children and students.

Vertical Gardens and Green Roofs: Integrating Nature into Built Environments

Vertical Gardens: Incorporate vertical gardens in building designs to enhance aesthetics, improve air quality, and provide thermal insulation.

- **Living Walls**: Equip buildings with living walls composed of diverse plant species. These walls can be self-sustaining with integrated irrigation systems, contributing to reduced energy consumption and carbon footprint.

- **Balcony and Facade Gardens**: Encourage residents and businesses to create balcony and facade gardens. These small-scale green initiatives collectively contribute to urban greenery, cooling effects, and biodiversity

Green Roofs: Green roofs offer substantial ecological, economic, and social benefits. Implementing green roofs on residential, commercial, and public buildings will mitigate urban heat island effects, manage stormwater, and provide recreational spaces.

- **Extensive Green Roofs**: Design low-maintenance green roofs with drought-resistant plants to cover large building areas, providing insulation and habitat for urban wildlife.
- **Intensive Green Roofs**: Develop green roofs with deeper soil layers capable of supporting larger plants, shrubs, and trees, creating rooftop parks accessible for public enjoyment and community activities.

Integrative Water Management Solutions

Sustainable Urban Drainage Systems (SUDS):

Implement SUDS across urban landscapes to manage stormwater sustainably, reduce flood risks, and promote groundwater recharge.

- **Permeable Pavements**: Construct walkways, parking areas, and streets with permeable materials that allow rainwater to infiltrate the ground, reducing surface runoff.
- **Rain Gardens and Bioswales**: Integrate rain gardens and bioswales into public spaces and residential areas. These systems capture and filter stormwater, enhancing water quality and providing habitat for aquatic plants and insects.

Rainwater Harvesting: Encourage the installation of rainwater harvesting systems in buildings. Collected rainwater can be used for irrigation, reducing the demand on municipal water supplies.

- **Storage Tanks and Cisterns**: Equip buildings with storage tanks and cisterns to collect and store rainwater for non-potable uses such as landscape irrigation and toilet flushing.

Enhancing Urban Biodiversity

Native Species Planting: Prioritize the planting of native species in urban green spaces to support local wildlife and maintain the ecological balance. Native plants require less maintenance, are more resilient to local climate conditions, and provide better habitat for native fauna.

- **Botanical Gardens and Arboretums**: Establish botanical gardens and arboretums showcasing native plant species. These spaces will serve as conservation sites for rare and endangered plants, as well as educational centers for the public.

Pollinator Gardens: Develop pollinator gardens throughout urban areas to support bees, butterflies, and other pollinators essential for biodiversity.

- **Floral Diversity**: Plant diverse flowering plants that bloom at different times of the year, ensuring a continuous nectar source for pollinators.

Economic and Social Benefits

Green Jobs and Economic Growth: Investing in green infrastructure projects will create jobs in landscaping, horticulture, environmental management, and maintenance. These initiatives will stimulate economic growth and provide sustainable livelihoods for residents.

- **Training and Employment Programs**: Implement training programs to equip residents with skills in urban gardening, green roof installation, and environmental conservation, ensuring a skilled workforce for green initiatives.

Community Engagement and Cohesion: Green spaces foster community cohesion and social interaction. Engaging residents in the creation and maintenance of green spaces will instill a sense of ownership and pride, enhancing community well-being and resilience.

- **Volunteer Programs**: Establish volunteer programs for community members to participate in planting and maintaining green spaces, promoting social interaction and collective responsibility.

Conclusion

Integrating green spaces and biodiversity into Ukraine's urban reconstruction not only addresses environmental challenges but also brings substantial social and economic benefits. By creating interconnected green networks, fostering urban biodiversity, and implementing innovative green infrastructure solutions, Ukraine can achieve a resilient, sustainable, and vibrant urban future. This approach will ensure that rebuilt cities are not only habitable but thrive with nature, providing a high quality of life for all residents.

This comprehensive framework sets a new standard for urban green space integration, creating a blueprint for resilient, inclusive, and sustainable urban development in the post-war context .

Section 3.3: Circular Economy Implementation

Introduction

In the quest for a sustainable post-war Ukraine, the circular economy emerges as a linchpin, transforming the traditional linear model of "take-make-dispose" into a regenerative system where waste is minimized, and resources are continuously reused. This section presents a comprehensive strategy to build a circular economy that minimizes waste, maximizes resource efficiency, and fosters economic resilience.

Establishing Material Banks

Centralized Hubs for Material Exchange: Develop centralized material banks that serve as repositories for reclaimed and reusable building materials. These banks will play a critical role in the sustainable rebuilding efforts by providing a steady supply of low-cost, high-quality materials salvaged from demolished or damaged structures.

- **Inventory and Distribution Systems**: Implement advanced inventory management systems using IoT and blockchain technologies to track material stocks and manage distribution efficiently. These systems will ensure transparency, reduce waste, and optimize resource allocation.

- **Collaboration with Local Enterprises**: Partner with local construction companies, NGOs, and municipal bodies to establish these material banks. Such collaborations will foster community involvement and create a network of stakeholders committed to sustainable practices.

Promoting Reuse and Recycling: Encourage the use of recycled materials in construction projects across Ukraine. Establish standards and guidelines for using recycled content to ensure quality and safety while promoting environmental sustainability.

- **Certification Programs**: Develop certification programs for recycled building materials to assure builders and consumers of their safety and performance. These certifications will boost market confidence and demand for recycled products.

Developing Neighborhood-Scale Waste-to-Resource Centers

Local Waste Processing Facilities: Create neighborhood-scale waste-to-resource centers that process organic and inorganic waste into valuable resources. These centers will significantly reduce the burden on centralized waste management systems and cut down on landfill usage.

- **Composting and Biogas Production**: Establish composting facilities for organic waste, converting it into valuable compost and biogas. These biogas systems can generate renewable energy, reducing reliance on fossil fuels and enhancing local energy security.

- **Materials Recovery Facilities (MRFs)**: Set up MRFs to sort, clean, and process recyclable materials. Advanced automation and AI-driven sorting technologies will improve efficiency and the quality of recovered materials.

Circular Business Models: Promote the development of circular business models that focus on product lifecycle extension, repair, and remanufacturing. Initiatives such as product-as-a-service (PaaS) and leasing models will encourage sustainable consumption patterns.

- **Incentives for Circular Practices**: Offer incentives to businesses adopting circular practices, such as tax breaks, grants, and low-interest loans. Government support will play a crucial role in catalyzing the transition to a circular economy.

Implementing City-Wide Circular Economy Initiatives

Public-Private Partnerships (PPPs): Leverage PPPs to drive city-wide circular economy initiatives. These partnerships can bring together the expertise, resources, and innovation needed to implement comprehensive recycling, waste management, and resource recovery programs.

- **Innovation Hubs**: Establish innovation hubs focused on circular economy research and development. These hubs will foster collaboration between academia, industry, and government to develop cutting-edge technologies and solutions tailored to Ukraine's specific needs.

Educational Campaigns: Conduct nationwide educational campaigns to raise awareness about the benefits of the circular economy. Encourage citizens to participate actively in recycling and sustainable consumption practices.

- **School Programs and Community Workshops**: Integrate circular economy principles into school curricula and community workshops. Educating the younger generation and engaging local communities will ensure the long-term sustainability of circular economy initiatives.

Digital Platforms for Circular Economy Management

Smart Waste Management Systems: Develop digital platforms using AI and IoT to enhance waste management efficiency. These platforms will provide real-time data on waste generation, collection, and processing, enabling smart decision-making and resource optimization.

- **Predictive Analytics**: Use predictive analytics to forecast waste trends and optimize collection routes. This will reduce operational costs, minimize environmental impact, and improve service delivery.

Blockchain for Transparency: Implement blockchain technology to ensure transparency and traceability in the circular economy. Blockchain can record transactions across the material lifecycle, from collection to processing and reuse, fostering trust and accountability.

- **Smart Contracts**: Utilize smart contracts to automate and enforce recycling agreements and incentive schemes. These contracts will ensure compliance and streamline transaction processes.

Policy and Regulatory Framework

Legislation for Circular Economy: Enact comprehensive legislation to support the circular economy transition. Policies should mandate recycling targets, extended producer responsibility (EPR), and eco-design requirements to minimize waste and maximize resource recovery.

- **Regulatory Bodies**: Establish regulatory bodies to oversee the implementation and enforcement of circular economy policies. These bodies will ensure compliance and provide guidance to businesses and municipalities.

International Collaboration: Collaborate with international organizations and experts to bring global best practices to Ukraine. Participation in international circular economy forums and networks will enhance knowledge sharing and innovation.

- **EU Support**: Engage with the European Union to secure funding and technical assistance for circular economy projects. The EU's support can accelerate Ukraine's transition by providing access to cutting-edge technologies and sustainable practices .

Benefits and Long-term Impact

Economic Resilience: The circular economy will contribute to economic resilience by creating new business opportunities, reducing resource dependency, and fostering innovation. The local production of materials and energy will insulate Ukraine's economy from global market fluctuations.

- **Job Creation**: Circular economy initiatives will create green jobs in recycling, resource recovery, and sustainable manufacturing, contributing to economic recovery and growth.

Environmental Sustainability: Implementing a circular economy will significantly reduce waste, lower greenhouse gas emissions, and conserve natural resources. This will enhance Ukraine's environmental sustainability and support global climate goals.

- **Reduced Landfill Usage**: By recovering valuable resources from waste, Ukraine can reduce landfill usage, mitigating associated environmental issues like soil and water contamination.

Social Cohesion: Engaging communities in circular economy practices will strengthen social cohesion and collective responsibility. Inclusive initiatives will ensure that all segments of the population benefit from sustainable development.

- **Community Well-being**: Cleaner, waste-free environments will enhance the quality of life for residents, fostering a sense of pride and community well-being.

Conclusion

The implementation of a circular economy is crucial for Ukraine's post-war reconstruction. By establishing material banks, developing waste-to-resource centers, leveraging digital platforms, and fostering international collaboration,

Ukraine can build a resilient, sustainable, and circular future. This comprehensive approach will not only support immediate recovery efforts but will also lay the foundation for long-term prosperity and environmental stewardship, embodying the principles of resilience, innovation, and community engagement at the heart of the nation's renewal.

Chapter 4: Long-Term Visionary Development (5-20 years)

Section 4.1: Advanced Transportation Systems

Vision for Transportation Networks of the Future

As Ukraine courageously steps into a new era, the vision for its transportation systems reflects an amalgamation of resilience, innovation, and sustainability. This section details the ambitious plans to overhaul Ukraine's transportation infrastructure, integrating advanced technologies and future-oriented designs to create an interconnected, efficient, and eco-friendly transport network pivotal for Ukraine's long-term prosperity.

Developing Underground Hyperloop Network

Revolutionizing Ground Transport: The hyperloop system stands as a beacon of futuristic transportation, promising unprecedented speed and efficiency. Ukraine's hyperloop network will connect major cities like Kyiv, Lviv, Kharkiv, and Odessa, drastically reducing travel times and spurring economic growth across regions.

- **High-Speed Connectivity**: Hyperloop pods, traveling through low-pressure tubes, will achieve speeds exceeding 760 mph, substantially minimizing intercity travel times and fostering enhanced economic integration.

- **Sustainable Infrastructure**: The hyperloop system will be powered by renewable energy sources such as solar and wind, integrated directly onto hyperloop tunnels and stations. This green-powered transportation will significantly reduce carbon emissions, aligning with Ukraine's sustainability goals.

- **Economic Impact**: The construction and operation of the hyperloop network will generate numerous job opportunities, stimulate local economies, and attract international businesses, boosting Ukraine's position as a global economic hub .

Urban Air Mobility Infrastructure

Taking to the Skies with Flying Taxis: Urban air mobility (UAM) introduces revolutionary aerial transportation solutions through flying taxis and cargo drones, alleviating urban congestion and enhancing mobility.

- **Flying Taxis**: Implementing an extensive network of flying taxis equipped with VTOL (Vertical Take-Off and Landing) technology will offer swift, on-demand transportation for urban dwellers and visitors.
- **Drone Logistics Ports**: Establish drone logistics ports to facilitate efficient cargo delivery in urban areas, ensuring rapid and eco-friendly transportation of goods. These hubs will be strategically located to optimize last-mile delivery, reducing traffic congestion and emissions.
- **Safety and Regulation**: Collaborate with international aviation authorities to establish rigorous safety standards and air traffic management systems, ensuring safe and reliable operations. Utilize AI-driven air traffic control to manage airspace dynamically, preventing collisions and optimizing flight paths 8:0†source .

Smart and Adaptable Road Infrastructure

Future-Proofing Roads and Highways: Building intelligent and adaptable road systems will be key to enduring energy efficiency and resilience against dynamic climatic conditions.

- **Self-Healing Materials**: Roads constructed with nanotechnology-enhanced, self-healing materials can autonomously repair minor damages and extend infrastructure life cycles, minimizing maintenance costs and disruptions.
- **Embedded Solar Panels**: Solar panel-embedded roads will generate renewable energy to power road infrastructure, including lighting, signage, and smart traffic systems. This innovation promises both sustainability and energy efficiency.
- **Wireless EV Charging**: Integrating wireless charging lanes for electric vehicles will revolutionize road travel in Ukraine, enabling continuous charging while driving and encouraging widespread adoption of EVs. This development will position Ukraine at the forefront of electric mobility .

Resilience and Environmental Integration

Designing Climate-Resilient Transport Systems: Adapting to climate change is essential for the longevity and reliability of Ukraine's transportation infrastructure.

- **Tidal Energy Sea Walls**: Coastal cities will benefit from tidal energy sea walls designed to protect against flooding and generate renewable energy. These structures will serve a dual purpose of defense and sustainability, promoting ecological balance in coastal ecosystems.

- **Green Transportation Corridors**: Develop green corridors that intertwine transportation networks with natural landscapes. This integration will reduce urban heat islands, improve air quality, and create aesthetic environments, contributing to public health and well-being.
- **Advanced Weather Monitoring**: Implement real-time weather monitoring and prediction systems using IoT and AI technologies to ensure transportation networks operate smoothly during extreme weather events. This proactive approach will enhance safety and minimize disruption risks 8:0†source .

Autonomous Vehicle Ecosystem

Leading the Charge in Autonomous Mobility: Autonomous vehicles (AVs) represent the future of transportation, offering significant improvements in safety, efficiency, and convenience.

- **Driverless Public Transit**: Deploy fully autonomous buses and shuttles in urban and suburban areas, providing reliable and efficient public transportation solutions. These vehicles will operate on pre-defined routes with minimal human intervention, reducing traffic congestion and transportation costs.
- **Connected Car Networks**: Develop smart infrastructure that supports vehicle-to-everything (V2X) communication, facilitating seamless interaction between AVs, traffic management systems, and city infrastructure. This interconnected system will optimize traffic flow, reduce accidents, and enhance urban mobility.
- **AI Traffic Management**: AI-driven traffic management platforms will dynamically adjust traffic signals, manage vehicle flow, and predict congestion patterns, transforming cities into smart, predictive environments. This will lead to remarkable improvements in travel times and fuel efficiencies, contributing to an inclusive and intelligent transportation ecosystem 8:0†source .

Conclusion

Reimagining Ukraine's transportation systems as part of its long-term visionary development involves embracing advanced technologies, sustainable practices, and resilient designs. By pioneering innovations such as the hyperloop network, urban air mobility, and self-healing roads, Ukraine will not only rebuild but redefine its transportation landscape. These transformative initiatives are set to propel Ukraine into a new era of connectivity, sustainability, and economic vitality, showcasing a resilient and forward-thinking nation ready to lead the world into the future.

Section 4.2: Next-Generation Energy Solutions

In the quest for energy resilience and sustainability, the reconstruction of Ukraine offers a unique opportunity to harness next-generation energy solutions. This ambitious vision sets the stage for a transformative energy landscape, combining pioneering technologies, renewable energy sources, and international collaborations to build a robust, sustainable, and future-proof energy infrastructure.

Fusion Power Plants: The Pinnacle of Clean Energy

Harnessing the Power of Stars: Fusion energy, often dubbed as the "holy grail" of clean energy, promises virtually limitless power with minimal environmental impact. By replicating the processes that power the sun, Ukraine can achieve a significant leap in energy independence and sustainability.

- **Strategic Development Sites**: Identify and develop strategic sites for fusion power plants, integrating them into the broader national grid. These facilities will provide a stable baseload power supply, crucial for ensuring energy security.

- **International Collaborations**: Leverage international expertise and partnerships with leading research institutions and countries pioneering in fusion technology. Establish joint research and development programs to accelerate technological advancements and deployment.

- **Economic and Environmental Impact**: Fusion power plants will not only reduce carbon emissions but will also create high-tech job opportunities and stimulate economic growth, positioning Ukraine as a leader in the global clean energy transition.

Space-Based Solar Energy: Tapping the Endless Potential

Collecting Solar Power from Space: Space-based solar power (SBSP) systems represent a revolutionary approach to harnessing solar energy. By capturing solar power in space, where sunlight is uninterrupted by atmospheric or weather conditions, Ukraine can achieve continuous and abundant energy generation.

- **Geostationary Solar Satellites**: Deploy solar satellites in geostationary orbit to collect and beam solar energy back to Earth using microwave or laser technology. Construct ground-based rectennas (rectifying antennas) to receive and convert this energy into usable electricity 8:0†source 8:0†source .

- **Infrastructure Investment**: Foster investments in space infrastructure, including the manufacturing of solar satellites and the development of ground-based receiving stations. Encourage private sector participation and international investment to share costs and benefits.

- **Policy and Regulatory Frameworks**: Establish clear policies and regulatory frameworks to govern the deployment and operation of SBSP systems. This includes international agreements on space usage and collaboration with global space agencies.

Advanced Geothermal Energy: Unlocking Earth's Subsurface Potential

Utilizing Geothermal Resources: Geothermal energy, derived from the Earth's internal heat, presents a stable and sustainable energy source. By tapping into geothermal reservoirs, Ukraine can diversify its energy mix and provide consistent power and heating solutions.

- **High-Efficiency Geothermal Plants**: Develop high-efficiency geothermal power plants in regions with significant geothermal potential. Utilize advanced drilling technologies and binary cycle power plants to maximize energy extraction and efficiency 8:0†source .
- **Enhanced Geothermal Systems (EGS)**: Invest in Enhanced Geothermal Systems (EGS), which enhance natural geothermal sites by engineering reservoirs in hot dry rocks. This technology expands the geographic applicability of geothermal energy, allowing for widespread deployment.
- **Direct Use Applications**: Promote the direct use of geothermal energy for heating residential and commercial buildings, greenhouses, and industrial processes. These applications can significantly reduce fossil fuel consumption and greenhouse gas emissions.

Hydrogen Economy: Pioneering Clean Fuel Alternatives

Developing Hydrogen as a Key Energy Carrier: Hydrogen, as a versatile and clean energy carrier, has the potential to revolutionize energy systems by providing a zero-emission fuel for various applications, including transportation, power generation, and industrial processes.

- **Green Hydrogen Production**: Focus on producing green hydrogen through electrolysis powered by renewable energy sources such as wind and solar. Establish large-scale electrolyzer installations to convert water into hydrogen and oxygen efficiently.
- **Hydrogen Infrastructure**: Develop comprehensive hydrogen infrastructure, including pipelines, storage facilities, and refueling stations. Encourage the adoption of hydrogen fuel cells in public transportation and heavy industries, reducing reliance on fossil fuels .
- **International Hydrogen Partnerships**: Engage in international partnerships to foster technology transfer, share best practices, and create a global hydrogen economy. Collaborative efforts can accelerate hydrogen adoption and drive down costs.

Smart Energy Grids: The Backbone of Next-Generation Energy Systems

Integrating Smart Grid Technologies: Smart grids are essential for managing and optimizing the distribution of energy from diverse and decentralized sources. By embracing smart grid technologies, Ukraine can enhance grid reliability, efficiency, and flexibility.

- **AI-Driven Load Management**: Implement AI-driven load management systems that optimize energy distribution based on real-time demand and supply conditions. These systems can predict consumption patterns and adjust distribution to minimize waste and prevent blackouts.

- **Decentralized Energy Generation**: Promote decentralized energy generation through microgrids and distributed renewable energy sources. This approach reduces the vulnerability of the national grid to targeted attacks or natural disasters and enhances energy security 20:13†source 20:16†source .

- **Blockchain for Energy Trading**: Utilize blockchain technology to facilitate transparent and secure energy trading between producers and consumers. Blockchain can streamline transactions, reduce costs, and ensure fair pricing in a decentralized energy market.

Sustainable Energy Storage Solutions

Battery and Beyond: Energy storage is critical for balancing supply and demand, particularly with the integration of intermittent renewable energy sources.

- **Advanced Battery Technologies**: Invest in advanced battery technologies, including solid-state batteries, lithium-sulfur batteries, and flow batteries. These storage solutions offer higher energy densities, longer lifespans, and better safety profiles compared to traditional lithium-ion batteries.

- **Grid-Scale Storage**: Develop grid-scale energy storage systems, such as pumped hydro storage and compressed air energy storage (CAES). These systems can store significant amounts of energy and provide stability to the grid during peak demand periods or supply disruptions.

- **Vehicle-to-Grid (V2G) Technology**: Encourage the adoption of Vehicle-to-Grid (V2G) technology, where electric vehicles (EVs) can feed stored energy back into the grid during peak hours. This not only enhances grid stability but also provides additional revenue streams for EV owners 8:0†source .

Conclusion

Ukraine's commitment to next-generation energy solutions is not just a path to resilience but a bold declaration of leadership in the global clean energy revolution. By leveraging fusion power, space-based solar energy, geothermal resources, hydrogen fuel, smart grids, and advanced energy storage, Ukraine can establish an energy infrastructure that is sustainable, secure, and capable of meeting future challenges. These initiatives will not only ensure national energy independence but also position Ukraine as a pioneer in the realm of innovative and sustainable energy solutions, inspiring the world towards a greener and more resilient future.

Section 4.3: Climate Resilience and Environmental Restoration

Introduction

As Ukraine moves toward rebuilding its cities and infrastructure, ensuring climate resilience and environmental restoration is paramount. This section lays out a comprehensive strategy to mitigate the impacts of climate change, restore ecosystems, and safeguard the environment while fostering sustainable urban development.

Coastal Defense and Climate Adaptation

Massive Seawalls with Integrated Tidal Energy Systems Given Ukraine's extensive coastline, protecting coastal cities from rising sea levels and storm surges is essential. Implementing massive seawalls with integrated tidal energy systems will serve a dual purpose of defense and energy generation.

- **Resilient Coastal Infrastructure**: Construct seawalls using advanced materials with high durability and flexibility to withstand extreme weather conditions. These structures will be embedded with sensors to monitor structural integrity and environmental conditions in real time.
- **Tidal Energy Integration**: Incorporate tidal turbines within the seawalls to harness renewable energy from tidal movements. This integration will generate sustainable power while reducing the carbon footprint of coastal defense structures.
- **Ecosystem-Compatible Design**: Design the seawalls to support marine ecosystems by incorporating artificial reefs and habitats for marine life. This approach ensures that coastal protection measures also contribute to biodiversity conservation .

Large-Scale Carbon Capture and Utilization

Carbon Capture Facilities To significantly reduce greenhouse gas emissions, developing large-scale carbon capture and utilization (CCU) facilities will be a keystone project in Ukraine's climate resilience strategy.

- **Direct Air Capture (DAC) Technology**: Utilize cutting-edge DAC technology to remove CO2 directly from the atmosphere. The captured carbon will be processed and stored or repurposed for industrial use, such as in construction materials or synthetic fuels.

- **Carbon Utilization Initiatives**: Collaborate with industries to develop applications for captured carbon, turning it into value-added products. These initiatives will create a circular carbon economy, fostering innovation and reducing dependency on fossil fuels.

- **Geological Storage Solutions**: Identify and develop geological formations suitable for long-term CO2 storage. Implement rigorous monitoring and verification systems to ensure the safety and efficacy of underground storage .

Climate-Responsive Urban Design

Green Building Standards Rebuilding urban areas with green building standards will enhance energy efficiency and climate resilience. These standards will guide the construction of new buildings and the retrofitting of existing structures.

- **Energy-Efficient Construction**: Use high-performance insulation, passive solar design, and energy-efficient HVAC systems to reduce energy consumption in buildings. Incorporate renewable energy systems such as solar panels and geothermal heat pumps.

- **Sustainable Materials**: Prioritize the use of sustainable and locally sourced materials with low environmental impact. Implement cradle-to-grave lifecycle assessments to ensure sustainability at every stage of construction and operation.

- **Climate-Responsive Architecture**: Design buildings to withstand extreme weather events, such as heatwaves and floods. Integrate features like green roofs, rain gardens, and permeable pavements to manage stormwater runoff and reduce urban heat island effects .

Reforestation and Urban Greening

Large-Scale Reforestation Projects Reforestation is crucial for enhancing carbon sequestration, restoring biodiversity, and mitigating the impacts of climate change.

- **National Reforestation Program**: Launch a nationwide reforestation program focusing on degraded and deforested areas. Prioritize native species to enhance biodiversity and ecosystem resilience.

- **Urban Greening Initiatives**: Develop urban forestry projects, including the planting of trees along streets, in parks, and on school campuses. Create green corridors to improve air quality, reduce noise pollution, and provide recreational spaces for residents.
- **Community Involvement**: Engage local communities in reforestation and urban greening activities. Establish community nurseries and tree-planting events to foster environmental stewardship and social cohesion .

Advanced Weather Monitoring Systems

Real-Time Climate Monitoring Implementing advanced weather monitoring systems is critical for predicting and responding to extreme weather events, ensuring the safety and resilience of urban areas.

- **IoT Sensor Networks**: Deploy a network of IoT sensors to monitor weather conditions, collect data on temperature, humidity, precipitation, and wind patterns. Integrate these sensors with AI-powered analytics platforms for real-time weather forecasting and risk assessment.
- **Early Warning Systems**: Develop robust early warning systems to alert communities about impending weather-related hazards. These systems will enable timely evacuations, resource mobilizations, and disaster response efforts.
- **Climate Data Sharing Platforms**: Create platforms for sharing climate data with the public and relevant stakeholders. This transparency will enhance community awareness and preparedness for climate-related challenges .

Ecosystem Restoration and Biodiversity Conservation

Wetland Restoration Projects Restoring wetlands is vital for water management, biodiversity conservation, and climate resilience.

- **Rehabilitating Degraded Wetlands**: Implement projects to restore and rehabilitate degraded wetlands. These efforts will enhance water filtration, flood control, and provide habitats for diverse species.
- **Constructed Wetlands**: Develop constructed wetlands in urban areas to treat wastewater, manage stormwater, and create green spaces. These wetlands will serve dual purposes of water purification and public recreation.

Biodiversity Corridors Creating biodiversity corridors will ensure the connectivity of habitats and support the movement and migration of wildlife.

- **Eco-Bridges and Tunnels**: Construct eco-bridges and tunnels across highways and urban areas to connect fragmented habitats. These struc-

tures will facilitate the safe passage of wildlife and reduce human-wildlife conflicts.
- **Landscape-Scale Conservation**: Implement landscape-scale conservation plans that integrate protected areas with sustainable land-use practices. Encourage agroforestry and sustainable agriculture to support biodiversity while benefiting local communities .

Conclusion

Building climate resilience and achieving environmental restoration are indispensable for Ukraine's sustainable future. By integrating seawalls with tidal energy systems, developing large-scale carbon capture and utilization facilities, implementing green building standards, and prioritizing reforestation and urban greening, Ukraine can effectively address climate challenges. Advanced weather monitoring systems and ecosystem restoration projects will further enhance resilience and ensure that Ukraine's rebuilt cities are not only habitable but thrive in harmony with nature. These initiatives will position Ukraine as a global leader in sustainable urban development and climate resilience, inspiring other nations to follow its exemplary path toward a resilient and sustainable future.

Chapter 5: Sector-Specific Reconstruction Strategies

Section 5.1: Industrial Revitalization

Introduction

In the vibrant framework of Ukraine's post-conflict reconstruction, the revitalization of the industrial sector plays an indispensable role. It builds the foundation for economic growth, sustainable development, and the restoration of livelihoods. This section envisions transforming defunct industrial landscapes into thriving hubs of innovation, sustainability, and productivity.

Converting Defunct Industrial Sites into Circular Economy Hubs

Strategic Reclamation and Repurposing The transformation of defunct and abandoned industrial sites into vibrant circular economy hubs is instrumental. These sites, once symbols of decay, will be repurposed to host sustainable industrial activities that emphasize resource efficiency and waste minimization.

- **Comprehensive Site Assessments**: Enlist multidisciplinary teams to conduct thorough assessments of each defunct industrial site, evaluating environmental contamination, structural integrity, and potential for redevelopment.

- **Sustainable Design Principles**: Incorporate eco-friendly designs and construction practices tailored to industrial reuse. Such designs will focus on minimizing energy consumption, reusing existing structures, and integrating renewable energy systems.
- **Resource Recovery Facilities**: Establish state-of-the-art facilities dedicated to the recovery and recycling of industrial byproducts and waste. These facilities will transform industrial waste into valuable resources, fostering a closed-loop economy.

Developing Smart Factories with IoT Integration and AI-Driven Production Lines

Next-Generation Manufacturing In the reimagined industrial landscape, smart factories will be the cornerstone of technological advancement and efficiency. Integrating Internet of Things (IoT) and Artificial Intelligence (AI) will revolutionize manufacturing processes.

- **IoT-Enabled Systems**: Equip factories with IoT sensors to monitor and control machinery, environmental conditions, and production processes in real-time. This setup will enhance operational efficiency, reduce downtime, and improve product quality.
- **AI-Driven Production Lines**: Implement AI-driven automation within production lines to optimize manufacturing processes, reduce labor costs, and increase production speed. Machine learning algorithms will predict maintenance needs, preventing costly equipment failures and minimizing interruptions.
- **Digital Twins**: Utilize digital twin technology to create virtual replicas of physical factories. These digital models will provide a platform for simulation, testing, and optimization of manufacturing processes without disrupting real-world operations.

Industrial Symbiosis Networks for Waste Exchange and Resource Efficiency

Fostering Collaborative Ecosystems Industrial symbiosis is a powerful strategy where different industries collaborate to utilize each other's byproducts, thereby minimizing waste and maximizing resource efficiency.

- **Network Formation**: Facilitate the formation of industrial symbiosis networks by connecting industries within close geographical proximity. These networks will enable the exchange of materials, energy, and water between industries, promoting mutual benefits and environmental sustainability.
- **Resource Mapping**: Develop comprehensive resource maps to identify potential synergies between different industries. These maps will highlight

opportunities for waste-to-resource exchanges, helping industries to reduce their environmental footprint and operating costs.

- **Stakeholder Collaboration**: Foster strong collaboration between industries, government bodies, and research institutions. This collaboration will support the development of innovative solutions, share best practices, and ensure regulatory compliance.

Encouraging Innovation and Start-Up Ecosystems in Industrial Parks

Nurturing Entrepreneurial Spirit Revitalized industrial zones will also serve as incubators for innovation and start-up ecosystems, driving technological advancement and economic growth.

- **Innovation Hubs and Incubators**: Establish innovation hubs and business incubators within industrial parks to support start-ups and small-medium enterprises (SMEs). These hubs will provide access to capital, mentorship, and state-of-the-art facilities.

- **Collaborative Research and Development (R&D)**: Promote collaborative R&D initiatives between start-ups, established industries, and academia. These partnerships will foster innovation, accelerate technological advancements, and bring new products to market more efficiently.

- **Funding and Incentives**: Develop funding mechanisms and incentives to attract and support start-ups. Government grants, tax incentives, and venture capital funds will provide the financial backing necessary for entrepreneurial success.

Implementing Green Technologies and Renewable Energy Integration

Sustainable Industrial Operations The integration of green technologies and renewable energy in industrial operations is key to sustainable development and reducing the carbon footprint of industrial activities.

- **Renewable Energy Systems**: Install solar panels, wind turbines, and geothermal energy systems within industrial parks to power operations sustainably. These renewable energy systems will significantly reduce reliance on fossil fuels and lower greenhouse gas emissions.

- **Energy Efficiency Initiatives**: Implement energy efficiency measures, including energy management systems, high-efficiency equipment, and waste heat recovery systems. These initiatives will optimize energy use, reduce costs, and enhance industrial sustainability.

- **Green Supply Chain Management**: Adopt green supply chain practices that prioritize environmentally friendly sourcing, production, and distribution processes. Encourage suppliers and partners to adhere to similar sustainable practices, creating a ripple effect throughout the supply chain.

Advanced Workforce Training and Development Programs

Building a Skilled Workforce for the Future The success of industrial revitalization hinges on a skilled and adaptable workforce. Comprehensive training and development programs are essential to equip workers with the skills needed in a modern, technology-driven industrial landscape.

- **Technical Training Programs**: Develop specialized training programs focused on advanced manufacturing techniques, IoT systems, AI integration, and sustainable practices. Collaborate with technical institutes and industry experts to ensure training is relevant and up-to-date.

- **Continuous Learning Platforms**: Establish continuous learning platforms that offer online courses, workshops, and certifications. These platforms will ensure that workers can continuously upgrade their skills and remain competitive in the evolving job market.

- **Partnerships with Educational Institutions**: Foster partnerships with universities and vocational schools to align curriculum with industry needs. Engage students in internships and apprenticeship programs, providing hands-on experience and a pathway to employment.

Conclusion

Revitalizing Ukraine's industrial sector is a monumental yet achievable task that promises transformative impacts on the nation's economy, sustainability, and social well-being. By repurposing defunct industrial sites, developing smart factories, fostering industrial symbiosis, nurturing start-up ecosystems, integrating green technologies, and investing in workforce development, Ukraine can forge a path toward a resilient and prosperous industrial future. This holistic approach ensures that industrial revitalization not only addresses immediate recovery needs but also lays a sustainable foundation for long-term growth and innovation.

Section 5.2: Agricultural Modernization

Introduction

The redevelopment of Ukraine's agricultural sector stands as a crucial step towards sustainable recovery and economic revitalization. Agriculture is the backbone of Ukraine's economy, and modernizing this sector will not only bolster food security but also enhance productivity, improve environmental sustainability, and foster rural development. This section outlines a comprehensive strategy to transform Ukraine's agricultural landscape through advanced technologies, sustainable practices, and community engagement.

Deployment of Autonomous Farm Equipment with Precision Agriculture Capabilities

Revolutionizing Farm Operations The deployment of autonomous farm equipment integrated with precision agriculture technologies will revolutionize farming in Ukraine, enhancing efficiency and productivity while reducing environmental impact.

- **Autonomous Machinery**: Introduce a fleet of autonomous tractors, harvesters, and drones equipped with GPS and AI-driven decision-making systems. These machines will conduct planting, watering, fertilizing, and harvesting operations with minimal human intervention, ensuring consistent and optimized agricultural practices.
- **Precision Agriculture Tools**: Utilize precision agriculture tools, including soil sensors, satellite imagery, and AI analytics, to monitor crop health, soil conditions, and weather patterns in real-time. This data-driven approach will enable farmers to apply water, fertilizers, and pesticides accurately, reducing waste and environmental footprints.

Development of Climate-Controlled Vertical Farming Towers

Year-Round Agricultural Production Implementing climate-controlled vertical farming towers will ensure year-round production of high-value crops, independent of weather conditions and seasons. These towers are designed to maximize space utilization and resource efficiency.

- **Vertical Hydroponics and Aeroponics**: Employ hydroponic and aeroponic systems within vertical farming structures to grow crops without soil, using nutrient-rich water solutions and mist. These systems consume significantly less water than traditional farming and enable faster plant growth.
- **LED Lighting and Climate Control**: Develop efficient LED lighting systems and climate control technologies to regulate temperature, humidity, and light exposure, creating optimal growing conditions for various crops. This controlled environment will boost crop yields and maintain high quality.

Implementation of Blockchain-Based Farm-to-Consumer Supply Chain Systems

Enhancing Transparency and Efficiency Blockchain technology will transform agricultural supply chains by enhancing transparency, traceability, and efficiency from farm to consumer.

- **Smart Contracts**: Use blockchain-based smart contracts to automate and secure transactions between farmers, suppliers, and retailers. These contracts ensure timely payments, reduce the risk of discrepancies, and streamline supply chain operations.

- **Traceability and Food Safety**: Implement blockchain systems to track the journey of agricultural products from farms to consumers, ensuring complete traceability. This transparency will enhance food safety, as consumers can verify the origins and quality of their food products, fostering trust in Ukrainian produce.

Building Sustainable Agro-Ecosystems Through Regenerative Agriculture Practices

Enhancing Soil Health and Biodiversity Adopting regenerative agriculture practices will restore soil health, increase biodiversity, and enhance ecosystem services, leading to resilient and sustainable agricultural systems.

- **Cover Cropping and Crop Rotation**: Encourage the use of cover crops and crop rotation to improve soil fertility, prevent erosion, and manage pests naturally. These practices will build healthier soils that retain more water and nutrients, reducing the need for chemical inputs.
- **Agroforestry**: Integrate agroforestry practices, where trees and shrubs are planted alongside crops and livestock. This diversification promotes biodiversity, enhances carbon sequestration, and provides additional income streams from timber, fruits, and nuts.

Advanced Workforce Training and Agricultural Education

Empowering the Next Generation of Farmers Providing advanced training and education programs will equip the agricultural workforce with the knowledge and skills needed to thrive in a modernized agricultural landscape.

- **Technical Training Programs**: Develop comprehensive training programs on advanced farming techniques, precision agriculture, and sustainable practices. Collaborate with agricultural universities and technical institutes to ensure the curriculum aligns with industry needs.
- **Digital Literacy and Technology Use**: Promote digital literacy and the use of agricultural technologies among farmers. This includes training on using farm management software, interpreting data analytics, and operating autonomous machinery and precision tools.

Community-Based Farming Cooperatives and Support Systems

Leveraging Collective Power for Sustainable Growth Forming community-based farming cooperatives will empower small and medium-sized farmers by providing access to shared resources, collective bargaining power, and support systems.

- **Cooperative Structures**: Establish cooperatives that pool resources for purchasing inputs, accessing advanced machinery, and marketing produce. These structures will enhance economies of scale, reduce costs, and increase market access for smallholders.

- **Extension Services and Support Networks**: Develop robust extension services and support networks to provide ongoing technical assistance, market information, and financial services to farmers. These networks will ensure that farmers receive the support they need to implement modern practices effectively .

Incentives for Sustainable Agricultural Practices

Encouraging Environmentally Friendly Farming Creating incentives for sustainable farming practices will drive adoption and ensure long-term environmental benefits.

- **Subsidies and Grants**: Offer subsidies and grants for farmers adopting sustainable practices such as organic farming, agroforestry, and precision agriculture. These financial incentives will reduce the initial costs and encourage widespread implementation.

- **Certification Programs**: Develop certification programs for sustainably produced goods, such as organic and fair-trade certifications. These programs will enhance marketability, allowing farmers to command premium prices for their products.

Conclusion

The modernization of Ukraine's agricultural sector is pivotal for sustainable development and economic recovery. By deploying autonomous farm equipment, developing vertical farming towers, implementing blockchain-based supply chain systems, and promoting regenerative agriculture practices, Ukraine can build a resilient and sustainable agricultural landscape. Advanced training and community-based support systems will empower farmers, while incentives for sustainable practices will drive long-term environmental benefits. Together, these initiatives will ensure that Ukraine's agriculture sector not only recovers but thrives, becoming a model for sustainable agricultural development globally.

Section 5.3: Cultural Heritage Preservation and Tourism

Introduction

Ukraine's rich cultural tapestry, woven through centuries of art, architecture, and tradition, is a testament to its enduring spirit and identity. The conflict has left indelible scars on these cultural assets, necessitating a robust and forward-thinking strategy for their preservation and revitalization. This section outlines a comprehensive plan to rehabilitate cultural heritage sites and leverage them to fuel tourism, fostering economic recovery and national pride.

Comprehensive Damage Assessment and Digital Archiving

Detailed Surveys and Mapping

Conduct thorough assessments of all historical and cultural sites affected by the conflict. Utilize advanced technologies such as drones, satellite imagery, and ground-penetrating radar to map damage accurately. These surveys will form the foundation for a structured restoration plan.

- **Visual and Structural Assessments**: Employ a combination of visual inspections and structural assessments to determine the extent of damage to each site. Use non-invasive techniques where possible to preserve the integrity of the artifacts.
- **Database Creation**: Develop a comprehensive database of all cultural assets, cataloging their condition, historical significance, and restoration needs. This database will serve as a centralized resource for all stakeholders involved in the restoration efforts.

Digital Archiving

In parallel with physical restoration, create digital archives of cultural heritage. This initiative will ensure that regardless of physical damage, the essence and knowledge of Ukraine's cultural heritage are preserved for future generations.

- **High-Resolution Scanning**: Implement high-resolution 3D scanning and photogrammetry to create digital replicas of artifacts and sites. These digital archives can be accessed globally, facilitating cultural exchange and virtual tourism.
- **Cloud-Based Storage**: Store digital archives in secure, cloud-based repositories. Partner with international technological firms to ensure data security and accessibility.

Restoration and Conservation Efforts

Restoration Planning

Develop detailed restoration plans tailored to the unique requirements of each cultural site. These plans should combine traditional restoration techniques with modern engineering and conservation methods.

- **Historical Accuracy**: Engage historians, archaeologists, and conservation experts to ensure that restorations maintain historical accuracy and respect the original craftsmanship and materials.
- **Sustainable Practices**: Integrate sustainable practices into restoration projects, using eco-friendly materials and processes. This approach will

mitigate environmental impact and enhance the resilience of restored sites.

International Collaboration

Leverage international expertise and resources for the restoration of Ukraine's cultural heritage. Forge partnerships with global cultural institutions, universities, and non-profits specializing in heritage conservation.

- **Knowledge Transfer Programs**: Establish knowledge transfer programs to enable local professionals to learn advanced restoration techniques. These programs will enhance local capacity and ensure sustainable conservation practices.
- **Funding and Grants**: Secure funding and grants from international bodies such as UNESCO, the European Union, and global heritage foundations. Transparent management and allocation of funds will be crucial to maintaining donor confidence and support.

Integrating Cultural Heritage with Tourism

Tourism Infrastructure Development

Develop robust tourism infrastructure around restored cultural sites to maximize their accessibility and appeal. This includes transportation links, visitor centers, and hospitality facilities.

- **Accessible Facilities**: Ensure that all tourist facilities are accessible to visitors with disabilities, promoting inclusive tourism. This will widen the tourist base and enhance the site's appeal.
- **Local Enterprise Support**: Encourage the establishment of local businesses such as cafes, artisanal shops, and guided tours around cultural heritage sites. These enterprises will benefit the local economy and provide authentic experiences for tourists.

Augmented and Virtual Reality Experiences

Harness augmented reality (AR) and virtual reality (VR) technologies to create immersive experiences that bring Ukraine's cultural heritage to life for visitors.

- **AR Guides**: Develop AR guides that provide interactive, real-time information about cultural sites through smartphones or wearable devices. These guides can offer historical context, architectural details, and storytelling elements that enrich the visitor experience.
- **VR Reconstructions**: Create virtual reality reconstructions of cultural sites, enabling global audiences to experience Ukraine's heritage from anywhere in the world. These VR experiences can also serve educational purposes, helping schools and universities integrate Ukrainian culture into their curricula.

Community Engagement and Education Programs

Cultural Education Initiatives

Implement educational programs to raise awareness and appreciation of Ukraine's cultural heritage among its citizens, particularly the younger generation.

- **School Curricula Integration**: Integrate cultural heritage education into school curricula, including field trips, heritage workshops, and interactive learning modules. These initiatives will instill a sense of pride and stewardship in young Ukrainians.
- **Public Awareness Campaigns**: Launch public awareness campaigns highlighting the importance of cultural preservation. Use media, community events, and social platforms to engage diverse audiences and foster a collective sense of responsibility.

Community-Driven Restoration Projects

Empower local communities to take an active role in the restoration and preservation of cultural heritage sites. Community engagement will ensure that restoration efforts reflect local values and traditions.

- **Volunteer Programs**: Establish volunteer programs that involve community members in restoration activities. Volunteers can assist with tasks such as site cleaning, documentation, and light maintenance under expert supervision.
- **Heritage Guardians**: Create a network of "heritage guardians" among community members who are trained to monitor and protect cultural sites. These guardians will act as custodians, ensuring the ongoing care and respect of heritage sites.

Leveraging Tourism for Economic Revival

Cultural Tourism Promotion

Promote cultural tourism as a key component of Ukraine's economic revival strategy. This includes marketing campaigns, partnerships with international travel agencies, and participation in global tourism fairs.

- **Destination Branding**: Develop a strong brand identity around Ukraine's cultural heritage that resonates with both domestic and international tourists. Highlight unique cultural narratives and historical significance in promotional materials.
- **Festival and Events**: Organize cultural festivals, heritage tours, and events that celebrate Ukrainian traditions and history. These events will attract tourists, create vibrant cultural scenes, and generate revenue for local businesses.

Sustainable Tourism Practices

Ensure that tourism development around cultural sites adheres to principles of sustainability and responsible tourism.

- **Environmental Protections**: Implement measures to protect natural environments surrounding cultural sites from over-tourism and degradation. This includes regulating visitor numbers, maintaining clean facilities, and preserving landscapes.
- **Cultural Sensitivity**: Promote cultural sensitivity among tourists through guidelines and educational programs that respect local customs, traditions, and heritage sites.

Conclusion

The preservation of cultural heritage and the development of tourism are vital strategies for Ukraine's reconstruction and economic rejuvenation. By combining meticulous restoration efforts, digital archiving, and innovative tourism practices, Ukraine can turn its cultural heritage into a powerful driver of national pride and economic growth. Engaging communities in these efforts ensures that restoration is both meaningful and sustainable, fostering a deep-rooted connection between the people and their heritage. Together, these initiatives will not only safeguard Ukraine's rich cultural legacy but also pave the way for a resilient and prosperous future.

Chapter 6: Financing and Resource Allocation

Section 6.1: Innovative Funding Mechanisms

Introduction

As Ukraine embarks on the monumental task of rebuilding its cities and infrastructure, it is imperative to establish innovative and robust funding mechanisms. These mechanisms will ensure the sustained flow of financial resources necessary for comprehensive reconstruction efforts while promoting transparency, accountability, and efficiency. This section outlines a strategic approach to harnessing diverse funding sources, leveraging international cooperation, and utilizing cutting-edge financial innovations to support Ukraine's post-war recovery.

Diverse Funding Sources

International Aid and Grants

International aid and grants remain pivotal to Ukraine's reconstruction, providing essential funding without the burden of repayment.

- **European Union Support**: The EU has established a substantial support mechanism for Ukraine, including an immediate aid package of up to 15 billion euros per month, which can be mobilized promptly to address urgent needs 54:1†source 54:9†source . Additionally, the EU has committed over 79 billion euros in various forms of support, ensuring a steady flow of financial resources for Ukraine's reconstruction 54:1†source 54:2†source 54:4†source .

- **Global Donor Conferences**: Organize global donor conferences to secure commitments from various countries, international organizations, and philanthropic entities. These conferences will highlight Ukraine's strategic recovery plans and facilitate coordinated international support.

Multilateral Development Banks

Multilateral development banks (MDBs) like the World Bank, the European Bank for Reconstruction and Development (EBRD), and the International Monetary Fund (IMF) play a critical role in providing financial resources and technical assistance.

- **World Bank and IMF Programs**: Engage with the World Bank and IMF to secure substantial financial packages designed for long-term reconstruction projects. These packages will include concessional loans, grants, and technical assistance to support infrastructure development and economic revitalization.
- **EBRD Investment**: Leverage EBRD investment programs focused on sustainable infrastructure, energy, and private sector development. These investments will drive economic growth and innovation, contributing to the resilience and diversification of Ukraine's economy.

Leveraging Private Sector Investments

Public-Private Partnerships (PPPs)

Public-private partnerships are essential for mobilizing private sector investments, sharing risks, and ensuring efficient project implementation.

- **Strategic PPP Frameworks**: Develop strategic frameworks for PPPs, outlining clear guidelines, roles, and responsibilities. This approach will attract private investment in critical sectors such as transportation, energy, and technology.
- **Incentive Structures**: Create attractive incentive structures, including tax breaks, subsidies, and guarantees, to encourage private investment in reconstruction projects. These incentives will mitigate risks and enhance the profitability of investments.

Green Bonds and Climate Finance

Green bonds and climate-related finance instruments will be crucial in funding sustainable and environmentally friendly reconstruction projects.

- **Issuance of Green Bonds**: Establish a national green bond program to raise capital for renewable energy projects, green infrastructure, and sustainable urban development. Green bonds will attract environmentally conscious investors and bolster Ukraine's commitment to sustainability.

- **Climate Funds**: Tap into international climate funds such as the Green Climate Fund (GCF) and the Global Environment Facility (GEF) to finance climate resilience and environmental restoration projects. These funds will support initiatives aimed at reducing carbon emissions, enhancing energy efficiency, and promoting biodiversity.

Tokenized Assets and Cryptocurrencies

Embrace blockchain technology and digital assets to create innovative funding mechanisms that ensure transparency and broaden investment opportunities.

- **Tokenized Real Estate Investment Platforms**: Develop platforms for tokenized real estate investments, allowing global investors to participate in Ukraine's reconstruction through fractional ownership of properties. This innovative approach will democratize access to real estate investment and generate significant capital inflows.

- **National Cryptocurrency for Reconstruction Financing**: Introduce a national cryptocurrency dedicated to reconstruction financing. This digital currency can be used to streamline transactions, enhance transparency, and engage tech-savvy investors in the funding process.

Enhanced Financial Management and Governance

Transparent Fund Distribution

Transparency in fund distribution is paramount to maintaining donor confidence and ensuring efficient use of resources.

- **Blockchain-Based Fund Management**: Implement blockchain technology for fund management, ensuring transparent tracking and allocation of resources. This system will provide real-time visibility into fund flows, reduce fraud, and enhance accountability.

- **Regular Audits and Reporting**: Conduct regular audits and provide comprehensive reports on the utilization of funds. Engage independent auditors and establish a dedicated oversight body to monitor financial activities and ensure adherence to best practices.

Anti-Corruption Measures

Robust anti-corruption measures are essential to safeguard financial integrity and build trust among donors and investors.

- **Anti-Corruption Frameworks**: Develop and enforce stringent anti-corruption frameworks, including whistleblower protection, anti-bribery laws, and conflict-of-interest regulations. These measures will create a zero-tolerance environment for corruption in reconstruction efforts 54:1†source 54:3†source 54:5†source .

- **International Collaboration**: Collaborate with international anti-corruption agencies and organizations to share best practices, conduct joint investigations, and build capacity for effective enforcement of anti-corruption measures.

Maximizing Resource Efficiency

Predictive Analytics and Resource Allocation

Utilize advanced data analytics to optimize resource allocation and ensure that investments yield the highest impact.

- **AI-Driven Predictive Models**: Develop AI-driven predictive models to identify priority areas for investment, forecast resource needs, and optimize budget allocations. These models will enhance decision-making processes and improve the effectiveness of reconstruction efforts.
- **Data-Driven Performance Metrics**: Establish data-driven performance metrics to assess the impact of funded projects. Regularly analyze and publish performance data to ensure that resources are directed towards the most effective and impactful initiatives.

International Collaboration and Knowledge Sharing

Global Knowledge Exchange Platforms

Foster international collaboration through knowledge exchange platforms that facilitate the sharing of best practices, innovative solutions, and technical expertise.

- **Reconstruction Best Practices Portal**: Create an online portal for sharing best practices in post-conflict reconstruction, drawing on global experiences and case studies. This portal will provide valuable insights and resources to support Ukraine's rebuilding efforts.
- **International Innovation Challenges**: Host international innovation challenges to identify and scale breakthrough technologies and solutions for reconstruction. These challenges will engage global innovators and drive the development of cutting-edge approaches to rebuilding.

Conclusion

Innovative funding mechanisms are the cornerstone of Ukraine's ambitious reconstruction agenda. By leveraging diverse funding sources, promoting private sector investments, and utilizing cutting-edge financial technologies, Ukraine can secure the resources necessary for comprehensive and sustainable reconstruction. Transparent fund distribution, robust anti-corruption measures, and international collaboration will ensure the effective and efficient use of these resources, driving Ukraine towards a resilient and prosperous future. The strategic approach outlined in this section not only addresses the immediate financial needs but also lays the foundation for long-term economic stability and growth.

Section 6.2: Resource Optimization Strategies

Introduction

In the aftermath of conflict, Ukraine's path to recovery requires an astute use of available resources. Optimizing resource allocation ensures that every dollar, every effort, is maximized for the greatest possible impact. This section delves into innovative strategies for resource optimization, combining cutting-edge technologies with practical tactics to ensure efficient, transparent, and effective use of funds and materials.

National Materials Exchange Platform

Centralized Resource Management

Creating a national materials exchange platform will streamline the distribution and reuse of construction materials, resources, and supplies across Ukraine. This centralized system will not only optimize resource utilization but also reduce waste and promote sustainability in reconstruction efforts.

- **Digital Marketplace**: Develop a digital marketplace where surplus materials from various reconstruction projects can be listed, traded, or donated. This platform will ensure that excess materials from one project can be efficiently redirected to another, minimizing waste and saving costs.

- **Blockchain Integration**: Use blockchain technology to provide a transparent and immutable ledger of all transactions on the platform. This will enhance trust among stakeholders, prevent fraud, and ensure that resources are used as intended .

- **Real-Time Inventory Management**: Implement real-time inventory management systems powered by IoT and AI, which will track the availability, condition, and location of materials. These systems will enable quick decision-making and efficient allocation of resources where they are most needed.

Predictive Models for Supply Chain Optimization

Utilizing Advanced Analytics

Leveraging machine learning and predictive analytics will revolutionize supply chain management in Ukraine's reconstruction efforts. These technologies will forecast demand, identify potential bottlenecks, and optimize logistics.

- **Demand Forecasting**: Use machine learning algorithms to analyze historical data and predict future demand for construction materials and essential supplies. This will help in planning and pre-ordering resources, thereby avoiding delays and shortages.

- **Optimized Logistics**: Implement AI-driven logistics solutions that optimize delivery routes and schedules, reducing transportation costs and emissions. These solutions will ensure timely delivery of materials to reconstruction sites, enhancing overall efficiency.

- **Scenario Planning**: Develop advanced scenario planning tools that simulate various supply chain disruptions and propose mitigation strategies. These tools will prepare stakeholders for unforeseen challenges, ensuring continuity and resilience in resource management.

Drone-Based Logistics Systems

Efficient and Timely Deliveries

Deploying drone-based logistics systems will address the pressing need for swift and precise delivery of materials to remote or hard-to-reach areas. Drones offer a flexible and scalable solution, particularly in regions with compromised infrastructure.

- **Last-Mile Delivery**: Utilize drones for last-mile delivery of critical supplies, ensuring that even the most remote areas receive essential materials promptly. This will be particularly useful for delivering medical supplies, emergency equipment, and specific construction materials to areas inaccessible by traditional means.

- **Automated Inventory Checks**: Employ drones equipped with advanced sensors to conduct automated inventory checks at construction sites and warehouses. These drones will provide real-time updates on stock levels, helping to maintain optimal inventory and prevent overstocking or shortages.

- **Environmental Monitoring**: Use drones to monitor environmental conditions around reconstruction sites, ensuring that construction activities comply with environmental regulations and sustainability goals.

International Coordination and Bulk Purchasing

Leveraging Scale for Cost Efficiency

Coordinating with international partners and engaging in bulk purchasing will significantly reduce costs and enhance the efficiency of reconstruction efforts.

- **Global Procurement Agreements**: Negotiate procurement agreements with international suppliers to purchase materials in bulk at reduced prices.

These agreements will leverage economies of scale, ensuring cost-effective procurement of essential supplies.

- **Joint Ventures and Consortia**: Form joint ventures and consortia with international firms and organizations to pool resources, share knowledge, and optimize procurement processes. This collaborative approach will bring advanced technologies and best practices to Ukraine's reconstruction efforts.

- **Aid Coordination**: Establish a robust framework for coordinating international aid, ensuring that donations and grants are used effectively and aligned with national priorities. Effective coordination will prevent duplication of efforts and ensure that resources are allocated to the most pressing needs.

Transparent Fund Distribution Mechanisms

Harnessing Technology for Accountability

Ensuring transparency and accountability in fund distribution is critical to maintaining donor confidence and preventing corruption.

- **Blockchain-Based Fund Management**: Implement blockchain technology for managing and tracking the distribution of funds. This transparent and secure system will record every transaction, ensuring that funds are used appropriately and efficiently.

- **AI-Driven Audits**: Use AI-driven audit systems to continuously monitor financial transactions and detect anomalies or suspicious activities. These systems will enhance oversight and ensure that all funds are accounted for and used as intended.

- **Public Dashboards**: Develop public dashboards that provide real-time updates on fund utilization, project progress, and financial audits. These dashboards will offer transparency to donors, stakeholders, and the general public, building trust and ensuring accountability.

Conclusion

Optimizing resource allocation is paramount to the successful reconstruction of Ukraine. By establishing a national materials exchange platform, leveraging predictive analytics, deploying drone-based logistics systems, coordinating international procurement, and ensuring transparent fund distribution, Ukraine can maximize the impact of every resource. These strategies will not only enhance efficiency and reduce costs but also build a foundation of trust and accountability, paving the way for a resilient and prosperous future.

Section 6.3: International Cooperation Frameworks

Introduction

Rebuilding Ukraine after the devastation of war is not an endeavor that can be tackled by the country alone. It requires a concerted global effort, mobilizing international resources, expertise, and goodwill. This section delineates the frameworks for international cooperation, outlining how Ukraine can synergize with global partners to secure the support necessary for sustainable and resilient reconstruction.

Concerted International Support

European Union's Commitment

The European Union stands as one of the most steadfast allies in Ukraine's reconstruction journey. The EU has mobilized significant financial resources, technical assistance, and policy support to aid in Ukraine's recovery.

- **Financial Support Mechanisms**: The EU has committed substantial financial aid to Ukraine, including an immediate package of up to 15 billion euros per month and a total support exceeding 79 billion euros. These funds are aimed at stabilizing the Ukrainian economy, rebuilding critical infrastructure, and fostering sustainable development 60:0†source .

- **Investment Frameworks**: The EU has established an investment framework for Ukraine, designed to stimulate investments in the country's recovery and reconstruction. This includes guarantees and grants of 14 billion euros announced during the Ukraine Recovery Conference in Berlin, focusing on energy infrastructure and private sector redevelopment 60:0†source .

- **Policy and Technical Cooperation**: The EU Commission is working closely with Ukrainian authorities to align policies, facilitate seamless integration into the European economic space, and implement reforms necessary for EU membership candidacy 60:0†source .

Leveraging Multilateral Organizations

World Bank and IMF Programs

Multilateral organizations like the World Bank and the International Monetary Fund (IMF) play a critical role in providing financial support and technical expertise required for large-scale reconstruction projects.

- **World Bank Engagement**: The World Bank offers comprehensive financial packages, including grants, concessional loans, and technical assistance geared towards infrastructure development, economic recovery, and social services revitalization. These projects are aimed at building back better, ensuring resilience against future threats 60:5†source .

- **IMF Structural Programs**: The IMF has designed emergency financial assistance programs totaling billions of dollars, which include structural reforms to enhance economic stability, governance, and fiscal management. These programs are pivotal for restoring macroeconomic stability and instilling confidence among international investors 60:5†source .

Bilateral and Multilateral Aid Coordination

Donor Coordination Platforms

Effective coordination among international donors is essential to maximize the impact of aid and avoid duplication of efforts.

- **Donor Conferences and Platforms**: Regular donor conferences facilitate pledges and commitments from various countries and organizations, ensuring that financial resources are aligned with Ukraine's reconstruction priorities. A donor coordination platform has been launched to guarantee cohesive support and accountability 60:0†source .
- **Joint Venture Agreements**: Establishing joint ventures with international companies and governments can pool resources and expertise to tackle complex reconstruction challenges. These partnerships will bring advanced technologies and innovative solutions to the rebuilding process 60:4†source .

Harnessing Global Financial Instruments

Green Bonds and International Climate Funds

Green bonds and international climate funds are instrumental for financing sustainable and resilient infrastructure projects.

- **Green Bond Issues**: Ukraine plans to issue green bonds to fund renewable energy projects, sustainable urban development, and environmental remediation efforts. These bonds will attract environmentally conscious investors committed to the global green agenda 60:4†source .
- **Accessing Climate Funds**: Ukraine will tap into global climate finance mechanisms such as the Green Climate Fund (GCF) and the Global Environment Facility (GEF). These funds will support projects aimed at climate adaptation, disaster risk reduction, and ecological restoration 60:0†source 60:5†source .

Strategic Partnerships for Capacity Building

International Technical Assistance

Technical assistance from developed nations and international organizations is crucial for building local capacity and transferring knowledge.

- **Expert Missions and Training**: International expert missions will conduct specialized training for Ukrainian engineers, urban planners, and policy makers. These missions will ensure that Ukrainian professionals are equipped with the latest techniques and best practices in reconstruction and sustainable development 60:2†source 60:5†source .

- **Exchange Programs**: Establish exchange programs with leading global institutions to facilitate the sharing of knowledge, technology, and innovation. These programs will include apprenticeships, internships, and fellowships for Ukrainian professionals 60:3†source .

Global Knowledge Exchange and Innovation

International Innovation Challenges

Hosting international innovation challenges will identify and scale breakthrough technologies and solutions tailored to Ukraine's reconstruction needs.

- **Competitions and Hackathons**: Organize global competitions and hackathons to crowdsource innovative ideas for urban reconstruction, sustainable energy solutions, and smart city technologies. These events will engage the global tech community and attract groundbreaking solutions 60:0†source .

- **Knowledge Portals**: Develop online knowledge portals that aggregate global best practices, case studies, and research on post-war reconstruction. These platforms will serve as valuable resources for policymakers, developers, and community leaders involved in Ukraine's rebuilding efforts 60:1†source .

Securing Long-term Commitments

Memoranda of Understanding (MoUs)

Securing long-term commitments from international partners through Memoranda of Understanding will ensure sustained support and collaboration.

- **Strategic MoUs**: Sign strategic MoUs with countries and organizations to formalize cooperation in key areas such as infrastructure development, economic support, and social services restoration. These agreements will outline the roles, responsibilities, and contributions of each partner, creating a clear framework for collaboration 60:0†source .

- **Regular Reviews and Updates**: Implement mechanisms for regularly reviewing and updating these MoUs to adapt to changing needs and emerging challenges. This flexibility will ensure that international support remains aligned with Ukraine's evolving reconstruction goals 60:1†source .

Conclusion

International cooperation is the cornerstone of Ukraine's ambitious reconstruction plans. By harnessing the support of the European Union, multilateral organizations, bilateral partners, and global financial instruments, Ukraine can secure the resources necessary for building a resilient and sustainable future. Strategic partnerships, donor coordination, capacity building, and knowledge exchange will drive the successful implementation of these plans, fostering a robust, inclusive, and innovative recovery process that stands as a model for the world.

Chapter 7: Implementation and Governance

Section 7.1: Project Management and Coordination

Introduction

In the grand vision for rebuilding Ukraine, effective project management and coordination are pivotal to ensure that reconstruction efforts are systematic, efficient, and impactful. This section outlines a comprehensive approach to managing the extensive array of projects, leveraging advanced technologies and best practices to orchestrate a seamless reconstruction process.

AI-Powered Project Management Systems

Architecture of Efficiency

Harnessing the power of artificial intelligence (AI) for project management will transform how reconstruction efforts are planned, executed, and monitored.

- **Centralized Command Systems**: Establish AI-powered centralized command systems to oversee the multiplicity of projects. These systems will integrate data from all reconstruction sites, providing real-time updates and predictive analytics to manage resources, schedules, and logistics.

- **Automated Workflow Optimization**: Implement AI algorithms to automate workflow processes, from scheduling to task allocation. This will minimize human error, accelerate project timelines, and ensure that resources are used optimally.

- **Predictive Analytics for Risk Management**: Utilize predictive analytics to identify potential risks and bottlenecks in project execution. AI-driven insights will enable proactive measures, reducing delays and preventing cost overruns .

Blockchain-Based Smart Contracts for Transparency

Ensuring Integrity and Trust

Deploying blockchain technology for managing procurement and contracts will enhance transparency, trust, and accountability in the reconstruction process.

- **Distributed Ledger Technology**: Implement blockchain-based distributed ledger technology to record all transactions and contract agreements. This immutable record will provide a transparent audit trail, ensuring that all financial flows and material allocations are traceable and tamper-proof.
- **Smart Contracts**: Utilize smart contracts to automate and enforce procurement agreements and project milestones. These self-executing contracts will ensure that payments are made only when predefined conditions are met, reducing the risk of fraud and ensuring that all parties adhere to their commitments .

Virtual War Room Environments for Real-Time Decision Making

Dynamic Coordination Hubs

Establishing virtual war room environments will support real-time decision-making and coordination among stakeholders involved in the reconstruction.

- **Interactive Dashboards**: Create interactive dashboards that provide a comprehensive overview of project statuses, resource allocations, and key performance indicators. These dashboards will be accessible to all stakeholders, enabling informed and timely decision-making.
- **Collaboration Platforms**: Develop digital collaboration platforms that facilitate communication and coordination among diverse teams. These platforms will support virtual meetings, document sharing, and collaborative planning, ensuring that all stakeholders are aligned and informed.
- **Scenario Simulation and Analysis**: Implement tools for simulating various scenarios and analyzing their potential impacts. These simulations will help decision-makers explore different strategies and select the most effective approaches for project implementation .

Integrated Monitoring and Evaluation Systems

Driving Performance through Data

Deploying integrated monitoring and evaluation systems will ensure continuous oversight and assessment of reconstruction projects.

- **IoT Sensor Networks**: Use Internet of Things (IoT) sensor networks to collect real-time data on construction progress, environmental conditions, and resource utilization. These sensors will provide accurate and timely information, enabling ongoing monitoring of project performance.
- **AI-Driven Impact Assessment**: Implement AI-driven impact assessment tools to evaluate the social, economic, and environmental outcomes

of reconstruction projects. These tools will analyze data from diverse sources, offering comprehensive insights into the effectiveness and sustainability of the initiatives.

- **Citizen Feedback Platforms**: Develop platforms for collecting and analyzing citizen feedback on reconstruction activities. These platforms will utilize sentiment analysis and data visualization to capture community perspectives, ensuring that projects align with local needs and expectations .

Capacity Building and Training Initiatives

Empowering Local Stakeholders

Building local capacity through training and development programs is essential for sustaining long-term reconstruction efforts.

- **National Online Learning Platforms**: Establish national online learning platforms that offer courses on project management, advanced construction techniques, and sustainable practices. These platforms will provide accessible and flexible learning opportunities for professionals involved in the reconstruction.
- **Virtual Reality Training Programs**: Develop virtual reality (VR) training programs that simulate real-world construction scenarios. These immersive programs will offer hands-on experience and skills development in a controlled and risk-free environment.
- **AI-Assisted Skill-Matching Systems**: Implement AI-assisted skill-matching systems to align workforce capabilities with project requirements. These systems will ensure that the right skills are deployed where they are most needed, enhancing efficiency and effectiveness .

Conclusion

Effective project management and coordination are the linchpins of successful reconstruction in Ukraine. By leveraging AI-powered systems, blockchain technology, virtual collaboration environments, and integrated monitoring tools, Ukraine can orchestrate a seamless and transparent reconstruction process. These innovative approaches will ensure that resources are used efficiently, projects are executed on time and within budget, and outcomes are sustainable and aligned with community needs. Empowering local stakeholders through capacity building and training initiatives will further sustain these efforts, ensuring a resilient and prosperous future for Ukraine.

Section 7.2: Capacity Building and Skill Development

Introduction

In the transformative journey of rebuilding Ukraine, a skilled and adaptable workforce is pivotal. Capacity building and skill development not only support immediate reconstruction efforts but also lay the foundation for long-term economic stability and innovation. This section underscores the strategic approach to equipping Ukraine's workforce with advanced skills, leveraging both national initiatives and international cooperation.

Establishing National Online Learning Platforms

Accessible and Inclusive Education

Creating comprehensive online learning platforms will democratize access to education, ensuring that all Ukrainians can participate in the reconstruction process regardless of their physical location.

- **Wide Range of Courses**: Develop a robust curriculum covering essential areas like advanced construction techniques, project management, sustainable practices, and digital skills. This extensive course offering will cater to the diverse needs of the workforce involved in rebuilding efforts.
- **Language Inclusivity**: Incorporate multiple languages, including Ukrainian, English, and Russian, to ensure broad accessibility. Utilize existing EU tools for skill profiling and language integration to support learning and professional development .
- **Flexible Learning Modules**: Design courses with flexible learning modules that accommodate various learning paces and schedules. These modules will allow learners to balance education with work and family commitments, promoting continuous skill development.

Virtual Reality Training Programs for Hands-On Experience

Immersive Learning Environments

Deploying virtual reality (VR) technology for training will provide immersive, hands-on experiences that enhance learning outcomes and practical skills.

- **Simulated Construction Sites**: Develop VR simulations of construction sites where trainees can practice advanced building techniques, safety protocols, and emergency responses in a controlled and risk-free environment. This immersive approach will build confidence and competence among the workforce.
- **Interactive Tutorials**: Offer interactive VR tutorials that guide users through complex procedures and best practices. These tutorials can cover a wide range of topics, from sustainable building practices to the operation of advanced machinery.

- **Collaboration with Technology Firms**: Partner with leading technology companies to create high-quality VR training programs. These collaborations will bring the latest innovations and expertise to the Ukrainian workforce, ensuring they are equipped with cutting-edge skills.

AI-Assisted Skill-Matching Systems

Optimizing Workforce Deployment

Implementing AI-assisted systems for skill matching will ensure that the right talents are deployed to the right projects, maximizing efficiency and impact.

- **Dynamic Skill Databases**: Develop dynamic databases that detail the skills and qualifications of the available workforce. AI algorithms will analyze these databases to identify the best matches for specific project needs.
- **Real-Time Matching**: Use AI for real-time matching of skills to job openings, ensuring swift and accurate placement. This system will also identify skill gaps and recommend targeted training programs to address them.
- **Talent Reserves**: Establish a talent reserve database that includes profiles of expatriates, refugees, and international volunteers willing to contribute to Ukraine's reconstruction. This global talent pool will enhance the capacity and diversity of the workforce.

International Exchange and Training Programs

Global Knowledge and Expertise Transfer

Fostering international exchange programs will facilitate the transfer of knowledge, technologies, and best practices, enriching Ukraine's reconstruction efforts.

- **Bilateral Exchange Programs**: Develop bilateral exchange programs with countries excelling in post-conflict reconstruction and urban development. These programs will enable Ukrainian professionals to gain firsthand experience and insights from international counterparts.
- **Joint Research Initiatives**: Initiate joint research projects with global universities and research institutions focusing on innovation in construction, sustainability, and disaster resilience. These collaborative research efforts will drive technological advancements and practical solutions tailored to Ukraine's needs.
- **Guest Lectures and Workshops**: Host guest lectures and workshops conducted by international experts in various fields. These sessions will provide valuable learning opportunities and foster a culture of continuous improvement and innovation .

Certification and Accreditation Programs

Ensuring Recognized Standards

Implementing robust certification and accreditation programs will ensure that training and education meet international standards and are recognized globally.

- **Professional Certifications**: Offer professional certifications in key areas such as green building, project management, and digital technologies. These certifications will enhance the employability and credibility of Ukrainian professionals on the global stage.

- **Accredited Training Providers**: Develop a network of accredited training providers that adhere to high standards of education and training. Regular audits and assessments will ensure the quality and relevance of the training programs.

- **Partnership with International Bodies**: Collaborate with international certification bodies to align Ukrainian training programs with global standards. This cooperation will facilitate mutual recognition of qualifications and support workforce mobility .

Community-Based Training and Development

Empowering Local Communities

Building local capacity through community-based training and development initiatives ensures that reconstruction efforts are inclusive and sustainable.

- **Field Training Centers**: Establish field training centers in urban and rural areas, providing hands-on training in construction, agriculture, and technology. These centers will serve as hubs for skill development tailored to local needs and conditions.

- **Training-of-Trainers Programs**: Implement training-of-trainers (ToT) programs to empower local leaders and educators to disseminate knowledge and skills within their communities. This approach will multiply the impact of training initiatives and foster community resilience.

- **Engagement of Local NGOs and CBOs**: Collaborate with local non-governmental organizations (NGOs) and community-based organizations (CBOs) to deliver training programs. These partnerships will leverage local networks and build trust within communities, ensuring successful implementation .

Conclusion

Capacity building and skill development are cornerstones of Ukraine's sustainable reconstruction. By establishing comprehensive online learning platforms, deploying immersive VR training programs, implementing AI-assisted skill-matching systems, fostering international exchanges, and delivering community-based training, Ukraine can cultivate a skilled workforce equipped to rebuild and innovate. These strategic initiatives will not only accelerate the reconstruction process but also ensure long-term economic resilience and growth, fostering a brighter future for all Ukrainians.

Section 7.3: Monitoring and Evaluation Systems

Introduction

The success of Ukraine's ambitious reconstruction efforts hinges not only on strategic planning and effective execution but also on continuous monitoring and evaluation. This section lays out a detailed framework for implementing state-of-the-art monitoring and evaluation (M&E) systems. These systems will ensure transparency, accountability, and adaptability throughout the reconstruction process, leveraging advanced technologies to provide real-time insights and facilitate evidence-based decision-making.

Deployment of IoT Sensor Networks

Real-Time Progress Monitoring

Utilizing the Internet of Things (IoT) will revolutionize how reconstruction projects are monitored, providing a constant stream of data on various parameters critical to project success.

- **Comprehensive Network of Sensors**: Establish a nationwide network of IoT sensors to track construction progress, environmental conditions, and resource utilization at every reconstruction site. These sensors will be strategically placed to cover key areas including structural integrity, environmental impact, and safety compliance.
- **Data Aggregation and Visualization**: Develop centralized platforms that aggregate sensor data and deploy advanced visualization tools. These platforms will enable project managers to monitor real-time data, identify trends, and detect anomalies. Interactive dashboards will facilitate easy access to critical metrics and support timely interventions.
- **AI-Enhanced Predictive Maintenance**: Implement AI-driven predictive maintenance systems that analyze sensor data to forecast equipment malfunctions and structural issues before they occur. This proactive approach will minimize downtime and ensure continuous progress on reconstruction projects.

AI-Driven Impact Assessment Tools

Evaluating Effectiveness and Sustainability

The integration of AI in impact assessment will provide deeper insights into the outcomes of reconstruction projects, ensuring that they meet their intended goals and contribute to long-term sustainability.

- **Machine Learning Algorithms for Impact Analysis**: Deploy machine learning algorithms to evaluate the social, economic, and environmental impacts of reconstruction initiatives. These algorithms will analyze diverse data sets, including demographic trends, economic indicators, and ecological metrics, to provide comprehensive impact assessments.

- **Scenario Planning and Simulation**: Use AI-powered tools to simulate various scenarios and their potential impacts. This capability will help planners and decision-makers test different strategies, predict outcomes, and choose the most effective path forward.

- **Regular Reporting and Feedback Loops**: Establish protocols for regular impact assessment reporting, ensuring that findings are communicated to all stakeholders. Feedback loops will be essential for adapting strategies based on real-time data and ongoing evaluation results.

Citizen Feedback Platforms

Engaging Communities in the Evaluation Process

Active citizen engagement is crucial for the accountability and responsiveness of the reconstruction efforts. Citizen feedback platforms will provide a channel for the public to contribute their perspectives and experiences.

- **Sentiment Analysis and Feedback Collection**: Develop digital platforms that use sentiment analysis to gauge public opinion on various reconstruction projects. These platforms will collect feedback through surveys, social media monitoring, and direct input, providing a comprehensive view of community sentiments.

- **Dialogue and Collaboration Tools**: Implement online forums and collaboration tools where citizens can discuss issues, share ideas, and propose solutions. These interactive platforms will foster a sense of ownership and participation among community members, ensuring that their voices are heard and considered in the decision-making process.

- **Transparency and Accountability**: Ensure that feedback collected from citizens is transparently reported and acted upon. Regular updates on how citizen input has influenced project decisions will build trust and strengthen community engagement.

Integration with National and International Standards

Aligning with Best Practices and Compliance

To ensure the highest standards of monitoring and evaluation, aligning with national and international frameworks is imperative.

- **Compliance with OECD Guidelines**: Adhere to the OECD's guidelines for good international engagement in fragile states and situations, focusing on principles of transparency, accountability, and inclusivity .

- **Adoption of Global M&E Standards**: Implement globally recognized M&E standards such as those from the UNDP and the World Bank. These standards will provide a robust framework for designing, implementing, and assessing reconstruction initiatives .

- **Collaboration with International Experts**: Engage international M&E experts to provide technical assistance, conduct independent evaluations, and share best practices. This collaboration will enhance the credibility and effectiveness of the evaluation processes.

Adaptive Frameworks for Continuous Improvement

Building Resilience and Flexibility

An adaptive monitoring and evaluation framework will ensure ongoing improvements and the ability to respond to emerging challenges and opportunities.

- **Dynamic Evaluation Models**: Develop dynamic evaluation models that can be adjusted as projects evolve. These models will account for changing conditions, new data inputs, and evolving priorities, ensuring that evaluation processes remain relevant and effective throughout the reconstruction period.

- **Continuous Learning and Adaptation**: Foster a culture of continuous learning by integrating lessons learned from ongoing evaluations into project planning and execution. Regular workshops, training sessions, and knowledge-sharing forums will support continuous improvement and innovation.

- **Benchmarking and Performance Metrics**: Establish clear benchmarks and performance metrics to measure progress against predefined goals. Regular benchmarking against these metrics will provide a clear view of achievements and areas needing improvement, driving better outcomes and accountability.

Conclusion

Implementing sophisticated monitoring and evaluation systems is essential for the success of Ukraine's reconstruction efforts. By leveraging IoT sensor networks, AI-driven impact assessment tools, and citizen feedback platforms, Ukraine can ensure that its rebuilding process is transparent, accountable, and adaptive. Aligning with international standards and fostering continuous improvement will further enhance the effectiveness and sustainability of these initiatives. This comprehensive approach will not only build a resilient infrastructure but also restore trust and hope among the Ukrainian people, paving the way for a prosperous and sustainable future.

Chapter 8: Resilience and Future-Proofing

Section 8.1: Multi-Hazard Resilience Strategies

In the reconstruction of Ukraine, fostering resilience against multiple hazards is paramount. This chapter delineates a comprehensive strategy to build cities capable of withstanding and adapting to a plethora of challenges—from natural disasters to socio-political upheavals. By integrating advanced technologies, innovative infrastructure designs, and community-driven initiatives, Ukraine can emerge stronger and more resilient.

Developing Adaptive Flood Defense Systems

Urban Flood Management

Urban areas in Ukraine are particularly vulnerable to flooding, requiring robust and adaptive flood defense strategies.

- **Real-Time Water Level Monitoring**: Deploy a nationwide network of IoT sensors to monitor water levels in real time. These sensors will be strategically placed along rivers, dams, and urban drainage systems. The data collected will feed into centralized control centers, providing instant updates and predictive analytics to preempt flood risks.

- **Dynamically Controlled Dam Systems**: Invest in adaptive dam systems capable of dynamically controlling water flow based on real-time data and predictive models. These systems will manage water levels during heavy rainfall, preventing urban flooding and reducing the risk of dam failures.

- **Green Infrastructure Integration**: Incorporate green infrastructure such as wetlands, green roofs, and permeable pavements to enhance natural water absorption and reduce surface runoff. Urban wetlands and retention ponds will serve as natural flood buffers, absorbing excess rainwater and mitigating flood impact.

Distributed Energy Storage Systems for Grid Resilience

Energy Security and Stability

Ensuring a stable energy supply is critical to the resilience of Ukrainian cities. Distributed energy storage systems can provide backup power, enhance grid reliability, and support the integration of renewable energy sources.

- **Neighborhood Microgrids**: Develop decentralized microgrids equipped with advanced energy storage solutions like lithium-ion and solid-state batteries. These microgrids will operate independently of the central grid during outages, ensuring a continuous power supply for critical infrastructure such as hospitals, emergency response centers, and water treatment facilities.

- **Second-Life Battery Integration**: Repurpose used electric vehicle (EV) batteries for grid-scale energy storage. By integrating these second-life batteries, Ukraine can create cost-effective storage solutions that stabilize the grid, store excess renewable energy, and provide emergency power during peak demand.
- **Virtual Power Plants (VPPs)**: Implement Virtual Power Plants that aggregate distributed energy resources—such as solar panels, wind turbines, and storage units—into a single, flexible operational entity. VPPs will optimize energy flow, respond to demand fluctuations, and provide grid services such as frequency regulation and load balancing.

Underground Shelter Networks

Multi-Use Facilities for Safety and Continuity

Building underground shelter networks equipped with modern amenities will provide safe havens during disasters and serve multiple community purposes.

- **Dual-Use Underground Facilities**: Design shelters that double as community centers, parking garages, or recreational facilities during normal times. These shelters should be fortified to withstand natural disasters, including earthquakes and bombings, ensuring they remain functional when needed.
- **Advanced Air Filtration Systems**: Equip underground shelters with state-of-the-art air filtration systems to protect against chemical, biological, radiological, and nuclear (CBRN) threats. These systems will ensure that air quality remains safe in emergencies, whether due to industrial accidents, terrorist attacks, or natural disasters.
- **Resource Stockpiling**: Stockpile essential resources such as food, water, medical supplies, and communication devices in these shelters. Regular audits and restocking programs will ensure that these supplies are sufficient and up-to-date, ready to support residents for extended periods.

Community-Based Hazard Preparedness Programs

Engaging Local Communities

Empowering communities with the knowledge and tools to respond to emergencies is fundamental to building resilience.

- **Resilience Training Workshops**: Conduct regular workshops and drills in local communities to educate residents on emergency preparedness, first aid, and disaster response. These workshops will build a culture of readiness and equip citizens with the skills needed to survive and assist others during crises.

- **Public Awareness Campaigns**: Launch public awareness campaigns using multimedia platforms to disseminate information on hazard risks, preparedness measures, and response actions. Engaging storytelling, local influencers, and interactive media will enhance public engagement and retention of critical information.

- **Neighborhood Resilience Committees**: Establish local resilience committees composed of community leaders, volunteers, and representatives from emergency services. These committees will coordinate preparedness activities, facilitate communication during emergencies, and act as liaisons between the public and authorities.

Advanced Early Warning Systems

Proactive Risk Management

Implementing advanced early warning systems will provide timely alerts and allow for proactive measures to mitigate the impact of disasters.

- **Multi-Hazard Early Warning Networks**: Develop integrated early warning systems that detect and alert for various hazards, including storms, floods, earthquakes, and chemical spills. These systems will utilize IoT sensors, satellite data, and AI algorithms to provide accurate and timely warnings to residents and authorities.

- **Mobile Alert Applications**: Create mobile applications that deliver real-time alerts and safety instructions to users' smartphones. These apps will use geolocation services to provide localized warnings and guide users to the nearest safe areas or shelters.

- **Public Alert Systems**: Enhance public alert systems through sirens, digital billboards, and radio broadcasts. These systems will ensure that everyone, including those without access to smartphones, receives critical information during emergencies.

Conclusion

Building a resilient Ukraine requires a multi-faceted approach that combines technological innovation, community engagement, and adaptive infrastructure. By implementing advanced flood defenses, distributed energy storage, underground shelters, community-based preparedness programs, and early warning systems, Ukraine can safeguard its citizens and ensure the continuity of its urban ecosystems. These strategies will not only respond to immediate threats but also build long-term resilience, enabling Ukraine to thrive in the face of future challenges.

Section 8.2: Cybersecurity and Digital Resilience

Introduction

In an era defined by digital transformation and increasing cyber threats, fortifying Ukraine's cybersecurity and ensuring digital resilience are paramount. These measures are not merely defensive but foundational to the sustainable reconstruction and modernization of Ukraine's urban infrastructure. This section outlines comprehensive strategies to enhance cybersecurity capabilities, integrate quantum encryption, and build self-healing networks, creating a robust digital ecosystem resilient to both cyberattacks and future technological challenges.

Building a National Cybersecurity Framework

Strategic National Cybersecurity Initiatives

Developing a robust national cybersecurity framework is essential. This framework will not only protect the nation's critical infrastructure but also establish protocols and standards for cybersecurity across all sectors.

- **Cybersecurity Task Force**: Establish a dedicated national cybersecurity task force to oversee the implementation of cybersecurity policies, coordinate responses to threats, and facilitate information sharing among government agencies, private sector entities, and international partners. This task force will act as the central body for all cybersecurity-related activities in Ukraine.

- **National Cybersecurity Strategy**: Develop and regularly update a national cybersecurity strategy that outlines the country's vision, goals, and action plans for enhancing cybersecurity measures. This strategy will address both short-term needs and long-term objectives, ensuring a proactive approach to emerging threats and technological advancements.

- **Regulatory Frameworks**: Implement regulatory frameworks that mandate cybersecurity standards for critical infrastructure sectors, including energy, transportation, healthcare, and finance. Compliance with these standards will be enforced through regular audits and assessments.

Implementing Quantum Encryption Technologies

Next-Generation Data Protection

The integration of quantum encryption technologies will revolutionize data security, making it virtually impregnable to conventional hacking methods.

- **Quantum Key Distribution (QKD)**: Deploy Quantum Key Distribution systems to secure communications across government networks, critical infrastructure, and private sector enterprises. These systems utilize the principles of quantum mechanics to generate and distribute cryptographic keys that are unbreakable by traditional and quantum computers.

- **Quantum-Safe Cryptography**: Upgrade existing cryptographic protocols to quantum-safe algorithms, ensuring that all sensitive data remains protected against future quantum computing threats. This transition will require comprehensive training programs for cybersecurity professionals to manage and implement quantum-safe solutions effectively.
- **Quantum Research and Development**: Invest in research and development of quantum technologies in collaboration with leading research institutions and international partners. Establish quantum research centers dedicated to advancing quantum computing and encryption technologies, positioning Ukraine at the forefront of technological innovation.

Developing AI-Powered Threat Detection Systems

Proactive Cyber Defense Mechanisms

AI-powered threat detection systems will enable real-time monitoring and defense against cyber threats, enhancing the proactive capabilities of Ukraine's cybersecurity infrastructure.

- **Machine Learning Algorithms**: Use advanced machine learning algorithms to analyze network traffic and detect anomalies indicative of potential cyber threats. These algorithms will continuously learn and adapt, improving their accuracy and effectiveness in threat detection over time.
- **Comprehensive Data Analytics Platforms**: Implement data analytics platforms that aggregate and analyze logs from various sources, including firewalls, servers, and endpoint devices. This centralized approach will provide a holistic view of the threat landscape and facilitate swift responses to detected threats.
- **Automated Incident Response**: Develop automated incident response systems that can take predefined actions when a threat is detected. These systems will isolate affected components, block malicious activities, and initiate recovery protocols without the need for human intervention.

Creating Self-Healing Networks

Resilient and Adaptive Infrastructure

Self-healing networks will ensure continuous operation and rapid recovery from cyberattacks or technical failures, significantly enhancing the resilience of Ukraine's digital infrastructure.

- **Autonomous Network Management**: Implement autonomous network management systems that can detect and repair faults automatically.

These systems will monitor network health in real-time, diagnose issues, and apply corrections without human oversight, minimizing downtime and maintaining network integrity.

- **Distributed Ledger Technology (DLT)**: Use distributed ledger technology (DLT) to create immutable records of network configurations and activities. This technology will enhance transparency and trust, ensuring that all changes and transactions within the network are securely documented and traceable.

- **Redundancy and Failover Mechanisms**: Design networks with built-in redundancy and failover mechanisms to ensure that critical services remain operational during cyberattacks or system failures. These mechanisms will dynamically reroute traffic and activate backup systems to maintain service continuity.

Enhancing Cybersecurity Workforce and Education

Building a Skilled and Resilient Workforce

A skilled and knowledgeable workforce is vital to the success of any cybersecurity initiative.

- **Comprehensive Training Programs**: Develop comprehensive training programs for cybersecurity professionals, focusing on advanced topics such as quantum encryption, AI in cybersecurity, and incident response. These programs should be accessible through online platforms and in-person workshops.

- **Cybersecurity Certifications**: Establish certification programs in collaboration with international certification bodies to ensure that cybersecurity professionals meet globally recognized standards. These certifications will validate skills and knowledge, enhancing the credibility and employability of Ukrainian professionals.

- **Public Awareness Campaigns**: Launch public awareness campaigns to educate citizens about cybersecurity best practices. These campaigns will emphasize the importance of strong passwords, safe online behaviors, and the recognition of phishing and other common cyber threats.

International Collaboration and Partnerships

Global Cybersecurity Alliances

International collaboration is critical to enhancing Ukraine's cybersecurity capabilities and staying ahead of evolving threats.

- **Bilateral and Multilateral Agreements**: Forge bilateral and multilateral agreements with other nations to collaborate on cybersecurity initiatives. These agreements will facilitate information sharing, joint threat intelligence operations, and coordinated responses to international cyber threats .

- **Participation in Global Forums**: Actively participate in global cybersecurity forums and organizations such as the Global Forum on Cyber Expertise (GFCE) and the International Telecommunication Union (ITU). These platforms provide opportunities for knowledge exchange, capacity building, and the development of global cybersecurity standards.
- **Cybersecurity Research Networks**: Establish international research networks dedicated to advancing cybersecurity technologies and practices. These networks will bring together experts from academia, industry, and government to collaborate on cutting-edge research and innovation.

Conclusion

Strengthening Ukraine's cybersecurity and digital resilience is not just a technical necessity but a strategic imperative for national security and sustainable development. By developing a robust national cybersecurity framework, implementing quantum encryption technologies, deploying AI-powered threat detection systems, creating self-healing networks, and enhancing cybersecurity education, Ukraine can build a digital fortress capable of withstanding the cyber challenges of today and tomorrow. These initiatives will ensure that Ukraine's digital infrastructure is secure, resilient, and primed for ongoing innovation and growth. Through international collaboration and a commitment to continuous improvement, Ukraine will emerge as a global leader in cybersecurity and digital resilience.

Section 8.3: Social Cohesion and Community Resilience

Introduction

The strength of a nation lies in the resilience and cohesion of its communities. As Ukraine embarks on the path of reconstruction, fostering social cohesion and community resilience becomes a cornerstone for sustainable development. This section outlines strategies to rebuild the social fabric, promote inclusivity, and empower communities to withstand future challenges, ensuring that the rebuilt Ukraine is not only physically strong but also socially integrated and resilient.

Establishing Time Banks and Skill-Sharing Platforms

Empowering Communities through Exchange

Time banks and skill-sharing platforms offer innovative ways to rebuild social capital and foster community cooperation.

- **Time Banks**: Implement time banks where community members can exchange services based on time rather than money. For example, an hour of teaching someone a skill could be exchanged for an hour of childcare.

Time banks encourage mutual aid and build trust within communities, strengthening social bonds.
- **Skill-Sharing Platforms**: Develop online and offline platforms that facilitate the sharing of skills and knowledge among community members. These platforms can support a wide range of activities, from professional training and educational workshops to cultural exchanges and hobby groups. This initiative will harness the diverse talents of the community, promoting continuous learning and collaboration.

Developing Mixed-Reality Community Spaces

Innovative Spaces for Interaction and Support

Creating mixed-reality community spaces will blend physical and virtual environments, offering new avenues for social interaction, support, and engagement.

- **Physical Community Centers**: Establish multifunctional community centers equipped with the latest technology, including augmented reality (AR) and virtual reality (VR) capabilities. These centers will serve as hubs for social activities, educational programs, and cultural events, fostering a sense of belonging and unity.
- **Virtual Spaces**: Develop virtual community spaces where members can interact, share experiences, and participate in communal activities regardless of physical location. These spaces can host virtual town halls, support groups, and collaborative projects, ensuring that no one is isolated.

Implementing Gamified Community Resilience Training Programs

Engaging and Educating through Gamification

Gamified training programs will make learning about resilience fun and engaging, enhancing community preparedness and response capabilities.

- **Resilience Training Games**: Create interactive games that simulate various emergency scenarios, teaching community members how to respond effectively. These games can cover a range of topics, including first aid, evacuation procedures, and resource management during disasters.
- **Community Challenges**: Organize community-wide challenges that encourage participants to complete resilience-building activities. These challenges can include emergency drills, neighborhood cleanup projects, and collaborative planning exercises. Rewards and recognition for participation will motivate community engagement and foster a culture of preparedness.

Inclusive and Participatory Governance

Ensuring Community Voices Are Heard

Inclusive and participatory governance practices will empower communities to take an active role in the reconstruction process, ensuring that all voices are heard and considered.

- **Participatory Planning Workshops**: Conduct regular workshops where community members can contribute to planning and decision-making processes. These workshops will address various aspects of reconstruction, from urban design and housing to public services and environmental management.
- **Local Planning Committees**: Establish local planning committees that include representatives from different segments of the community, including marginalized groups. These committees will work closely with government authorities and planners to ensure that reconstruction efforts are inclusive and equitable .

Promoting Social Cohesion through Community Programs

Building Stronger, More United Communities

Community programs focused on rebuilding social cohesion will help heal divisions and foster a unified national identity.

- **Cultural and Recreational Activities**: Organize cultural events, sports tournaments, and recreational activities that bring together people from different backgrounds. These activities will provide opportunities for social interaction, cultural exchange, and mutual understanding.
- **Intergenerational Projects**: Develop projects that encourage interaction between different age groups, such as mentorship programs, storytelling sessions, and collaborative arts projects. These initiatives will bridge generational gaps, preserving cultural heritage and fostering mutual respect.

Citizen Feedback Mechanisms

Ensuring Accountability and Continuous Improvement

Robust citizen feedback mechanisms will ensure that community needs and concerns are addressed, promoting transparency and accountability in the reconstruction process.

- **Feedback Platforms**: Develop digital platforms where citizens can provide feedback on reconstruction projects and public services. These platforms will utilize user-friendly interfaces and mobile accessibility to reach a wide audience.
- **Regular Consultations**: Hold regular town hall meetings and public consultations to gather input and report on progress. These forums will

provide a space for dialogue between citizens, government officials, and other stakeholders, fostering a collaborative approach to rebuilding.

Supporting Vulnerable Populations

Targeted Assistance for Those in Need

Special attention must be given to vulnerable populations to ensure that everyone benefits from reconstruction efforts.

- **Tailored Support Programs**: Implement support programs designed for specific vulnerable groups, such as people with disabilities, elderly residents, and families with young children. These programs will provide targeted assistance, including accessible housing, healthcare services, and educational opportunities.

- **Community-Based Services**: Enhance community-based services that address the needs of vulnerable populations. This includes mobile healthcare units, home visit programs, and community support networks that offer personalized care and assistance 8:0†source .

Conclusion

Rebuilding social cohesion and community resilience is fundamental to the sustainable reconstruction of Ukraine. By establishing time banks and skill-sharing platforms, developing mixed-reality community spaces, implementing gamified training programs, and promoting inclusive governance, Ukraine can strengthen the social fabric of its communities. These initiatives, combined with robust feedback mechanisms and targeted support for vulnerable populations, will ensure that the new Ukraine is a cohesive, resilient, and inclusive society. This holistic approach will not only address immediate recovery needs but also build a foundation for enduring social stability and unity.

Chapter 9: Technology Integration

Section 9.1: Smart City Technologies

Smart City Vision for Post-War Ukraine

In the transformation journey towards a resilient and innovative Ukraine, integrating smart city technologies is paramount. These technologies will not only streamline urban management but also enhance the quality of life for all citizens. This section presents a comprehensive plan to deploy cutting-edge smart city solutions, redeveloping urban infrastructure with intelligence, efficiency, and sustainability as cornerstones.

Implementing IoT and Data-Driven Solutions

Harnessing the Power of the Internet of Things (IoT)

IoT is the backbone of smart city technologies, enabling interconnected systems that communicate and function autonomously.

- **IoT-Enabled Urban Management**: Deploying IoT sensors across the city will facilitate real-time monitoring and management of urban infrastructure. These sensors will be placed on streets, buildings, utilities, and public spaces to collect data on traffic patterns, air quality, energy usage, and more.

- **Adaptive Traffic Management**: Implement smart traffic management systems that use IoT data to optimize traffic flow, reduce congestion, and improve public transportation efficiency. These systems will dynamically adjust traffic signals and provide live updates to commuters through mobile apps and digital displays.

- **Smart Grids for Energy Efficiency**: Install smart grids equipped with IoT devices to monitor and manage energy consumption in real-time. These grids will integrate renewable energy sources, optimize distribution, and balance demand, reducing energy costs and environmental impact.

Developing Integrated Digital Platforms

Unified City Management through Digital Platforms

Creating integrated digital platforms will streamline government services, improve citizen engagement, and enhance transparency.

- **City-Wide Digital Twin**: Develop a digital twin of the city—a comprehensive, virtual replica that simulates all physical and social elements. This digital twin will be instrumental in planning, monitoring, and managing urban operations, providing a real-time, interactive dashboard for city administrators.

- **Online Public Services**: Establish a unified digital platform for public services, where citizens can access government services online, including applications for permits, tax payments, and public records. This platform will simplify bureaucratic processes, increase accessibility, and improve service delivery.

Leveraging Big Data and AI for Urban Planning

Data-Driven Decision Making

Harnessing big data and AI will revolutionize urban planning and decision-making processes, making them more informed, efficient, and proactive.

- **Urban Data Analytics Hub**: Create an urban data analytics hub that consolidates data from various sources, including IoT sensors, public services, and citizen feedback. Advanced analytics tools and AI algorithms will process this data to generate actionable insights for urban planners, policymakers, and developers.
- **Predictive Urban Modeling**: Implement predictive modeling tools that use big data and AI to forecast urban growth, infrastructure needs, and environmental impacts. These models will simulate different scenarios, helping planners to optimize land use, allocate resources effectively, and plan sustainable development projects.

Enhancing Connectivity and Cybersecurity

Building Robust and Secure Networks

Ensuring high-speed connectivity and robust cybersecurity is essential for the functioning of smart cities.

- **6G Network Deployment**: Roll out advanced 6G networks to provide ultra-fast, reliable connectivity across urban areas. These networks will support the massive data exchange required by IoT devices, autonomous vehicles, and other smart city technologies.
- **Quantum-Encrypted Communication**: Deploy quantum encryption technologies to secure communications within the city's digital infrastructure. Quantum encryption ensures the highest level of data protection, safeguarding critical information from cyber threats.

Smart Public Spaces and Infrastructure

Innovating Urban Landscapes

Transforming public spaces with smart technologies will enhance urban living and sustainability.

- **Smart Poles and Lighting**: Install smart poles equipped with multifunctional capabilities, including 5G connectivity, environmental sensors, and EV charging stations. Smart lighting systems will adjust brightness based on real-time conditions, improving energy efficiency and public safety.
- **Intelligent Waste Management**: Implement IoT-based waste management systems to monitor trash levels in real-time, optimize collection routes, and reduce operational costs. These systems will ensure cleaner urban environments and promote recycling and sustainable waste practices.

Encouraging Innovation and Community Engagement

Fostering a Culture of Innovation

Promoting innovation and engaging the community are crucial for the success of smart city initiatives.

- **Innovation Hubs and Start-Up Incubators**: Establish innovation hubs and incubators to support start-ups and tech firms working on smart city solutions. These spaces will provide resources, mentorship, and funding opportunities to foster innovation and drive economic growth.
- **Citizen Participation Platforms**: Develop digital platforms for citizen participation, enabling residents to provide feedback, participate in decision-making, and collaborate on community projects. These platforms will empower citizens, foster transparency, and build a smarter, more inclusive city.

Conclusion

Integrating smart city technologies is pivotal to ushering in a new era of urban living in Ukraine. By deploying IoT solutions, creating integrated digital platforms, leveraging big data and AI, enhancing connectivity and cybersecurity, innovating public spaces, and encouraging community engagement, Ukraine can rebuild its cities into modern, resilient, and liveable spaces for all. This comprehensive approach will not only address immediate reconstruction needs but also pave the way for sustainable development and innovation, positioning Ukraine as a leader in smart urban transformation.

References

- **Government and International Guidelines**:
  - Global Facility for Disaster Reduction and Recovery (GFDRR) guidelines on post-disaster needs assessment.
  - World Bank's "Building Back Better: Achieving Resilience through Stronger, Faster, and More Inclusive Post-Disaster Reconstruction."
  - UN-Habitat's "Sustainable Housing Reconstruction in the Context of Climate Change."
  - ITU's "United for Smart Sustainable Cities."
- **Case Studies and Examples**:
  - Singapore's Smart Nation initiative.
  - Medellín's transformation through social urbanism.
  - Germany's "Building to COP26" report from the World Green Building Council.

Note: Make sure to properly cite the references and adapt them according to specific sections to maintain a coherent and persuasive narrative.

Section 9.2: Digital Public Services

As Ukraine rebuilds, integrating digital public services is key to creating an efficient, transparent, and modern governance system. These services will play a crucial role in ensuring accessible, responsive, and citizen-centric administration. This section outlines a comprehensive plan to implement digital public services, leveraging cutting-edge technologies and best practices to streamline government operations, enhance citizen engagement, and rebuild trust in public institutions.

Unified Digital Government Platform

Centralized Access to Services

Creating a unified digital government platform will centralize access to all public services, making interactions with government agencies seamless and efficient.

- **Single Sign-On (SSO)**: Develop a Single Sign-On system that allows citizens to access all government services through one secure login. This unified system will simplify the user experience, reduce login fatigue, and enhance security by minimizing the number of credentials that require management.

- **Integrated Services Portal**: Establish an integrated online portal where citizens can access various services such as tax filing, business registration, social benefits, and more. This portal will feature user-friendly navigation, responsive design, and multilingual support to cater to the diverse needs of Ukrainian citizens.

- **Mobile Accessibility**: Ensure that all digital services are mobile-friendly to increase accessibility. The development of mobile applications will provide additional convenience and functionality, enabling citizens to interact with government services on the go.

Blockchain-Enabled Public Records and Transactions

Ensuring Transparency and Trust

Blockchain technology will revolutionize the way public records and transactions are managed, ensuring transparency, security, and immutability.

- **Blockchain-Based Land Registry**: Implement a blockchain-based land registry system to manage property records. This system will guarantee the authenticity and integrity of property transactions, reducing fraud and disputes over land ownership .

- **Digital Identity Management**: Develop a blockchain-enabled digital identity system that securely stores citizens' identity information. This system will provide a tamper-proof digital ID, streamlining verification processes for various public and private sector services.

- **Transparent Procurement Process**: Utilize blockchain for public procurement to ensure transparent and fair bidding processes. This system will record all procurement activities on an immutable ledger, preventing corruption and ensuring accountability .

AI-Powered Public Service Delivery

Enhancing Efficiency and Responsiveness

Artificial Intelligence (AI) will enhance public service delivery by automating routine tasks, enabling predictive analytics, and providing personalized citizen services.

- **AI Chatbots and Virtual Assistants**: Deploy AI-powered chatbots and virtual assistants to handle routine inquiries and service requests. These systems will provide instant responses, freeing up human resources for more complex tasks and streamlining service delivery.
- **Predictive Analytics for Social Services**: Implement AI-driven predictive analytics to identify citizens in need of social services, such as unemployment benefits or healthcare support. This proactive approach will ensure timely assistance and improve the allocation of resources.
- **Personalized Service Recommendations**: Use AI algorithms to analyze citizen data and provide personalized service recommendations. These tailored suggestions will enhance the relevance and effectiveness of public services, improving citizen satisfaction.

E-Governance and Open Data Initiatives

Promoting Transparency and Citizen Engagement

E-governance and open data initiatives will promote transparency, foster citizen engagement, and enable data-driven decision-making.

- **Open Data Platforms**: Develop open data platforms that provide public access to government datasets, including budget allocations, spending, public policies, and more. These platforms will enable researchers, journalists, and citizens to analyze and utilize the data, fostering transparency and accountability.
- **Participatory Budgeting**: Implement e-governance tools that allow citizens to participate in the budgeting process. Citizens can propose projects, vote on funding allocations, and track the implementation of approved projects, ensuring that public spending aligns with community needs and priorities.
- **Feedback and Grievance Redressal Systems**: Create digital platforms for collecting citizen feedback and addressing grievances. These systems will use data analytics to identify common issues, prioritize responses,

and monitor the resolution of complaints, enhancing trust in government responsiveness.

Cybersecurity and Data Protection

Safeguarding Public Services

Ensuring the cybersecurity and data protection of digital public services is critical to maintaining public trust and service continuity.

- **Comprehensive Cybersecurity Framework**: Develop a comprehensive cybersecurity framework that includes policies, guidelines, and best practices for protecting digital public services. This framework will address threat detection, incident response, and data recovery, ensuring resilience against cyber threats.

- **End-to-End Encryption**: Implement end-to-end encryption for all digital communications and transactions involving public services. This measure will protect sensitive information from unauthorized access and data breaches.

- **Regular Security Audits**: Conduct regular security audits and vulnerability assessments of digital public services. These audits will identify potential security gaps and ensure that protective measures are up-to-date and effective.

Capacity Building for Digital Transformation

Empowering Public Sector Employees

Capacity building initiatives are essential for equipping public sector employees with the skills and knowledge required for the digital transformation of public services.

- **Training Programs**: Develop comprehensive training programs on digital literacy, cybersecurity, and the use of AI and blockchain technologies. These programs will ensure that public sector employees are well-equipped to manage and operate digital public services effectively.

- **Change Management**: Implement change management strategies to support the transition to digital public services. These strategies will address resistance to change, provide clear communication of goals and benefits, and offer support throughout the transformation process.

- **Collaborative Networks**: Establish collaborative networks that connect public sector employees with tech experts, researchers, and peers from other countries. These networks will facilitate knowledge exchange, best practices sharing, and continuous learning.

Conclusion

Integrating digital public services is a transformative step in Ukraine's reconstruction journey. By developing a unified digital government platform, leveraging blockchain technology, deploying AI-powered service delivery, and promoting e-governance and open data initiatives, Ukraine can create a modern, efficient, and transparent public administration. Ensuring robust cybersecurity and building capacity for digital transformation will further cement these efforts, enabling Ukraine to rebuild not just its infrastructure but also trust in its public institutions. These digital innovations will play a crucial role in shaping a resilient, inclusive, and sustainable future for Ukraine.

Section 9.3: Data Analytics for Urban Planning

The Transformative Power of Data Analytics

In the grand endeavor to rebuild Ukraine, data analytics stands as a cornerstone for informed decision-making and strategic planning. This section explores how harnessing the power of data can transform urban planning, making Ukrainian cities more efficient, resilient, and sustainable. By leveraging big data, predictive analytics, and AI-driven insights, Ukraine can navigate the complexities of reconstruction with precision and foresight.

Establishing Urban Data Platforms

Centralized Data Repositories

Creating centralized urban data platforms is crucial for consolidating diverse data sources and enabling comprehensive analysis.

- **Data Integration**: Develop platforms that aggregate data from various sources, including satellite imagery, IoT sensors, public records, and citizen feedback. These repositories will provide a holistic view of urban dynamics, supporting informed decision-making.
- **Interoperable Systems**: Ensure that data platforms are interoperable, allowing seamless data exchange between different governmental departments and agencies. This integration will break down silos, fostering collaborative efforts in urban planning and development 17:4†source 17:4†source .

Leveraging Big Data and Predictive Analytics

From Data to Actionable Insights

Big data and predictive analytics will enable urban planners to anticipate challenges, optimize resource allocation, and enhance service delivery.

- **Predictive Modeling for Urban Growth**: Use predictive analytics to model future urban growth, identifying areas that will require infrastructure upgrades, new housing developments, and expanded public services. These models will help planners allocate resources efficiently and avoid bottlenecks in urban expansion.

- **Risk and Impact Assessment**: Implement AI-driven risk assessment tools that analyze historical data to predict the impact of natural disasters, economic changes, and population shifts. These assessments will guide the development of resilient urban infrastructure and disaster preparedness plans.

- **Traffic and Mobility Management**: Utilize data from traffic sensors, public transportation systems, and mobile apps to optimize traffic flow and reduce congestion. Predictive analytics will help in designing efficient transportation networks that accommodate future mobility demands 17:4†source .

Advanced Scenario Planning and Simulation

Digital Twins for Urban Resilience

Creating digital twins of cities will revolutionize urban planning by providing a dynamic, real-time replica of urban environments.

- **Virtual Urban Models**: Develop digital twins that simulate urban infrastructure, environmental conditions, and social dynamics. These models will allow planners to test various scenarios, from natural disaster responses to urban development projects, ensuring that plans are robust and adaptive.

- **Scenario Simulations**: Conduct advanced scenario planning using digital twins to evaluate the effectiveness of different strategies. Simulations will provide insights into potential outcomes, helping planners make data-driven decisions that enhance urban resilience and sustainability 17:4†source 17:4†source .

Data-Driven Infrastructure Management

Optimizing Urban Infrastructure

Data analytics will play a pivotal role in managing and maintaining urban infrastructure, ensuring it meets the needs of a growing population.

- **Infrastructure Monitoring**: Implement real-time monitoring systems that collect data on the condition of roads, bridges, utilities, and public buildings. Predictive maintenance algorithms will analyze this data to identify maintenance needs before issues become critical, reducing downtime and repair costs.

- **Energy and Resource Efficiency**: Use data analytics to optimize the consumption and distribution of energy and resources. Smart grids, water management systems, and waste management solutions will be fine-tuned based on data insights, enhancing efficiency and reducing environmental impact.

- **Public Health and Safety**: Develop data-driven public health initiatives by analyzing health records, environmental data, and social determinants of health. Predictive models will help in planning healthcare services, managing pandemics, and addressing public health challenges proactively 17:4†source .

Enhancing Citizen Engagement through Data

Participatory Planning and Feedback Loops

Engaging citizens in urban planning processes through data-driven platforms will enhance transparency, inclusivity, and community trust.

- **Interactive Data Dashboards**: Create interactive dashboards that present urban data in an accessible format for citizens. These dashboards will enable residents to explore data on city services, environmental conditions, and ongoing projects, fostering informed participation.

- **Crowdsourced Data Collection**: Develop mobile applications and online platforms that allow citizens to report issues, provide feedback, and contribute local data. These crowdsourced insights will enrich urban data repositories and ensure that plans reflect community needs and preferences.

- **Feedback and Improvement Cycles**: Establish feedback mechanisms where citizen input is analyzed and integrated into urban planning processes. Regular updates on how feedback has influenced decisions will build trust and encourage continued engagement 17:4†source 17:4†source .

Data Governance and Privacy Considerations

Ethical and Secure Data Practices

Ensuring ethical and secure management of urban data is essential to protect citizen privacy and build public trust.

- **Data Governance Frameworks**: Develop comprehensive data governance frameworks that outline policies for data collection, storage, sharing, and usage. These frameworks will ensure that data practices comply with legal standards and ethical guidelines.

- **Privacy Protection Mechanisms**: Implement robust privacy protection mechanisms, including data anonymization, encryption, and access controls. Transparency in data practices and clear communication of privacy policies will reassure citizens that their data is handled responsibly.

- **Ethical Use of AI**: Establish ethics committees to oversee the use of AI and data analytics in urban planning. These committees will address concerns related to bias, fairness, and the societal impact of AI-driven decisions, ensuring that technologies serve all citizens equitably 17:4†source .

Conclusion

The integration of data analytics into urban planning is transformative, enabling Ukraine to rebuild its cities with intelligence, precision, and resilience. By establishing urban data platforms, leveraging big data and predictive analytics, creating digital twins, and fostering citizen engagement, Ukraine can ensure that its urban planning processes are data-driven and future-proof. Ethical data governance and privacy considerations will further enhance trust and transparency, paving the way for sustainable and inclusive urban development. Through these innovative approaches, Ukraine will not only restore but also reimagine its urban landscapes for a brighter, more resilient future.

Chapter 10: Housing Reconstruction

Section 10.1: Temporary Housing

Introduction

In the immediate aftermath of conflict, ensuring that displaced populations have access to safe, secure, and dignified temporary housing is paramount. Ukraine faces the daunting task of providing immediate shelter to millions while laying the groundwork for a resilient and sustainable future. This section presents a comprehensive blueprint for developing temporary housing solutions that are rapid to deploy, adaptable, and environmentally sustainable.

Emergency Shelters with Advanced 3D Printing

Rapid Deployment of 3D-Printed Shelters

In the critical hours and days following displacement, speed is of the essence. Harnessing the power of advanced 3D printing technologies can facilitate the rapid deployment of durable shelters.

- **Local Material Utilization**: Use locally sourced materials such as concrete and recycled materials to 3D-print emergency shelters on-site. This approach not only accelerates construction but also reduces transportation costs and environmental impact .
- **Modular Design**: Design shelters with modular components that can be quickly printed and assembled. Modular shelters offer flexibility, allowing for easy expansion or modification based on the needs of the displaced populations.

- **Energy-Efficient Systems**: Integrate solar panels and energy-efficient systems into the design of 3D-printed shelters. These systems will provide off-grid power solutions, ensuring that shelters are self-sufficient and reducing the burden on local infrastructure.

Conversion of Vacant Buildings into Temporary Housing

Adaptive Reuse of Existing Structures

Another critical strategy for rapidly creating temporary housing is the adaptive reuse of existing vacant buildings. This approach maximizes the use of existing resources and infrastructure, offering a quicker transition to safe housing for displaced individuals.

- **Comprehensive Assessment**: Conduct thorough assessments of potential buildings, such as schools, office buildings, and warehouses, to ensure they meet safety and habitability standards. Use advanced diagnostic tools to evaluate structural integrity and necessary retrofits.
- **IoT-Enabled Resource Management**: Implement IoT technology to manage resources and monitor conditions within converted buildings. Automated systems will optimize lighting, heating, and cooling, ensuring comfort and efficiency while reducing operational costs .
- **Community Integration**: Repurpose buildings to include communal facilities such as kitchens, healthcare clinics, and recreational areas, fostering a sense of community and providing essential services within close proximity.

Development of Smart Refugee Camps

Innovative and Sustainable Refugee Camps

Building smart refugee camps equipped with modern technologies will enhance the living conditions and security of displaced populations.

- **Smart Infrastructure**: Deploy IoT-enabled infrastructure to manage water, sanitation, energy, and waste. Sensors will monitor resource usage and environmental conditions, ensuring efficient management and quick responses to issues.
- **Integrated Health Monitoring**: Establish health monitoring systems equipped with telemedicine capabilities to provide continuous healthcare access. These systems will track health metrics and alert medical professionals to potential outbreaks or health concerns, ensuring timely intervention.
- **Education and Skill Development**: Integrate educational facilities within camps, utilizing digital learning platforms to provide uninterrupted education for children and skill development programs for adults. Access

to education and training will empower residents and prepare them for eventual reintegration into society .

Sustainable Designs and Materials

Eco-Friendly and Durable Housing Solutions

Sustainability is a critical component of temporary housing solutions, ensuring that they are not only expedient but also environmentally responsible.

- **Recycled and Biodegradable Materials**: Use recycled and biodegradable materials for construction to minimize environmental impact. These materials should be durable and suited to the local climate, providing long-term shelter without excessive waste.

- **Renewable Energy Integration**: Equip temporary housing units with renewable energy sources such as solar panels and wind turbines. These systems will provide reliable and sustainable power, reducing the reliance on fossil fuels and enhancing energy resilience.

- **Water and Waste Management**: Implement systems for rainwater harvesting and waste-to-energy conversion. These systems will ensure that camps are self-sustainable, reducing their ecological footprint and supporting environmental health.

International Cooperation and Coordination

Leveraging Global Support and Expertise

Effective international cooperation is vital for the successful implementation of temporary housing solutions. Coordination with international organizations, NGOs, and donor countries will ensure efficient resource allocation and expertise sharing.

- **Donor Coordination Mechanisms**: Establish mechanisms for coordinating international aid and investments. Utilize platforms that ensure transparency and accountability, facilitating trust and maximizing the impact of resources provided by global partners .

- **Knowledge Transfer and Capacity Building**: Collaborate with international experts to transfer knowledge and build local capacities in areas such as construction, resource management, and humanitarian response. Training programs and workshops will empower local stakeholders to manage and maintain temporary housing solutions effectively.

- **Funding and Resource Mobilization**: Mobilize funding from international donors, financial institutions, and private sector partners. Develop comprehensive fundraising strategies, showcasing the humanitarian impact and long-term benefits of temporary housing initiatives to attract sustained financial support.

Community-Centric Approaches

Engaging and Empowering Local Communities

Involving the affected communities in the planning and implementation of temporary housing projects ensures that solutions are tailored to their needs and fosters a sense of ownership and resilience.

- **Participatory Planning**: Engage community members in the planning process through workshops, consultations, and feedback mechanisms. This inclusive approach ensures that housing solutions reflect the preferences and priorities of the displaced populations.

- **Empowerment Programs**: Develop programs to empower residents, such as leadership training, community governance structures, and self-help groups. These programs will build capacity within the camps, enabling residents to take proactive roles in managing their living environment.

- **Cultural Sensitivity**: Ensure that housing designs and community structures respect local cultures and traditions. Cultural sensitivity in the development process will enhance acceptance and integration, promoting social cohesion and well-being.

Conclusion

The implementation of innovative and sustainable temporary housing solutions is a critical step in Ukraine's journey towards recovery and resilience. By leveraging advanced technologies such as 3D printing, IoT-enabled systems, and renewable energy, Ukraine can provide immediate, dignified, and environmentally responsible shelter for its displaced populations. International cooperation, community engagement, and sustainable practices will ensure that these solutions are effective, scalable, and aligned with the long-term goals of rebuilding a resilient and vibrant Ukraine .

Section 10.2: Permanent Housing

Introduction

As Ukraine transitions from immediate stabilization to long-term recovery, the development of permanent housing solutions becomes a critical focus. This section outlines a comprehensive strategy to design and construct energy-efficient, resilient housing units that adhere to modern urban planning principles. These efforts aim to create sustainable neighborhoods capable of providing safety, comfort, and resilience to future challenges for all Ukrainian citizens.

Energy-Efficient Residential Buildings

Designing for Sustainability and Efficiency

Permanent housing initiatives must prioritize energy efficiency to reduce operational costs and environmental impact, thus contributing to Ukraine's broader sustainability goals.

- **Passive Design Strategies**: Implement passive design strategies in residential buildings to maximize natural lighting and ventilation. This includes optimal building orientation, thermal mass utilization, and incorporation of large windows to reduce reliance on artificial lighting and air conditioning.
- **High-Performance Insulation**: Use high-performance insulation materials, such as aerogels and phase-change materials, to enhance the thermal efficiency of buildings. These materials will keep homes warmer in winter and cooler in summer, reducing energy consumption for heating and cooling.
- **Renewable Energy Systems**: Integrate renewable energy systems, such as solar panels, wind turbines, and geothermal heat pumps, into residential buildings. These systems will provide sustainable power and heating, contributing to energy independence and reduced carbon footprints.

Resilient Housing Designs

Building for Safety and Durability

Incorporating resilience into housing designs will ensure that homes can withstand natural disasters and other challenges, providing long-term safety and security for residents.

- **Earthquake-Resistant Structures**: Develop housing units with earthquake-resistant designs, utilizing flexible foundations, shear walls, and advanced materials like carbon fiber reinforcements. These structures will minimize damage during seismic events and protect inhabitants.
- **Flood-Resilient Construction**: Implement flood-resilient construction techniques in areas prone to flooding. Elevated foundations, waterproof materials, and effective drainage systems will prevent water ingress and damage, ensuring housing durability in adverse conditions.
- **Fire-Resistant Materials**: Use fire-resistant materials, such as concrete, steel, and fire-retardant treated wood, in the construction of homes. These materials will enhance the safety of buildings, reducing the spread of fires and protecting lives and property.

Community-Focused Urban Planning

Creating Sustainable and Livable Neighborhoods

Permanent housing development must adopt a holistic approach to urban planning, ensuring that neighborhoods are not only functional but also vibrant and inclusive.

- **Mixed-Use Developments**: Develop mixed-use neighborhoods that integrate residential, commercial, and recreational spaces. This approach promotes walkability, reduces commuting times, and fosters community interaction, creating a more dynamic urban environment.

- **Green Spaces and Biodiversity Corridors**: Incorporate ample green spaces and biodiversity corridors into urban designs. Parks, community gardens, and green rooftops will provide residents with recreational opportunities, improve air quality, and support urban biodiversity.

- **Public Transportation Accessibility**: Ensure that new residential areas are well-connected to public transportation networks. Proximity to bus stops, train stations, and cycling paths will encourage the use of sustainable transportation options, reducing traffic congestion and emissions.

Smart Housing Technologies

Leveraging Technology for Modern Living

Integrating smart technologies into housing units will enhance comfort, security, and energy efficiency, transforming homes into intelligent living spaces.

- **Smart Home Systems**: Install smart home systems that allow residents to control lighting, heating, security, and appliances through mobile apps or voice commands. These systems will optimize energy use, improve convenience, and enhance home security.

- **Internet of Things (IoT) Integration**: Utilize IoT devices to monitor and manage home environments. Smart thermostats, water sensors, and energy meters will provide real-time data and analytics, enabling residents to make informed decisions about resource consumption.

- **AI-Assisted Maintenance**: Implement AI-assisted maintenance systems that predict and alert residents to potential issues before they become critical. These systems will track the condition of structural components and appliances, scheduling maintenance tasks to prevent costly repairs and extend the lifespan of housing units.

Financial Strategies for Housing Development

Securing Investments and Funding

Effective financial strategies are essential to support the large-scale development of permanent housing projects.

- **Public-Private Partnerships (PPPs)**: Encourage public-private partnerships to mobilize resources and expertise from both the government and private sector. These collaborations will share risks and benefits, ensuring efficient project delivery and sustainable outcomes.

- **Affordable Housing Programs**: Develop affordable housing programs that provide financial assistance, subsidies, and incentives to low-income families and vulnerable populations. These programs will ensure that all citizens have access to safe and secure housing.
- **International Funding and Grants**: Leverage international funding and grants from organizations such as the European Union, World Bank, and United Nations. These funds will support large-scale housing projects, enabling the reconstruction of resilient communities.

Regulatory and Policy Frameworks

Ensuring Compliance and Quality

Establishing robust regulatory and policy frameworks will ensure that housing development meets high standards of quality, safety, and sustainability.

- **Building Codes and Standards**: Develop and enforce stringent building codes and standards that incorporate best practices for energy efficiency, resilience, and sustainability. Regular inspections and compliance checks will ensure adherence to these standards.
- **Incentives for Green Building**: Provide incentives for developers to adopt green building practices, such as tax breaks, grants, and expedited permitting processes. These incentives will encourage the construction of environmentally friendly and energy-efficient housing.
- **Community Engagement in Policy Making**: Involve local communities in the development of housing policies and plans. Public consultations, workshops, and feedback channels will ensure that policies reflect the needs and preferences of residents, promoting buy-in and support for housing projects.

Conclusion

The development of permanent housing is a vital component of Ukraine's reconstruction strategy, aiming to provide safe, resilient, and sustainable homes for its citizens. By focusing on energy efficiency, resilient designs, community-focused urban planning, smart technologies, and robust financial and regulatory frameworks, Ukraine can rebuild its housing infrastructure to meet the highest standards of quality and sustainability. These efforts will not only address the immediate housing needs but also lay the foundation for a prosperous and resilient future .

Section 10.3: Sustainable Neighborhoods

Introduction

In the grand vision of rebuilding Ukraine, the development of sustainable neighborhoods is essential. These neighborhoods will not only provide a high quality of life for residents but also embody principles of environmental stewardship, social cohesion, and economic resilience. This section lays out a comprehensive strategy for creating neighborhoods that are self-sustaining, vibrant, and adaptable to future challenges.

Integrated Green Spaces and Biodiversity

Creating Green Urban Sanctuaries

The integration of green spaces and biodiversity corridors is fundamental to the sustainability and livability of neighborhoods. These spaces enhance the environment, provide recreational areas, and support urban biodiversity.

- **Urban Forests and Parks**: Develop extensive urban forests and parks that serve as green lungs for neighborhoods. These areas will provide recreational spaces, improve air quality, and support local wildlife. Implement tree-planting programs focusing on native species to enhance biodiversity and ecosystem resilience.

- **Community Gardens and Urban Agriculture**: Encourage the development of community gardens and urban agriculture. These spaces will not only provide fresh produce for residents but also foster community interaction and education about sustainable living practices .

- **Green Roofs and Vertical Gardens**: Integrate green roofs and vertical gardens into building designs to reduce urban heat island effects, enhance insulation, and improve air quality. These green installations will also contribute to the aesthetic appeal of the neighborhoods.

Energy-Efficient Housing and Renewable Systems

Ensuring Sustainable Energy Consumption

Energy efficiency and the integration of renewable energy systems are key to creating sustainable housing solutions within neighborhoods.

- **Solar and Wind Energy Systems**: Equip homes with solar panels and small wind turbines to harness renewable energy. These systems will reduce dependence on fossil fuels, lower energy bills, and contribute to the overall sustainability of the community.

- **Energy Storage Solutions**: Develop neighborhood-scale energy storage solutions, such as battery storage systems, to store excess energy generated from renewable sources. These storage systems will ensure a stable energy supply, even during peak demand or power outages.

- **Energy-Efficient Appliances and Systems**: Encourage the use of energy-efficient appliances and systems, such as LED lighting, smart thermostats, and high-efficiency HVAC systems. These technologies will reduce energy consumption and enhance the comfort and sustainability of homes.

Sustainable Water Management

Innovative Water Solutions

Effective water management is crucial for sustainable neighborhoods, ensuring that water resources are used efficiently and responsibly.

- **Rainwater Harvesting and Greywater Recycling**: Implement rainwater harvesting systems to collect and store rainwater for non-potable uses, such as irrigation and toilet flushing. Integrate greywater recycling systems to reuse water from sinks, showers, and washing machines, reducing overall water consumption.

- **Permeable Pavements and Green Infrastructure**: Use permeable pavements and green infrastructure, such as rain gardens and bioswales, to manage stormwater runoff. These systems will reduce flooding risks, recharge groundwater, and improve water quality.

- **Smart Water Management Systems**: Deploy IoT-enabled water management systems to monitor water usage and detect leaks in real-time. These systems will optimize water distribution, reduce waste, and ensure the efficient use of water resources.

Inclusive and Affordable Housing

Ensuring Accessibility for All

Creating inclusive and affordable housing is essential to fostering diverse and equitable neighborhoods.

- **Affordable Housing Initiatives**: Develop affordable housing initiatives that provide financial assistance, subsidies, and incentives for low-income families. Ensure that affordable housing units are integrated within neighborhoods, promoting social diversity and inclusion.

- **Universal Design Principles**: Adhere to universal design principles that ensure accessibility for people of all ages and abilities. This includes features such as ramps, wide doorways, and step-free access, making homes and public spaces inclusive for everyone.

- **Co-housing and Shared Living Models**: Encourage co-housing and shared living models that combine private living spaces with shared communal facilities. These models promote social interaction, resource sharing, and affordability, creating close-knit and supportive communities.

Transportation and Mobility Solutions

Promoting Sustainable Mobility

Efficient and sustainable transportation solutions are vital for reducing emissions and enhancing connectivity within neighborhoods.

- **Public Transit Accessibility**: Ensure that neighborhoods are well-connected by public transit, with easy access to bus, tram, and train services. Develop transit-oriented development strategies that prioritize housing and amenities within walking distance of transit stops.

- **Cycling and Walking Infrastructure**: Develop extensive cycling and walking infrastructure, including bike lanes, pedestrian paths, and secure bike parking. These investments will encourage active transportation, reducing reliance on cars and improving public health.

- **Electric Vehicle Charging Stations**: Install electric vehicle (EV) charging stations throughout neighborhoods to support the adoption of electric vehicles. Provide incentives for residents to switch to EVs, contributing to reduced air pollution and greenhouse gas emissions.

Social Infrastructure and Community Services

Building Strong and Supportive Communities

Robust social infrastructure and community services are essential for the well-being and cohesion of neighborhoods.

- **Health and Wellness Centers**: Develop health and wellness centers that provide medical, dental, and mental health services. These centers will ensure that residents have access to comprehensive healthcare, promoting overall well-being.

- **Community Centers and Libraries**: Establish community centers and libraries that offer a variety of programs and resources, including education, recreation, and cultural activities. These facilities will serve as hubs for social interaction and community building.

- **Schools and Childcare Services**: Ensure that neighborhoods have access to high-quality schools and childcare services. Develop partnerships with educational institutions to provide a range of educational opportunities, from early childhood to adult learning.

Economic Opportunities and Local Business Support

Fostering Economic Resilience

Supporting local businesses and creating economic opportunities are key to the vitality and resilience of neighborhoods.

- **Business Incubators and Start-Up Support**: Establish business incubators and provide support for start-ups, including mentorship, funding, and access to resources. Encourage the development of local enterprises that contribute to the neighborhood economy.

- **Local Markets and Retail Hubs**: Develop local markets and retail hubs that provide convenient access to goods and services. Promote local entrepreneurship and support small businesses by creating a favorable business environment and providing marketing assistance.

- **Job Training and Employment Programs**: Implement job training and employment programs that equip residents with the skills needed to succeed in the local job market. Partner with local businesses and educational institutions to offer apprenticeships, internships, and vocational training.

Conclusion

Developing sustainable neighborhoods is pivotal to the reconstruction of Ukraine, ensuring that newly built communities are environmentally responsible, socially inclusive, and economically resilient. By integrating green spaces, energy-efficient housing, innovative water management, inclusive design, sustainable mobility, and robust social infrastructure, Ukraine can create vibrant neighborhoods that stand as models of sustainability and resilience. These neighborhoods will not only provide safe and comfortable living spaces but also embody the values of community, sustainability, and innovation, paving the way for a prosperous and sustainable future for all Ukrainian citizens.

Chapter 11: Public Services

Section 11.1: Healthcare Systems

Introduction

In the wake of conflict, rebuilding Ukraine's healthcare infrastructure is paramount to ensuring the well-being and resilience of its population. A comprehensive approach to healthcare system reconstruction will not only address immediate medical needs but also lay the groundwork for a robust, sustainable, and inclusive healthcare framework. This section details a strategic plan to modernize Ukraine's healthcare systems, incorporating advanced technologies, innovative practices, and international cooperation to deliver high-quality healthcare for all.

Rebuilding and Modernizing Healthcare Facilities

Strategic Restoration and Upgrading

Reconstructing healthcare facilities damaged during the conflict is a critical priority. This involves not just rebuilding but upgrading to meet modern standards and future needs.

- **Comprehensive Healthcare Facility Assessment**: Conduct thorough assessments of existing healthcare facilities, using drones, satellite imagery, and on-the-ground evaluations to determine the extent of damage and needs for restoration.
- **Modular Healthcare Units**: Deploy modular healthcare units as temporary solutions to provide immediate medical services while permanent facilities are being rebuilt. These units should be equipped with essential medical equipment and telemedicine capabilities to ensure continuity of care.
- **Upgrading Infrastructure**: Rebuild and upgrade hospitals, clinics, and primary care centers with state-of-the-art medical technologies, energy-efficient designs, and expanded capacities to better serve the population in both urban and rural areas .

Telemedicine and Digital Health Integration

Leveraging Technology for Accessible Healthcare

Integrating telemedicine and digital health solutions will expand access to medical services, particularly in remote and underserved areas.

- **Nationwide Telemedicine Network**: Establish a nationwide telemedicine network that connects patients with healthcare providers regardless of geographic barriers. This network will include virtual consultations, remote diagnostics, and telemonitoring, enhancing access to specialized care.
- **Electronic Health Records (EHR)**: Implement a secure, interoperable electronic health records system to streamline patient data management, improve continuity of care, and facilitate information sharing among healthcare providers. Blockchain technology will be used to ensure data security and integrity .
- **Mobile Health (mHealth) Applications**: Develop mHealth applications to provide patients with tools for self-management of health conditions, access to health information, and reminders for medication and appointments. These apps will empower patients and improve health outcomes through proactive management.

Training and Capacity Building for Healthcare Professionals

Empowering the Workforce

Building a skilled and resilient healthcare workforce is essential for the sustainability of the healthcare system.

- **Continuous Medical Education (CME)**: Implement continuous medical education programs for healthcare professionals, focusing on the latest medical advancements, telemedicine, and emergency care. Online learning platforms and virtual simulations will facilitate ongoing training and skill development.

- **International Exchange Programs**: Establish exchange programs with international medical institutions to facilitate knowledge transfer and enhance the skills of Ukrainian healthcare workers. These programs will include internships, fellowships, and collaborative research opportunities.

- **Recognition of Qualifications**: Expedite the recognition of qualifications for Ukrainian healthcare professionals displaced by the conflict, enabling them to contribute to healthcare services in host countries and upon return to Ukraine .

Enhancing Public Health and Preventive Care

Proactive Health Management

A focus on public health and preventive care will improve population health outcomes and reduce the burden on healthcare facilities.

- **National Vaccination Campaigns**: Launch national vaccination campaigns to ensure widespread immunization against communicable diseases, leveraging mobile clinics and community health workers to reach all regions.

- **Health Education and Awareness**: Develop health education programs to raise awareness about preventive care, healthy lifestyles, and disease prevention. Utilize multimedia platforms, community workshops, and school-based programs to disseminate information.

- **Community Health Initiatives**: Encourage community-based health initiatives that promote physical activity, mental health, and nutritional well-being. Programs such as fitness classes, mental health support groups, and nutrition counseling will foster healthier communities.

International Cooperation and Funding

Global Partnerships for Health

International cooperation is vital for the successful reconstruction of Ukraine's healthcare system.

- **European Health Networks**: Collaborate with European health networks and institutions to access expertise, technology, and funding. The

European Union's commitment to supporting Ukraine includes financial aid for healthcare infrastructure and services .

- **Global Health Partnerships**: Engage with global health organizations such as the World Health Organization (WHO), the International Red Cross, and Médecins Sans Frontières (MSF) to receive technical assistance, medical supplies, and funding for healthcare projects.

- **Innovative Financing Mechanisms**: Explore innovative financing mechanisms, including health impact bonds and international grants, to secure funding for long-term healthcare projects. Transparent fund management and accountability measures will ensure the efficient use of resources.

Building Resilient Healthcare Systems

Preparedness for Future Challenges

Rebuilding efforts must also focus on resilience, ensuring that the healthcare system can withstand and respond to future crises.

- **Emergency Response Infrastructure**: Develop robust emergency response infrastructure, including disaster-ready hospitals, mobile medical units, and emergency supply stockpiles. These resources will enhance the healthcare system's ability to respond to natural disasters, conflicts, and pandemics.

- **Healthcare System Redundancy**: Create redundancies within the healthcare system by establishing multiple centers of care that can operate independently. This decentralization will ensure continuity of care in case of localized disruptions.

- **Surveillance and Early Warning Systems**: Implement advanced surveillance and early warning systems to detect emerging health threats. Real-time data analytics and AI-driven monitoring will enable rapid response to infectious disease outbreaks and other public health emergencies .

Conclusion

Reconstructing Ukraine's healthcare system is a vital step in the nation's recovery and resilience journey. By modernizing healthcare facilities, integrating telemedicine, building workforce capacity, enhancing public health initiatives, fostering international cooperation, and ensuring system resilience, Ukraine can establish a healthcare system that is not only responsive to current needs but also adaptable to future challenges. These strategic efforts will ensure that all Ukrainian citizens have access to high-quality, sustainable healthcare, fostering a healthier and more resilient society.

Section 11.2: Educational Institutions

Introduction

Reconstructing Ukraine's educational institutions is a cornerstone of the nation's recovery and future resilience. The rebuilding process must aim not only to restore the physical infrastructure of schools and universities but also to modernize and innovate the educational landscape, ensuring that all Ukrainian children and youth have access to high-quality, inclusive, and future-proof education. This section outlines a comprehensive strategy to rebuild and enhance educational institutions across Ukraine, leveraging advanced technologies, inclusive practices, and international cooperation.

Rebuilding and Modernizing Educational Infrastructure

Strategic Restoration and Innovation

The restoration and modernization of educational infrastructure are crucial for providing safe, inclusive, and engaging learning environments.

- **Comprehensive Damage Assessment**: Conduct thorough assessments of damaged educational facilities using drones, satellite imagery, and on-ground teams to map destruction and prioritize reconstruction efforts based on severity and strategic importance.
- **Innovative Reconstruction Designs**: Incorporate modern architectural designs and sustainable construction practices in the rebuilding of schools and universities. Facilities should feature adaptable classrooms, state-of-the-art laboratories, and energy-efficient systems to support diverse educational needs.
- **Focus on Safety and Resilience**: Ensure that new educational buildings are resilient to natural disasters and other hazards. Utilize earthquake-resistant designs, flood-proofing techniques, and fire-resistant materials to safeguard students and staff in future emergencies .

Integrating Digital Technologies in Education

Leveraging Technology for Enhanced Learning

Incorporating digital technologies will transform Ukraine's education system, making it more accessible, efficient, and innovative.

- **E-Learning Platforms**: Develop e-learning platforms that provide access to a wide range of educational resources, including interactive lessons, digital textbooks, and multimedia tools. These platforms will support both in-class and remote learning, ensuring continuity of education regardless of external disruptions.
- **Digital Classrooms**: Equip classrooms with digital learning tools such as interactive whiteboards, tablets, and virtual reality (VR) kits. These

tools will enhance student engagement, foster interactive learning, and enable immersive educational experiences .

- **AI-Powered Educational Tools**: Implement AI-powered tools to personalize learning experiences, offering tailored educational content and adaptive assessments based on individual student needs and progress. This approach will support differentiated instruction and improve learning outcomes.

Inclusive and Equitable Education

Ensuring Access for All Students

Fostering inclusivity and equity in education is essential for rebuilding a just and fair education system.

- **Universal Design for Learning (UDL)**: Apply Universal Design for Learning principles to create flexible learning environments that accommodate diverse learners, including students with disabilities. This includes providing multiple means of representation, engagement, and expression in the curriculum.
- **Language Support Programs**: Develop language support programs for internally displaced students and those from minority backgrounds. These programs will offer bilingual education, language classes, and culturally relevant teaching materials to facilitate integration and academic success .
- **Scholarships and Financial Aid**: Establish scholarship programs and financial aid for disadvantaged students to ensure that financial barriers do not impede access to education. Collaborate with international donors and NGOs to fund these initiatives.

Teacher Training and Professional Development

Empowering Educators

Investing in teacher training and professional development is critical to elevating the quality of education and fostering innovative teaching practices.

- **Continuous Professional Development (CPD)**: Implement ongoing professional development programs for teachers, focusing on the integration of digital technologies, inclusive teaching strategies, and resilience education. Online training modules, workshops, and collaborative learning communities will facilitate CPD.
- **International Teacher Exchange Programs**: Establish teacher exchange programs with educational institutions abroad to foster knowledge transfer and expose Ukrainian educators to global best practices. These

exchanges will enhance teaching skills and broaden pedagogical perspectives.

- **Teacher Support Networks**: Create support networks for educators to share resources, experiences, and solutions to common challenges. These networks will provide mentorship, collaborative opportunities, and emotional support, helping teachers adapt to the evolving educational landscape.

Community and Parental Engagement

Building Strong Educational Communities

Strong partnerships between schools, families, and communities are essential for creating supportive and enriching educational environments.

- **Parental Involvement Programs**: Develop programs that encourage active parental involvement in their children's education. Workshops, seminars, and volunteer opportunities will empower parents to support their children's learning and collaborate with educators.
- **Community-School Partnerships**: Foster partnerships between schools and local communities to enhance educational experiences. Community leaders, businesses, and organizations can contribute resources, expertise, and real-world learning opportunities for students.
- **Student and Family Support Services**: Establish comprehensive support services for students and families, including counseling, social services, and after-school programs. These services will address the holistic needs of students, supporting their academic and personal development.

International Cooperation and Funding

Leveraging Global Support

International cooperation is pivotal for the reconstruction and modernization of Ukraine's educational institutions.

- **Collaborations with International Organizations**: Partner with international organizations such as UNESCO, UNICEF, and the European Union to gain access to expertise, resources, and funding for educational projects. These collaborations will help implement evidence-based practices and innovative solutions.
- **Erasmus+ Program**: Utilize the flexibility of the Erasmus+ program to support the education of refugee students and the integration of displaced academic staff. This program will provide mobility opportunities, capacity building, and collaborative projects with European educational institutions.

- **Educational Aid and Grants**: Secure educational aid and grants from international donors and financial institutions to fund the reconstruction and development of schools and universities. Ensure transparent and accountable management of these funds to build donor confidence and support sustainable initiatives.

Conclusion

Rebuilding Ukraine's educational institutions is a vital endeavor that requires a multifaceted and innovative approach. By modernizing infrastructure, integrating digital technologies, ensuring inclusivity, empowering educators, engaging communities, and leveraging international cooperation, Ukraine can establish a resilient and forward-looking education system. These efforts will equip Ukrainian children and youth with the knowledge, skills, and opportunities needed to thrive in a rapidly changing world, fostering a brighter and more prosperous future for the nation.

Section 11.3: Government Buildings and Public Transport

Introduction

The reconstruction of Ukraine's government buildings and public transport systems is crucial for restoring essential services, ensuring effective governance, and facilitating mobility. This section outlines a strategic plan to rebuild and modernize these critical infrastructures, focusing on resilience, sustainability, and technological innovation. By integrating advanced construction methods, smart technologies, and community-centered designs, Ukraine can create efficient and durable public facilities and transport networks that support the nation's recovery and long-term development.

Rebuilding Government Buildings

Modern and Resilient Public Facilities

Reconstructing government buildings is essential to re-establish effective public administration and deliver essential services to citizens.

- **Damage Assessment and Prioritization**: Conduct comprehensive assessments of damaged government buildings using drones, satellite imagery, and on-the-ground inspections to determine the extent of damage and prioritize reconstruction based on functionality and strategic importance .

- **Sustainable Building Designs**: Incorporate sustainable design principles in the reconstruction of government buildings. Utilize energy-efficient materials, renewable energy systems, and smart building technologies to reduce operational costs and environmental impact. Features such as green roofs, solar panels, and rainwater harvesting systems will enhance sustainability.

- **Resilience and Security**: Ensure that new government buildings are designed to withstand natural disasters and security threats. Implement earthquake-resistant structures, flood-proofing, and advanced security systems to protect critical infrastructure and ensure the safety of public servants and citizens .

Enhancing Public Transport Systems

Accessible and Sustainable Mobility

Rebuilding and modernizing public transport systems is vital for economic recovery and improving the quality of life for all Ukrainians.

- **Restoration of Key Transport Infrastructure**: Focus on the immediate restoration of key transport infrastructure, including roads, railways, and airports damaged during the conflict. Utilize self-healing materials for road construction and advanced engineering techniques for bridges and tunnels to ensure durability and longevity.

- **Smart Public Transportation**: Develop smart public transportation systems that incorporate IoT and AI technologies for efficient management and operation. Implement real-time tracking of buses and trains, digital ticketing systems, and dynamic route optimization to enhance service reliability and user convenience .

- **Electrification and Sustainability**: Electrify public transport fleets to reduce emissions and promote sustainability. Invest in electric buses, trams, and trains, along with the necessary charging infrastructure. Additionally, create dedicated lanes for electric vehicles and integrate cycling and pedestrian paths into urban planning to support multimodal transport options.

Integrated Transport Hubs

Seamless Connectivity

Creating integrated transport hubs will enhance connectivity and streamline the movement of people and goods.

- **Multimodal Transport Centers**: Develop multimodal transport centers that connect various forms of transport, such as buses, trains, and bicycles. These centers will facilitate seamless transfers and improve overall mobility in urban and rural areas .

- **Smart Traffic Management Systems**: Implement smart traffic management systems powered by AI and big data analytics. These systems will optimize traffic flow, reduce congestion, and enhance safety by adjusting traffic signals, monitoring road conditions, and predicting traffic patterns.

Green Public Spaces and Transit-Oriented Development

Sustainable Urban Planning

Integrating green public spaces and promoting transit-oriented development (TOD) will create vibrant, livable communities.

- **Green Corridors and Urban Parks**: Incorporate green corridors and urban parks within transport planning. These spaces will provide environmental benefits, recreational opportunities, and improve mental health for residents. Urban parks near transit hubs will encourage the use of public transport and reduce car dependency .
- **Transit-Oriented Development (TOD)**: Plan and develop high-density, mixed-use neighborhoods around transit hubs to promote walkability and reduce the need for car travel. TOD will integrate residential, commercial, and recreational spaces, making cities more sustainable and reducing urban sprawl .

International Collaboration and Funding

Global Partnerships and Support

International cooperation is essential for the successful reconstruction of government buildings and transport systems.

- **Partnerships with International Organizations**: Collaborate with international organizations such as the European Union, World Bank, and United Nations to access expertise, technology, and funding. These partnerships will provide critical support for large-scale infrastructure projects .
- **Innovative Financing Mechanisms**: Explore innovative financing mechanisms, including public-private partnerships (PPPs), green bonds, and international grants. These financial tools will mobilize resources and ensure the sustainability of reconstruction efforts.

Community Involvement and Feedback

Engaging Citizens in Reconstruction

Involving the community in the reconstruction process ensures that projects align with local needs and garners public support.

- **Community Consultations**: Conduct regular community consultations to gather input on the design and functionality of government buildings and public transport systems. Public feedback will ensure that infrastructure developments meet the needs and expectations of residents .

- **Participatory Planning**: Implement participatory planning approaches that empower citizens to take part in decision-making processes. Create platforms for continuous dialogue between planners, government officials, and the public to foster transparency and trust.

Conclusion

Rebuilding Ukraine's government buildings and public transport systems is foundational to the nation's recovery and future success. By integrating resilient and sustainable designs, leveraging smart technologies, and fostering community engagement, Ukraine can create efficient, accessible, and durable public infrastructure. These efforts will not only restore essential services but also support economic revitalization and improve the quality of life for all citizens, paving the way for a resilient and prosperous Ukraine.

Chapter 12: Economic Revitalization

Section 12.1: Business Support and Incentives

Introduction

The economic revitalization of Ukraine is a cornerstone of the nation's recovery and sustainable development plan. Central to this endeavor is a robust strategy to support existing businesses in rebuilding and to attract new investments. This section details comprehensive measures designed to bolster the private sector, stimulate economic growth, and foster a vibrant business environment. By providing targeted support and clear incentives, Ukraine can rebuild a more resilient and dynamic economy that benefits all citizens.

Immediate Support for Existing Businesses

Shock Absorption and Restart Grants

The immediate aftermath of conflict leaves many businesses grappling with severe financial strains. To mitigate these impacts and support recovery:

- **Emergency Financial Assistance**: Deploy emergency grants and low-interest loans to help businesses address immediate needs, such as repairing damaged properties, replacing lost inventory, and covering operational costs. This financial injection will ensure that businesses can resume operations quickly and effectively.

- **Tax Relief and Credits**: Implement temporary tax relief measures, including deferrals and reductions, to ease the financial burden on businesses.

Offer tax credits for expenditures related to rebuilding and modernization efforts, incentivizing rapid recovery and investment in resiliency measures.
- **Public Procurement Opportunities**: Prioritize local businesses in public procurement processes for reconstruction projects. This approach will ensure that government spending supports domestic enterprises, creating immediate business opportunities and fostering local economic growth.

Creating a Conducive Business Environment

Regulatory Reforms and Business-Friendly Policies

Establishing a business-friendly environment is essential for attracting investments and fostering economic activities:

- **Streamlining Regulations**: Simplify business regulations and reduce bureaucratic red tape to facilitate easier and faster business formation, registration, and operation. Introduce one-stop-shop services to provide a single access point for all business-related procedures, enhancing efficiency and reducing administrative burdens.
- **Transparent Governance**: Ensure transparent governance by implementing digital platforms for business licensing and permitting procedures. Utilize blockchain technology to create an immutable record of business transactions, licenses, and permits, promoting accountability and reducing corruption risks.
- **Land and Property Rights**: Secure land and property rights through clear and enforceable regulations. Develop a blockchain-based land registry system to provide transparent and tamper-proof records of property ownership, reducing disputes and attracting real estate investments.

Incentivizing New Investments

Attracting Domestic and International Investors

Encouraging new investments is critical for economic growth and job creation:

- **Investment Promotion Agencies**: Establish dedicated investment promotion agencies tasked with attracting and facilitating domestic and international investments. These agencies will provide potential investors with essential information, support services, and incentives to invest in Ukraine.
- **Special Economic Zones (SEZ)**: Develop Special Economic Zones offering tax incentives, relaxed regulations, and infrastructure support to attract foreign direct investment (FDI). SEZs will create concentrated areas of economic activity, driving innovation, industrial growth, and technology transfer.

- **Public-Private Partnerships (PPPs)**: Promote public-private partnerships to leverage private sector expertise and financing for public projects. PPP frameworks will facilitate collaboration on infrastructure development, renewable energy projects, and technological advancements

Support for Small and Medium Enterprises (SMEs)

Empowering the Backbone of the Economy

Small and medium enterprises are vital to Ukraine's economic fabric. Tailored support measures will ensure their resilience and growth:

- **Microfinance Programs**: Develop microfinance programs to provide SMEs with access to small loans and financial services. These programs will help entrepreneurs, particularly those in rural areas, to start and scale their businesses, driving inclusive economic growth.
- **Business Incubators and Accelerators**: Establish business incubators and accelerators to nurture start-ups and early-stage companies. These institutions will offer mentorship, training, and funding opportunities, creating a nurturing ecosystem for innovation and entrepreneurship.
- **Export Support Programs**: Develop export support programs to assist SMEs in accessing international markets. Provide training on export procedures, market research, and networking opportunities with global trade partners, enhancing the competitiveness of Ukrainian products abroad .

Leveraging Technology and Innovation

Fostering a Knowledge-Based Economy

Harnessing technology and innovation will drive economic diversification and resilience:

- **Technology Hubs and Research Parks**: Create technology hubs and research parks that bring together academia, industry, and government to foster innovation and research. These hubs will support tech start-ups, facilitate knowledge transfer, and drive advancements in fields such as AI, biotechnology, and clean energy.
- **Digital Infrastructure Development**: Invest in robust digital infrastructure, including high-speed internet, 5G networks, and cloud computing services. These investments will support the digital transformation of businesses, enhance productivity, and enable new business models.
- **Skill Development Programs**: Implement skill development programs focused on digital literacy, coding, cybersecurity, and advanced manufacturing techniques. Collaborate with tech companies and educational insti-

tutions to offer training and certifications, ensuring a skilled workforce for the knowledge-based economy.

Engaging the Diaspora and International Communities

Harnessing Global Expertise and Resources

The global Ukrainian diaspora and international communities are invaluable assets for economic revitalization:

- **Diaspora Investment Initiatives**: Launch initiatives to attract investments from the Ukrainian diaspora. Offer diaspora bonds, investment matching programs, and exclusive business opportunities to encourage their participation in the country's economic development.
- **International Collaboration Networks**: Develop international collaboration networks that connect Ukrainian businesses with global markets, investors, and expertise. These networks will facilitate exports, joint ventures, and technology partnerships.
- **Global Talent Attraction**: Implement programs to attract highly skilled professionals from the diaspora and international communities. Provide incentives such as relocation packages, tax benefits, and professional development opportunities to lure talent back to Ukraine.

Conclusion

Rebuilding Ukraine's economy requires a multifaceted approach that encompasses immediate business support, regulatory reforms, investment incentives, SME empowerment, technological innovation, and international collaboration. By implementing these strategies, Ukraine can create a thriving, resilient economy that supports sustainable growth and improves the livelihoods of all its citizens. These efforts will transform Ukraine into a vibrant hub of economic activity, driving prosperity and stability in the post-war era.

Section 12.2: Industrial Parks and Technology Hubs

Introduction

The development of industrial parks and technology hubs is instrumental in revitalizing Ukraine's economy and ensuring sustainable growth. These centers of innovation and productivity will attract new investments, foster technological advancements, and create substantial employment opportunities. This section presents a strategic blueprint for establishing industrial parks and technology hubs that align with Ukraine's long-term development goals, leveraging best practices in sustainable and inclusive urban planning.

Strategic Development of Industrial Parks

Catalyzing Industrial Growth and Innovation

Industrial parks serve as engines of economic growth, providing the infrastructure and environment necessary for industrial activities to thrive.

- **Site Selection and Planning**: Conduct comprehensive feasibility studies to identify optimal locations for industrial parks based on factors such as proximity to transportation networks, availability of resources, and existing industrial bases. Utilize geographic information systems (GIS) to map potential sites and plan layouts that maximize efficiency and minimize environmental impact.

- **Sustainable Infrastructure**: Develop industrial parks incorporating sustainable infrastructure, including green buildings, renewable energy systems, and advanced waste management solutions. Prioritize the use of eco-friendly materials and technologies to create environmentally responsible industrial zones.

- **Cluster Development**: Encourage the development of industry clusters within the parks to foster synergy and innovation. By grouping related industries together, businesses can benefit from shared resources, collaborative research and development, and enhanced supply chain efficiency.

Establishing Technology Hubs

Fostering Innovation and Technological Advancement

Technology hubs are critical for driving innovation and supporting the development of a knowledge-based economy.

- **Innovation and Research Centers**: Establish technology hubs with dedicated innovation and research centers, focusing on cutting-edge fields such as artificial intelligence, biotechnology, and renewable energy. These centers will serve as incubators for start-ups, offering resources, mentorship, and funding opportunities to emerging tech firms.

- **Collaboration with Academia**: Foster strong partnerships between technology hubs and academic institutions to promote knowledge transfer and collaborative research. Universities and research institutions can provide critical expertise, while technology hubs offer real-world applications for academic innovations.

- **Digital Infrastructure**: Invest in robust digital infrastructure, including high-speed internet, cloud computing services, and cybersecurity systems. These investments will support the digital transformation of businesses and enable them to compete in the global market.

Attracting Investments and International Partnerships

Mobilizing Financial Resources and Expertise

Attracting investments and forging international partnerships are essential for the success of industrial parks and technology hubs.

- **Investment Promotion Agencies**: Establish investment promotion agencies to actively seek and facilitate domestic and international investments. These agencies will provide potential investors with detailed information on investment opportunities, regulatory frameworks, and available incentives.

- **Public-Private Partnerships (PPPs)**: Promote public-private partnerships to leverage private sector expertise and financing. PPPs can be instrumental in developing large-scale infrastructure projects, ensuring efficient management, and sharing risks and rewards.

- **Special Economic Zones (SEZs)**: Create Special Economic Zones offering tax incentives, regulatory relaxations, and infrastructure support to attract foreign direct investment. SEZs will serve as innovation hotspots, driving industrial growth and technological advancements.

Supporting Small and Medium Enterprises (SMEs)

Empowering SMEs as Engines of Growth

Small and medium enterprises are vital to Ukraine's economic resilience and diversification.

- **Incubators and Accelerators**: Develop business incubators and accelerators within industrial parks and technology hubs to support the growth of SMEs. These institutions will provide mentorship, training, and access to capital, fostering a vibrant entrepreneurial ecosystem.

- **Microfinance Programs**: Implement microfinance programs to offer financial services and small loans to SMEs. These programs will enable entrepreneurs to launch and expand their businesses, contributing to job creation and economic diversification.

- **Export Support Initiatives**: Establish export support initiatives to help SMEs access international markets. Provide training on export procedures, market research, and networking opportunities with global trade partners, enhancing the competitiveness of Ukrainian products abroad .

Leveraging Advanced Technologies and Innovation

Driving Efficiency and Competitiveness

Incorporating advanced technologies and innovative practices will enhance the efficiency and competitiveness of industrial parks and technology hubs.

- **Smart Manufacturing**: Implement smart manufacturing technologies, including IoT-enabled machinery, AI-driven production processes, and automation. These technologies will optimize manufacturing efficiency, reduce operational costs, and enhance product quality.
- **Sustainable Practices**: Promote sustainable industrial practices such as circular economy principles, energy-efficient processes, and waste minimization. Encourage businesses to adopt green technologies and practices that reduce their environmental footprint.
- **Collaborative Platforms**: Create digital platforms that facilitate collaboration among businesses, researchers, and policymakers. These platforms will support knowledge sharing, joint ventures, and innovation partnerships, driving collective growth and advancement.

Ensuring Social and Environmental Responsibility

Building Inclusive and Sustainable Communities

Social and environmental responsibility must be integral to the development of industrial parks and technology hubs.

- **Local Community Engagement**: Engage local communities in the planning and development process through consultations and participatory approaches. Ensure that development projects align with the needs and aspirations of local residents, fostering social cohesion and support.
- **Environmental Safeguards**: Implement robust environmental safeguards to protect natural resources and minimize pollution. Conduct regular environmental impact assessments and enforce compliance with environmental regulations.
- **Inclusive Employment Practices**: Promote inclusive employment practices that provide opportunities for all segments of society, including women, youth, and marginalized groups. Develop vocational training programs to equip the local workforce with the skills needed for employment in industrial and tech sectors 17:0†source .

Conclusion

The establishment of industrial parks and technology hubs is a strategic lever for Ukraine's economic revitalization. By fostering innovation, attracting investments, empowering SMEs, and leveraging advanced technologies, Ukraine can build a resilient and dynamic economy that supports sustainable growth and prosperity. Ensuring social and environmental responsibility in these developments will create inclusive and vibrant communities, aligning economic progress with the principles of sustainability and equity. Through these comprehensive efforts, Ukraine can transform its economic landscape, driving forward towards a future of innovation and resilience.

Section 12.3: Job Training Programs

Introduction

The revitalization of Ukraine's economy hinges significantly on the availability of a skilled workforce that can meet the demands of an evolving job market. Job training programs are essential not only for empowering displaced individuals and returning citizens but also for fostering innovation and competitiveness within the Ukrainian economy. This section outlines a comprehensive strategy for implementing job training programs that address both immediate needs and long-term economic goals, ensuring that the workforce is equipped with the skills necessary for sustainable development and resilience.

Comprehensive Workforce Assessment

Identifying Skill Gaps and Opportunities

A thorough understanding of the current workforce's skills and the demands of the job market is vital for designing effective training programs.

- **Workforce Surveys**: Conduct detailed surveys to assess the skills of the existing workforce and identify gaps that need to be filled to meet the demands of a modern economy. Utilize data analytics to interpret the results and tailor training programs accordingly.

- **Sector-Specific Needs Analysis**: Work with industry leaders and economic planners to identify the specific skills required in sectors poised for growth, such as technology, green energy, construction, and healthcare.

- **Talent Reserve Initiatives**: Establish talent reserves that document the skills and experiences of Ukrainian citizens, both within the country and in the diaspora. This database will be instrumental in matching skills with job opportunities and identifying areas where additional training is needed.

Implementation of Training and Educational Programs

Building a Future-Ready Workforce

Deploying comprehensive training and educational programs will ensure that the Ukrainian workforce is prepared for current and future challenges.

- **Technical and Vocational Education and Training (TVET)**: Expand TVET programs to provide hands-on skills training in areas such as advanced manufacturing, IT, renewable energy, and healthcare. These programs should be flexible, modular, and aligned with industry standards.

- **Digital Literacy and STEM Education**: Promote digital literacy and science, technology, engineering, and mathematics (STEM) education at all levels. Implement coding bootcamps, online courses, and school curriculums that emphasize these critical areas, preparing students and workers for high-tech jobs .

- **Language and Soft Skills Training**: Offer programs in language acquisition, communication, teamwork, and problem-solving. These soft skills are crucial for job success and will enhance the adaptability of the workforce in diverse environments .

Public-Private Partnerships (PPP)

Leveraging Collaboration for Enhanced Training

Public-private partnerships can provide significant resources, expertise, and opportunities for workforce development.

- **Collaborative Training Centers**: Establish collaborative training centers in partnership with leading businesses and educational institutions. These centers will offer state-of-the-art facilities and industry-aligned training programs, ensuring that participants receive relevant and practical education.
- **Employer-Led Apprenticeships**: Develop apprenticeship programs led by employers in key industries. These programs will combine on-the-job training with academic learning, providing apprentices with valuable work experience and a pathway to employment .
- **Funding and Support**: Secure funding from private sector partners to support training programs and provide financial assistance to participants. This could include scholarships, grants, and stipends to ensure that training is accessible to all.

International Cooperation and Exchange Programs

Gaining Global Perspectives and Skills

International cooperation and exchange programs can enrich Ukraine's workforce with diverse skills and experiences.

- **Global Training Partnerships**: Forge partnerships with international organizations and institutions to facilitate knowledge transfer and provide access to cutting-edge training programs. Engage in exchange programs that allow Ukrainian workers and students to gain experience abroad and bring back valuable insights .
- **Recognition of International Qualifications**: Work with international bodies to ensure the recognition of Ukrainian qualifications abroad and vice versa. This will enable Ukrainian workers to access job opportunities in the international market, and attract foreign talent to Ukraine.

- **Digital Learning Platforms**: Utilize global e-learning platforms to offer a wide range of courses and certifications. These platforms provide flexible learning opportunities that can be accessed from anywhere, making education more inclusive and adaptable .

Support Systems for Transition to Employment

Ensuring Smooth Integration of Workers

Providing robust support systems will facilitate the transition of trained individuals into the workforce.

- **Job Placement Services**: Establish job placement services that assist trainees in finding employment that matches their skills. These services will offer resume writing workshops, interview coaching, and job matching services, helping candidates navigate the job market effectively.
- **Mentorship and Guidance Programs**: Implement mentorship programs that connect trainees with industry professionals. Mentors will provide guidance, support, and networking opportunities, helping trainees build confidence and career pathways.
- **Continuous Learning and Development**: Promote a culture of continuous learning by offering opportunities for ongoing professional development. Encourage workers to pursue additional certifications and advanced training to stay current with industry trends and advancements .

Monitoring and Evaluation

Ensuring Program Effectiveness

Regular monitoring and evaluation are essential to ensure that job training programs are effective and meet their intended goals.

- **Data-Driven Evaluation**: Use data analytics to monitor the progress and outcomes of training programs. Track metrics such as employment rates, salary increases, and job satisfaction to assess program impact and identify areas for improvement.
- **Feedback Mechanisms**: Establish feedback mechanisms that allow participants to share their experiences and suggestions. This feedback will inform program adjustments and ensure that training remains relevant and effective .
- **Continuous Program Improvement**: Implement a continuous improvement process based on evaluation results. Regularly update curricula, adopt new training methodologies, and incorporate advancements in technology to keep programs aligned with industry needs.

Conclusion

Implementing comprehensive job training programs is fundamental to the economic revitalization of Ukraine. By assessing workforce needs, deploying targeted training programs, leveraging public-private partnerships, engaging in international cooperation, and providing robust support systems, Ukraine can build a skilled and adaptable workforce ready to drive sustainable economic growth. Continuous monitoring and improvement will ensure the effectiveness of these programs, empowering individuals and communities to rebuild and prosper in a resilient and dynamic Ukrainian economy.

Chapter 13: Environmental Remediation

Section 13.1: Contaminated Sites Cleanup

Introduction

The impact of conflict on Ukraine's environment has been severe, particularly in terms of land contamination from military activities, industrial spills, and the remnants of war. Cleaning up these contaminated sites is essential not only for ecological restoration but also for the health and safety of the population. This section outlines a comprehensive strategy for identifying, assessing, and remediating contaminated sites across Ukraine, leveraging advanced technologies, international cooperation, and community engagement to restore the environment and prevent future harm.

Comprehensive Site Assessment and Prioritization

Mapping Contaminated Areas

A meticulous assessment of contaminated sites is the first step towards effective remediation.

- **Satellite Imagery and Drone Surveys**: Utilize high-resolution satellite imagery and drone surveys to identify and map contaminated areas. These technologies provide a broad overview and pinpoint hotspots that require detailed investigation.

- **Ground-Based Sampling and Analysis**: Conduct ground-based sampling of soil, water, and air to determine the extent and type of contamination. Advanced analytical techniques, including gas chromatography and mass spectrometry, will identify pollutants and their concentrations.

- **Risk Assessment Framework**: Develop a risk assessment framework to evaluate the potential health and environmental risks posed by each site. Prioritize remediation efforts based on the severity of contamination, proximity to populated areas, and ecological sensitivity.

Advanced Remediation Technologies

Employing Cutting-Edge Solutions

Implementing advanced remediation technologies will ensure the efficient and effective cleanup of contaminated sites.

- **Bioremediation and Phytoremediation**: Use bioremediation techniques to degrade hazardous substances through the action of microorganisms. Additionally, phytoremediation employs plants to absorb, concentrate, and detoxify pollutants from the soil and water, leveraging natural processes for sustainable cleanup.

- **Thermal Desorption**: Apply thermal desorption to treat soils and sediments contaminated with volatile organic compounds (VOCs) and semi-volatile organic compounds (SVOCs). This method heats contaminated material to vaporize pollutants, which are then captured and treated.

- **Chemical Oxidation**: Employ in-situ chemical oxidation (ISCO) to inject oxidizing agents directly into contaminated soil and groundwater. This process breaks down complex pollutants into less harmful compounds, providing an efficient solution for cleaning up persistent organic pollutants.

Mobile and Modular Cleanup Units

Flexible and Efficient Solutions

Deploying mobile and modular cleanup units will provide flexible and scalable solutions for various contamination scenarios.

- **Mobile Treatment Plants**: Establish mobile treatment plants that can be transported to different sites for on-site remediation. These units will handle a variety of contaminants, including heavy metals, petroleum hydrocarbons, and industrial solvents.

- **Modular Bio-Reactors**: Develop modular bio-reactors that can be assembled on-site to treat contaminated water and soil using biological processes. These systems are adaptable and can be scaled up or down based on site-specific needs and the extent of contamination.

International Cooperation and Best Practices

Leveraging Global Expertise

International cooperation is crucial for accessing the expertise, technology, and funding necessary for large-scale environmental remediation.

- **International Technical Assistance**: Engage with international organizations and experts from countries experienced in post-conflict environmental remediation. Collaborative efforts will bring in proven techniques and technological innovations, enhancing the effectiveness of Ukraine's cleanup initiatives .

- **Knowledge Exchange Programs**: Establish knowledge exchange programs to share best practices in contamination cleanup and environmental restoration. Host international workshops and seminars to disseminate knowledge and foster collaboration among global environmental scientists and engineers.

- **Funding and Grants**: Secure international funding and grants from bodies like the European Union, World Bank, and United Nations to support remediation projects. Transparent fund management will ensure efficient use of resources and build confidence among donors .

Community Engagement and Awareness

Fostering Local Involvement

Community involvement is essential for the success and sustainability of environmental remediation efforts.

- **Public Awareness Campaigns**: Launch public awareness campaigns to educate local communities about the risks of contaminated sites and the importance of remediation efforts. Use multimedia platforms and local media to reach a broad audience.

- **Community Participation Programs**: Develop programs that encourage community participation in cleanup activities. These initiatives not only enhance local ownership but also provide employment opportunities and skills development for residents.

- **Transparent Communication**: Maintain transparent communication channels to keep the public informed about remediation progress and findings. Regular updates and open forums will build trust and encourage continued community support.

Sustainable Remediation Practices

Prioritizing Long-Term Environmental Health

Incorporating sustainability into remediation practices will ensure long-term environmental health and resilience.

- **Eco-Friendly Technologies**: Prioritize the use of eco-friendly remediation technologies that minimize ecological disruption and enhance natural recovery processes. Techniques like natural attenuation and enhanced bioremediation promote the self-healing properties of ecosystems.

- **Revegetation and Habitat Restoration**: Implement revegetation projects to restore native plant communities and improve habitat quality.

These efforts will enhance biodiversity, stabilize soil, and prevent erosion, contributing to the overall resilience of the environment.

- **Monitoring and Maintenance**: Develop long-term monitoring programs to assess the effectiveness of remediation efforts and ensure sustained recovery. Regular maintenance and adaptive management strategies will address any emerging issues and optimize the benefits of cleanup activities.

Conclusion

The cleanup of contaminated sites is a critical component of Ukraine's postwar environmental remediation strategy. By leveraging advanced technologies, international cooperation, community engagement, and sustainable practices, Ukraine can effectively address pollution, protect public health, and restore ecological integrity. These comprehensive efforts will not only heal the wounds inflicted by conflict but also pave the way for a greener, healthier, and more resilient Ukraine.

Section 13.2: Reforestation and Urban Greening

Introduction

Reforestation and urban greening are critical to Ukraine's sustainable recovery, enhancing environmental resilience, improving public health, and promoting social well-being. These initiatives serve as a dual solution for environmental remediation and urban revitalization, offering substantial benefits such as carbon sequestration, biodiversity support, and the creation of vibrant public spaces. This section details a multifaceted approach to reforesting and greening urban areas, incorporating innovative techniques, community engagement, and international best practices.

Strategic Reforestation Initiatives

Reviving Forest Ecosystems

Reforestation is essential not only for environmental health but also for economic and social resilience. Comprehensive reforestation programs will restore degraded landscapes, enhance biodiversity, and contribute to climate change mitigation.

- **Native Species Planting**: Prioritize the planting of native tree species to restore natural ecosystems and support local wildlife. Native species are better adapted to the local climate and soil conditions, ensuring higher survival rates and ecological harmony.
- **Afforestation Programs**: Implement large-scale afforestation programs in urban peripheries and degraded lands. These programs will create new

forests, enhance green corridors, and serve as buffers against environmental hazards such as floods and landslides.

- **Community Forests**: Develop community-managed forests, involving local populations in the planning, planting, and maintenance of forest areas. Community forests foster local stewardship, provide livelihoods, and create a sense of ownership among residents.

Urban Greening Projects

Transforming Urban Landscapes

Urban greening transforms cityscapes into vibrant, healthy, and sustainable environments. Integrating green spaces within urban areas improves air quality, enhances urban biodiversity, and provides recreational opportunities.

- **Green Roofs and Vertical Gardens**: Promote the installation of green roofs and vertical gardens on buildings. These green installations reduce the urban heat island effect, improve insulation, and provide habitat for urban wildlife.
- **Park Revitalization**: Rejuvenate existing parks and develop new urban parks to offer recreational spaces for relaxation and physical activities. Incorporate playgrounds, sports facilities, and community gardens to cater to diverse needs 17:0†source .
- **Street Greening**: Enhance streetscapes by planting trees and creating green buffer zones along roadsides. Street greening improves air quality, provides shade, and enhances the aesthetic appeal of urban areas.

Innovative Greening Techniques

Leveraging Advanced Technologies

Adopting innovative greening techniques and technologies will maximize the environmental and social benefits of reforestation and urban greening efforts.

- **Drones for Reforestation**: Utilize drone technology for seed dispersal to accelerate reforestation efforts in inaccessible or large areas. Drones can plant trees at higher speeds and with greater precision, ensuring efficient coverage.
- **Hydroponic and Aquaponic Systems**: Integrate hydroponic and aquaponic systems in urban farming projects. These soil-less farming methods save water, reduce land use, and can be implemented in urban settings to produce fresh vegetables and fish, contributing to food security.
- **Smart Irrigation Systems**: Implement smart irrigation systems that use IoT sensors and AI to monitor soil moisture levels and optimize water

use. These systems ensure efficient watering, reduce waste, and support healthy plant growth.

Community Involvement and Education

Engaging Citizens in Green Initiatives

Community involvement is crucial for the success and sustainability of reforestation and urban greening projects.

- **Educational Programs**: Develop educational programs in schools and community centers to raise awareness about the benefits of trees and green spaces. Hands-on activities, such as tree planting events and garden projects, will engage citizens and foster environmental stewardship.
- **Volunteer Initiatives**: Encourage volunteer participation in greening projects. Organize community planting days, clean-up events, and greening maintenance activities to build social cohesion and a sense of community responsibility.
- **Public-Private Partnerships**: Form partnerships with businesses, NGOs, and government agencies to support urban greening projects. These collaborations can provide funding, expertise, and resources, enhancing the scope and impact of green initiatives.

International Cooperation and Best Practices

Learning from Global Successes

International cooperation and the adoption of best practices are essential for the effective implementation of reforestation and urban greening projects.

- **Global Reforestation Networks**: Join international reforestation networks to share knowledge, resources, and best practices. Collaborate with global organizations involved in large-scale reforestation efforts to gain insights and support.
- **Case Studies and Pilot Projects**: Study successful reforestation and urban greening projects from around the world and adapt relevant practices to the Ukrainian context. Implement pilot projects to test and refine strategies before scaling them up.
- **International Funding and Support**: Secure international funding and technical support from organizations such as the World Bank, United Nations Environment Programme (UNEP), and the European Union. These resources will enable the implementation of large-scale projects and ensure their sustainability .

Monitoring and Maintenance

Ensuring Long-Term Sustainability

Continuous monitoring and maintenance are critical to the long-term success of reforestation and urban greening projects.

- **GIS and Remote Sensing**: Use geographic information systems (GIS) and remote sensing technologies to monitor the health and growth of trees and green spaces. These tools provide accurate data for assessing progress and making informed management decisions.

- **Maintenance Programs**: Establish maintenance programs that include regular watering, pruning, and pest control. Engage local communities and employ maintenance staff to ensure that green spaces are well-maintained and thrive over time.

- **Impact Assessment**: Conduct regular impact assessments to evaluate the ecological, social, and economic benefits of reforestation and urban greening projects. Use the findings to improve strategies and demonstrate the value of green initiatives to stakeholders.

Conclusion

Reforestation and urban greening are pivotal to Ukraine's environmental remediation and sustainable urban development. By implementing thoughtful and innovative strategies, engaging communities, and leveraging international cooperation, Ukraine can transform its landscapes into vibrant, resilient, and green environments. These efforts will contribute significantly to the country's recovery, enhancing the quality of life for its citizens and fostering a legacy of sustainability and ecological stewardship.

Section 13.3: Sustainable Waste Management

Introduction

Effective waste management is a cornerstone of sustainable urban reconstruction. In the aftermath of conflict, debris, hazardous materials, and general waste present significant challenges that must be addressed to protect public health, restore environmental integrity, and lay the groundwork for resilient urban development. This section outlines a comprehensive strategy to implement sustainable waste management practices across Ukrainian cities, focusing on innovative technologies, community engagement, and international cooperation to transform waste from a burden into a resource.

Comprehensive Waste Assessment

Identifying and Categorizing Waste

A systematic assessment of the various types and quantities of waste generated is critical to developing effective management strategies.

- **Debris and Rubble**: Conduct thorough surveys to assess the extent of construction and demolition waste. Use drones and ground teams to map debris sites and quantify materials that can be recycled or repurposed.
- **Hazardous Waste**: Identify hazardous wastes such as asbestos, lead-based paints, and contaminated soils. Utilize specialized detection technologies to ensure these materials are safely handled and disposed of according to international safety standards .
- **Municipal Solid Waste (MSW)**: Assess the capacity and condition of existing MSW infrastructure. Document the types and volumes of household waste, industrial waste, and organic matter to optimize collection and treatment processes.

Advanced Waste Processing Technologies

Leveraging Innovation for Effective Waste Management

Incorporating advanced technologies will enhance the efficiency and sustainability of waste management operations.

- **Autonomous Sorting Facilities**: Establish automated sorting facilities equipped with robotics and AI to separate recyclable materials from mixed waste streams. These technologies ensure high accuracy and efficiency in material recovery, reducing reliance on manual sorting.
- **Waste-to-Energy (WTE) Plants**: Develop waste-to-energy plants that convert non-recyclable waste into electricity and heat. Employ advanced thermal treatments like gasification and pyrolysis to maximize energy recovery and minimize emissions 16†EU-Commission-Ukraine.docx†source .
- **Material Recovery Facilities (MRFs)**: Deploy MRFs that leverage cutting-edge technologies to process and reclaim valuable materials from waste. These facilities will play a crucial role in supporting circular economy initiatives by providing a steady supply of recycled materials for construction and manufacturing.

Community Involvement and Education

Engaging Citizens in Sustainable Waste Practices

Active community participation is vital for the success of sustainable waste management programs.

- **Public Awareness Campaigns**: Launch comprehensive public awareness campaigns to educate citizens about recycling, composting, and proper waste disposal. Use diverse media platforms, including social media, local newspapers, and community events, to reach a wide audience.
- **Citizen Participation Programs**: Develop programs that encourage residents to participate in waste reduction and recycling initiatives. Or-

ganize neighborhood clean-up events, recycling drives, and composting workshops to build a culture of sustainability.

- **School Education Programs**: Implement education programs in schools to teach children about the importance of waste management and environmental stewardship. Hands-on activities, such as creating school gardens and recycling projects, will instill lifelong sustainable habits from an early age.

Circular Economy Initiatives

Transforming Waste into Resources

Promoting a circular economy will ensure that waste is seen not as a problem but as a valuable resource.

- **Product-as-a-Service Models**: Encourage businesses to adopt product-as-a-service models, where consumers rent or lease products rather than purchase them outright. This approach reduces waste, promotes product longevity, and enhances material recovery.
- **Urban Mining Programs**: Implement urban mining programs to extract valuable metals and materials from e-waste and other discarded products. These programs will support the recycling industry and reduce the need for raw material extraction.
- **Material Banks**: Establish material banks to collect and store reusable construction materials from demolition sites. These banks will enable the efficient reuse of materials in new construction projects, reducing waste and conserving resources 13†EU-Commission-Ukraine.docx†source .

International Collaboration and Best Practices

Learning and Adopting Global Standards

International cooperation will provide valuable insights, technologies, and funding for sustainable waste management.

- **Global Waste Management Partnerships**: Engage in partnerships with global organizations and governments to learn best practices and innovative waste management solutions. Collaborations with entities like the World Bank, European Union, and UN Environment Programme will provide access to expertise and resources.
- **Adoption of International Standards**: Implement international waste management standards and guidelines to ensure that practices in Ukraine align with global best practices. This alignment will enhance the effectiveness and sustainability of waste management operations.
- **International Funding and Grants**: Secure funding from international donors and financial institutions to support large-scale waste management

projects. Transparent and accountable use of funds will build confidence among international partners and ensure the long-term success of these initiatives 16†EU-Commission-Ukraine.docx†source .

Monitoring and Evaluation Systems

Ensuring Continuous Improvement

Developing robust monitoring and evaluation systems will ensure that waste management practices are continuously improved and adapted to changing needs.

- **IoT-Enabled Waste Monitoring**: Deploy IoT devices to monitor waste collection, processing, and disposal in real time. These systems will provide data on waste volumes, types, and treatment efficiency, enabling timely adjustments to operations.
- **Performance Metrics and KPIs**: Establish key performance indicators (KPIs) to measure the success of waste management programs. Regularly review metrics such as recycling rates, waste diversion rates, and energy recovery efficiency to assess performance.
- **Feedback and Adaptive Management**: Create feedback mechanisms that allow citizens and stakeholders to report issues and suggest improvements. Use this feedback to make data-driven decisions and continuously refine waste management strategies for better outcomes .

Conclusion

Implementing sustainable waste management practices is fundamental to Ukraine's urban reconstruction and environmental remediation efforts. By leveraging advanced technologies, fostering community engagement, promoting a circular economy, and adhering to international standards, Ukraine can transform its waste management systems into models of sustainability and efficiency. These comprehensive efforts will not only mitigate immediate waste-related challenges but also contribute to long-term environmental health, public well-being, and economic resilience. Through sustained commitment and innovative approaches, Ukraine can lead the way in sustainable waste management, setting an example for post-conflict recovery worldwide.

Chapter 14: Funding and Resource Allocation

Section 14.1: Donor Coordination

Ensuring Synergy and Efficiency in International Support

In the monumental task of rebuilding Ukraine, seamless coordination with international donors and financial institutions is paramount. This section outlines a strategic framework to harness global support efficiently, ensuring that the multitude of financial aid and technical assistance initiatives align with Ukraine's comprehensive reconstruction agenda. The approach emphasizes creating robust systems for collaboration, transparency, and accountability to maximize the impact of international contributions.

Establishing a Centralized Donor Coordination Platform

Unified Coordination Mechanism

To effectively manage the influx of international support, Ukraine will establish a centralized donor coordination platform. This platform will serve as the nerve center for all international aid and investment activities.

- **Interagency Collaboration**: Integrate efforts across various government agencies, including the Ministry of Reconstruction, the Ministry of Finance, and the Ministry of Foreign Affairs, to ensure unified communication and plan execution. This interagency collaboration will streamline processes and eliminate bureaucratic delays .

- **International Donor Coordination Platform (IDCP)**: Launch the IDCP to facilitate real-time information sharing and collaboration between Ukraine, international donors, and financial institutions. The IDCP will provide a comprehensive database of all ongoing and planned projects, ensuring that resources are allocated efficiently and duplications are avoided .

Strategic Donor Engagement

Proactive and Strategic Relationships

Building strong, strategic relationships with international donors is essential for securing sustained support and aligning efforts with Ukraine's reconstruction priorities.

- **Bilateral and Multilateral Agreements**: Formalize partnerships with international organizations such as the European Union (EU), World Bank, International Monetary Fund (IMF), and United Nations (UN) through bilateral and multilateral agreements. These agreements will define specific roles, responsibilities, and funding commitments, ensuring coordinated and cohesive support .

- **Donor Conferences**: Organize regular donor conferences to present Ukraine's reconstruction progress, funding needs, and impact metrics. These conferences will serve as platforms for securing commitments, fostering transparency, and renewing donor confidence. High-level representation from Ukraine will underscore the government's commitment to accountability and effective use of resources .

Transparent Fund Management Systems

Ensuring Accountability and Trust

Transparent fund management is critical to maintaining donor trust and ensuring that financial resources are used effectively and efficiently.

- **Blockchain-Based Fund Tracking**: Implement blockchain technology to create a transparent, immutable ledger for tracking all financial transactions related to reconstruction efforts. This system will enhance transparency by providing real-time visibility into fund flows and allocations, thereby reducing the risk of fraud and corruption .
- **Regular Audits and Reporting**: Conduct regular audits in collaboration with international audit firms and oversight agencies. These audits will verify that funds are being used as intended and provide accountability to donors. Detailed reports will be published and made accessible to all stakeholders, ensuring continuous oversight and management .

Maximizing Impact Through Strategic Planning

Data-Driven Decision Making

Data-driven strategies will enhance the effectiveness of donor-funded projects and ensure that resources are directed where they are most needed.

- **Advanced Data Analytics**: Utilize advanced data analytics to assess needs, track progress, and evaluate the impact of reconstruction projects. Integrating data from various sources will provide comprehensive insights, enabling evidence-based decision-making and strategic allocation of donor funds .
- **Impact Assessment Framework**: Develop and maintain an impact assessment framework to measure the outcomes of donor-funded projects. This framework will include key performance indicators (KPIs) related to economic recovery, infrastructure development, public service restoration, and community resilience. Regular assessments will identify successes, areas for improvement, and best practices to be scaled or replicated .

Leveraging International Best Practices

Drawing from Global Experiences

Adopting international best practices will ensure that Ukraine's reconstruction efforts benefit from global expertise and proven methodologies.

- **Global Knowledge Exchange**: Engage in knowledge exchange programs with countries that have successfully navigated post-conflict reconstruction. Workshops, training sessions, and study tours will facilitate the transfer of knowledge and best practices in urban planning, infrastructure development, and governance .

- **Case Studies and Pilot Projects**: Implement pilot projects based on successful international case studies. These projects will serve as models for scaling best practices across Ukraine, ensuring that innovative solutions are adapted to local contexts and needs.

Enhancing Capacity for Fund Management

Building Long-Term Sustainability

Investing in capacity building for Ukrainian institutions will ensure the long-term success and sustainability of reconstruction efforts.

- **Training Programs**: Develop and implement comprehensive training programs for government officials and project managers on fund management, international financial regulations, and best practices in transparency and accountability. Partner with international donors to provide expertise and resources for these programs.
- **Institutional Strengthening**: Strengthen the capacities of local institutions involved in reconstruction efforts. This includes enhancing technical skills, improving governance structures, and establishing new units dedicated to monitoring and evaluation.

Fostering Continuous Dialogue and Evaluation

Adaptation and Continuous Improvement

Establishing mechanisms for continuous dialogue and evaluation will ensure that reconstruction efforts remain responsive and adaptive to evolving needs.

- **Regular Review Meetings**: Hold regular review meetings with key stakeholders, including international donors, financial institutions, and local authorities. These meetings will provide opportunities to assess progress, address challenges, and adjust strategies as necessary.
- **Feedback Loops and Adaptive Management**: Develop feedback loops that incorporate input from local communities, project beneficiaries, and other stakeholders. Adaptive management practices will allow for real-time adjustments based on feedback and evaluation findings, ensuring flexibility and responsiveness in implementation.

Conclusion

Coordinating with international donors and financial institutions is a linchpin in Ukraine's comprehensive strategy for sustainable post-war urban reconstruction. Through the establishment of centralized coordination platforms, strategic donor engagement, transparent fund management, and the integration of global best practices, Ukraine will ensure that international support is effectively mobilized and utilized. These efforts, underpinned by capacity building and continuous evaluation, will pave the way for a resilient, prosperous, and sustainably rebuilt Ukraine.

Section 14.2: Transparent Fund Distribution

Building Trust Through Transparency

Ensuring transparent fund distribution is critical for the effective and ethical use of resources in Ukraine's reconstruction efforts. A robust framework for transparent allocation and utilization of funds will foster trust among international donors, local stakeholders, and the broader Ukrainian population. This section details the strategies and mechanisms to achieve transparent fund distribution, drawing on international best practices and leveraging advanced technologies to uphold the highest standards of accountability.

Establishing Robust Financial Oversight Mechanisms

Creating Audit and Compliance Frameworks

A detailed and systematic approach to financial oversight is essential for monitoring and verifying the use of reconstruction funds.

- **Independent Audit Committees**: Form independent audit committees to oversee the use of funds. These committees, composed of financial experts, auditors, and legal advisors, will conduct regular audits and provide detailed reports on fund utilization, ensuring compliance with international standards .

- **Regular Financial Reporting**: Implement mandatory financial reporting requirements for all entities receiving reconstruction funds. These reports will detail the allocation, disbursement, and utilization of funds, and will be made publicly accessible to enhance transparency.

- **External Audits**: Engage international audit firms to perform regular external audits. These firms will bring global expertise and impartiality, adding an additional layer of accountability and trust.

Leveraging Blockchain Technology

Ensuring Immutable Records and Transparency

Blockchain technology can provide a secure and transparent method for tracking financial transactions and fund allocations.

- **Blockchain-Based Fund Tracking**: Implement blockchain systems to create an immutable ledger of all transactions related to reconstruction funds. This ledger will be publicly accessible, allowing stakeholders to trace the flow of funds from donors to end recipients, thus preventing fraud and misappropriation 16†EU-Commission-

Ukraine.docx†source 17†EU-Commission-Ukraine.docx†source 18†EU-Commission-Ukraine.docx†source .

- **Smart Contracts**: Utilize smart contracts to automate the disbursement of funds. These contracts will be executed only when predefined conditions are met, ensuring that funds are released in accordance with specific project milestones and objectives 2:0†EU-Commission-Ukraine.docx†source 2:19†EU-Commission-Ukraine.docx†source .

Transparent Allocation and Disbursement Processes

Streamlined and Accountable Procedures

Developing clear and transparent procedures for fund allocation and disbursement will ensure that resources are directed efficiently where they are most needed.

- **Standardized Application Processes**: Create standardized application processes for accessing reconstruction funds. These processes should be simple, clear, and accessible to all potential beneficiaries, ensuring equal opportunity for funding.
- **Allocation Committees**: Establish allocation committees with representatives from government, international donors, civil society, and local communities. These committees will review funding applications and allocate resources based on transparent criteria and strategic priorities 5†EU-Commission-Ukraine.docx†source 19†EU-Commission-Ukraine.docx†source .
- **Real-Time Monitoring Systems**: Implement real-time monitoring systems to track the progress of funded projects. These systems will provide ongoing oversight and ensure that funds are being used as intended, enabling timely interventions if issues arise.

Public Accountability Platforms

Engaging Citizens and Enhancing Trust

Public accountability is crucial for maintaining trust and ensuring that the reconstruction process is inclusive and transparent.

- **Online Transparency Portals**: Develop online transparency portals where detailed information about fund distribution and project progress is published. These portals will allow citizens to see how funds are being used, fostering greater public trust and engagement 11†EU-Commission-Ukraine.docx†source 20†EU-Commission-Ukraine.docx†source .
- **Feedback Mechanisms**: Establish feedback mechanisms that allow citizens to report concerns or irregularities related to fund distribution. These mechanisms will include hotlines, web forms, and community meetings,

providing multiple channels for feedback and ensuring that concerns are addressed promptly.

International Best Practices and Standards

Adopting Proven Models

Learning from global experiences and adopting international best practices will enhance the effectiveness and credibility of fund distribution mechanisms.

- **OECD Principles**: Adhere to the OECD's "Principles for Good International Engagement in Fragile States and Situations" to ensure that reconstruction efforts are conducted transparently and ethically 2:0†EU-Commission-Ukraine.docx†source .
- **World Bank Guidelines**: Follow the World Bank's guidelines on post-disaster needs assessment and transparent fund distribution to ensure that funds are allocated efficiently and effectively 5†EU-Commission-Ukraine.docx†source .
- **European Union Support Frameworks**: Leverage the European Union's frameworks for financial support and oversight, ensuring that funds are used for their intended purposes and that all expenditures are thoroughly documented and audited 2†EU-Commission-Ukraine.docx†source 2:16†EU-Commission-Ukraine.docx†source .

Conclusion

Transparent fund distribution is a cornerstone of Ukraine's post-war reconstruction. By establishing robust financial oversight mechanisms, leveraging blockchain technology, ensuring transparent processes, engaging the public, and adhering to international best practices, Ukraine can ensure the ethical and efficient use of reconstruction funds. These efforts will build trust among donors, enhance public support, and ultimately contribute to the successful rebuilding of a resilient, sustainable, and inclusive Ukraine.

Section 14.3: Anti-Corruption Measures

Ensuring Integrity and Trust in Reconstruction Efforts

The successful reconstruction of Ukraine depends on the integrity of financial management and the assurance that funds are used as intended. Implementing robust anti-corruption measures is critical to building trust among international donors, local stakeholders, and the general public. This section outlines comprehensive strategies to prevent, detect, and address corruption in all aspects of the reconstruction process, leveraging advanced technologies, strengthening institutions, and fostering a culture of transparency and accountability.

Establishing a Comprehensive Anti-Corruption Framework

Creating a Culture of Accountability

A well-structured anti-corruption framework is essential for overseeing the ethical use of funds and resources in reconstruction efforts.

- **Anti-Corruption Task Force**: Establish an Anti-Corruption Task Force within the Ministry of Finance, comprising members from various governmental bodies, law enforcement agencies, and civil society organizations. This task force will coordinate anti-corruption initiatives, conduct investigations, and ensure compliance with anti-corruption laws and regulations.

- **National Anti-Corruption Strategy**: Develop a comprehensive National Anti-Corruption Strategy that delineates clear policies, objectives, and action plans for tackling corruption during the reconstruction phase. This strategy will include specific measures for prevention, detection, enforcement, and public awareness.

- **Whistleblower Protection Mechanisms**: Implement robust whistleblower protection laws to encourage reporting of corrupt activities. Ensure that individuals who report corruption are safeguarded against retaliation and that their complaints are thoroughly investigated.

Leveraging Technology for Anti-Corruption

Utilizing Advanced Tools for Transparency and Monitoring

The application of advanced technologies can significantly enhance the effectiveness of anti-corruption measures.

- **Blockchain Technology**: Use blockchain technology to create immutable records of all financial transactions related to reconstruction funds. This technology will ensure transparency and traceability, making it difficult to alter or hide financial activities .

- **AI and Machine Learning**: Implement AI and machine learning algorithms to analyze financial data for patterns indicative of corrupt behavior. These technologies can detect anomalies and flag suspicious transactions for further investigation, providing real-time oversight and intervention capabilities.

- **Digital Platforms for Public Accountability**: Develop digital platforms where citizens can track the allocation and usage of funds. These platforms should provide detailed financial data, project statuses, and allow for public feedback, enhancing transparency and public trust.

Strengthening Legal and Institutional Frameworks

Enhancing Regulatory and Enforcement Capabilities

A robust legal and institutional framework is essential for enforcing anti-corruption measures and ensuring compliance.

- **Strengthening Anti-Corruption Legislation**: Update and strengthen existing anti-corruption laws to address current challenges and incorporate international best practices. Ensure that these laws provide clear definitions, stringent penalties, and effective enforcement mechanisms.

- **Capacity Building for Law Enforcement**: Invest in capacity-building programs for law enforcement agencies, including specialized training in financial crime investigation and anti-corruption enforcement. Equip these agencies with the necessary tools and resources to effectively combat corruption.

- **Judicial Independence**: Ensure the independence and integrity of the judiciary by protecting judges from political pressure and interference. Establish special anti-corruption courts with trained judges to handle corruption cases swiftly and impartially.

Engaging Civil Society and International Partners

Promoting Collaborative Anti-Corruption Efforts

Collaboration with civil society organizations and international partners is crucial for a holistic approach to anti-corruption.

- **Civil Society Engagement**: Engage civil society organizations in anti-corruption efforts by involving them in monitoring, advocacy, and education initiatives. These organizations can provide valuable insights, raise public awareness, and hold authorities accountable.

- **International Cooperation**: Strengthen cooperation with international anti-corruption bodies such as Transparency International, the International Anti-Corruption Academy, and the United Nations Office on Drugs and Crime (UNODC). Collaborate on joint investigations, share best practices, and participate in international anti-corruption forums.

- **Donor Involvement**: Involve international donors in anti-corruption initiatives by incorporating anti-corruption clauses in funding agreements. Donors should require regular audits, adherence to transparency standards, and reporting of any suspected corruption.

Monitoring and Evaluation

Ensuring Continuous Improvement and Accountability

Ongoing monitoring and evaluation are critical to the success of anti-corruption measures.

- **Regular Audits and Reporting**: Conduct regular audits of all reconstruction projects and financial transactions. Publish audit reports and make them accessible to the public to ensure transparency and accountability.

- **Performance Metrics**: Develop key performance indicators (KPIs) to measure the effectiveness of anti-corruption initiatives. Regularly review these metrics to identify areas for improvement and ensure that anti-corruption efforts are achieving their desired outcomes.

- **Feedback and Adaptation**: Create mechanisms for continuous feedback from stakeholders, including government officials, civil society, and the public. Use this feedback to adapt and refine anti-corruption strategies, ensuring that they remain relevant and effective.

Conclusion

Anti-corruption measures are a critical component of Ukraine's reconstruction strategy. By establishing a comprehensive anti-corruption framework, utilizing advanced technologies, strengthening legal and institutional capacities, engaging civil society and international partners, and ensuring continuous monitoring, Ukraine can build a transparent, accountable, and resilient reconstruction process. These efforts will not only restore trust but also pave the way for a sustainable and prosperous future, free from the scourge of corruption.

Chapter 15: Community Engagement

Section 15.1: Participatory Planning

Building Inclusive and Responsive Urban Reconstruction

In the wake of the immense destruction wrought by conflict, the regeneration of Ukraine's cities must be grounded in inclusive and participatory planning processes. Engaging local communities in decision-making ensures that reconstruction reflects the needs, desires, and aspirations of the people it serves. This section details a strategic framework for participatory planning that empowers citizens, fosters social cohesion, and enhances the legitimacy and effectiveness of reconstruction initiatives.

Establishing Local Planning Committees

Empowering Communities through Structured Engagement

Local planning committees are essential for harnessing community input and ensuring that reconstruction efforts are responsive to local needs.

- **Formation of Committees**: Establish local planning committees composed of community leaders, residents, civil society representatives, and local government officials. These committees will serve as the primary platform for community engagement in planning and decision-making processes .

- **Capacity Building**: Provide training and resources to committee members to enhance their capacity for effective participation. Training programs will cover topics such as urban planning, project management, and conflict resolution, equipping members with the skills needed to contribute meaningfully to the reconstruction process.

- **Inclusive Representation**: Ensure that planning committees represent the full diversity of the community, including women, youth, elderly, and marginalized groups. This inclusivity will ensure that the voices of all community members are heard and considered 11†EU-Commission-Ukraine.docx†source .

Conducting Community Consultations

Facilitating Open and Transparent Dialogue

Community consultations are vital for gathering input, building consensus, and fostering a sense of ownership among residents.

- **Public Meetings and Workshops**: Organize regular public meetings and workshops to discuss reconstruction plans and gather community feedback. These forums will provide opportunities for residents to share their perspectives, raise concerns, and propose solutions .

- **Town Hall Meetings**: Hold town hall meetings to facilitate direct dialogue between community members and decision-makers. These meetings will ensure transparency and accountability, allowing citizens to hold authorities accountable for their actions and decisions .

- **Focus Groups and Surveys**: Conduct focus groups and surveys to collect detailed input on specific issues or projects. These tools will provide valuable insights into community preferences and priorities, informing more nuanced and tailored reconstruction plans .

Utilizing Digital Platforms for Engagement

Harnessing Technology for Broad-Based Participation

Digital platforms offer innovative ways to engage citizens and facilitate participatory planning.

- **Online Portals and Forums**: Develop online portals and forums where residents can access information, submit feedback, and participate in discussions. These platforms will enable continuous engagement and ensure that even those unable to attend in-person meetings can contribute.

- **Mobile Applications**: Implement mobile applications that allow residents to report issues, provide feedback, and receive updates on reconstruction progress. These apps will offer convenient, real-time channels for communication and participation.

- **Virtual Reality (VR) and Augmented Reality (AR)**: Use VR and AR technologies to create immersive simulations of proposed projects. These virtual tools will help residents visualize changes and provide more informed feedback, enhancing their understanding and engagement.

Ensuring Transparency and Accountability

Building Trust through Open Governance

Transparent and accountable practices are essential for maintaining public trust and ensuring the legitimacy of participatory planning processes.

- **Public Disclosure of Plans and Budgets**: Publish detailed plans, budgets, and timelines for reconstruction projects. This transparency will allow residents to see how funds are being used and hold authorities accountable for delivering on their commitments.

- **Monitoring and Reporting Mechanisms**: Establish robust monitoring and reporting mechanisms to track the progress of projects and the implementation of community inputs. Regular reports will be shared with the public, providing updates and demonstrating responsiveness to community feedback 20†EU-Commission-Ukraine.docx†source.

- **Independent Oversight Bodies**: Create independent oversight bodies to review and audit reconstruction projects. These bodies, comprised of experts and community representatives, will ensure that funds are used effectively and ethically, and that projects meet high standards of quality and inclusivity.

Encouraging Participatory Budgeting

Involving Citizens in Financial Decision-Making

Participatory budgeting empowers citizens to have a direct say in how reconstruction funds are allocated.

- **Citizen Panels**: Form citizen panels to review budget proposals and make recommendations on funding allocations. These panels will represent diverse community interests and ensure that spending reflects local priorities 11:9†source.

- **Budgetary Workshops**: Conduct workshops to educate citizens on the budgeting process and the financial aspects of reconstruction projects. These workshops will equip residents with the knowledge needed to make informed decisions and engage meaningfully in budgeting discussions.

- **Voting Mechanisms**: Implement voting mechanisms that allow citizens to vote on budget priorities and specific funding proposals. This democratic process will enhance community ownership and ensure that resources are directed towards the most valued projects .

Fostering Social Cohesion through Shared Projects

Building Stronger Communities through Collaborative Efforts

Joint projects and initiatives can rebuild social fabric and foster a sense of unity and purpose among residents.

- **Community-Driven Initiatives**: Support community-driven reconstruction initiatives that involve residents in the design and implementation of local projects. These initiatives will strengthen community bonds and empower residents to take an active role in rebuilding their own neighborhoods .
- **Public Art and Cultural Projects**: Promote public art and cultural projects that reflect the community's heritage and identity. These projects will not only beautify public spaces but also provide a platform for collective expression and reconciliation .
- **Volunteer Programs**: Develop volunteer programs that encourage residents to contribute their time and skills to reconstruction efforts. Volunteer activities, such as tree planting, park cleanups, and construction projects, will enhance community spirit and build a culture of civic engagement .

Conclusion

Participatory planning is a cornerstone of Ukraine's reconstruction strategy, ensuring that the rebuilding process is inclusive, transparent, and responsive to the needs of its citizens. By establishing local planning committees, conducting community consultations, leveraging digital platforms, ensuring transparency, encouraging participatory budgeting, and fostering social cohesion, Ukraine can create a resilient and vibrant urban landscape that reflects the aspirations of its people. These efforts will not only rebuild infrastructure but also restore community trust, unity, and hope for a brighter future.

Section 15.2: Social Cohesion Programs

Unifying Efforts for a Resilient Community

As Ukraine embarks on the journey of reconstruction, fostering social cohesion is crucial for healing the nation's wounds and building a resilient, inclusive society. Social cohesion programs aim to bridge divides, promote mutual understanding, and support the integration of diverse communities, including internally displaced persons (IDPs) and returning refugees. This section lays out a comprehensive plan for social cohesion, leveraging community-based initiatives, international partnerships, and innovative strategies to rebuild trust, unity, and social fabric.

Developing Social Cohesion Frameworks

Strategic Planning and Community Involvement

A strategic framework is essential to guide the implementation of social cohesion programs effectively.

- **Community Needs Assessment**: Conduct thorough assessments to understand the specific needs, challenges, and aspirations of various community groups. Utilize surveys, focus groups, and consultations to gather comprehensive data and insights.
- **Inclusive Policy Development**: Involve community leaders, local organizations, and stakeholders in developing policies and action plans for social cohesion. This participatory approach ensures that programs are tailored to the unique context and needs of each community.
- **Integration of Conscious Efforts**: Ensure that social cohesion is a cross-cutting objective integrated into all reconstruction and development initiatives. This holistic approach will ensure consistent efforts to promote unity and inclusivity across various sectors.

Community-Driven Initiatives

Empowering Residents to Shape Their Future

Empowering communities to take an active role in rebuilding their social fabric fosters ownership and responsibility.

- **Local Community Centers**: Establish community centers that serve as hubs for social activities, educational programs, and support services. These centers will provide safe spaces for interaction, collaboration, and learning.
- **Volunteer Programs**: Develop volunteer programs that encourage residents to participate in community service and local development projects. Volunteering not only addresses immediate needs but also strengthens bonds among community members.
- **Cultural and Recreational Activities**: Organize cultural events, sports tournaments, and recreational activities that celebrate diversity and foster mutual understanding. These activities will provide opportunities for people from different backgrounds to connect and build relationships.

Supporting Vulnerable Groups

Ensuring Inclusivity and Equity

Special attention must be given to vulnerable groups to ensure that social cohesion efforts are inclusive and equitable.

- **Support for IDPs and Refugees**: Provide targeted support for internally displaced persons and returning refugees, including access to housing, employment, education, and healthcare. Implement programs that facilitate their integration into local communities and support social and economic recovery.

- **Programs for Children and Youth**: Develop programs specifically for children and youth to promote their well-being and positive development. Initiatives such as after-school programs, mentorship schemes, and youth leadership training will empower young people and foster a sense of belonging.

- **Assistance for Elderly and Disabled Individuals**: Establish services and programs that cater to the needs of elderly and disabled individuals, ensuring they have access to support and opportunities to participate in community life. This includes accessible infrastructure, home care services, and social inclusion initiatives.

Leveraging International Partnerships

Gaining Global Support and Expertise

International cooperation can provide valuable resources, expertise, and support for social cohesion programs.

- **Partnerships with International Organizations**: Collaborate with international organizations such as the European Union, United Nations, and Global Citizen to gain access to best practices, funding, and technical assistance for social cohesion initiatives 0†EU-Commission-Ukraine.docx†source 1†EU-Commission-Ukraine.docx†source .

- **Exchange Programs**: Implement international exchange programs that enable community leaders and practitioners to learn from successful social cohesion efforts in other countries. These exchanges will facilitate knowledge transfer and inspire innovative approaches.

- **Global Advocacy Campaigns**: Engage in global advocacy campaigns to raise awareness about Ukraine's reconstruction efforts and garner international solidarity and support. These campaigns can mobilize resources and foster a sense of global community.

Monitoring and Evaluation

Ensuring Effectiveness and Adaptation

Continuous monitoring and evaluation are vital to ensure the effectiveness of social cohesion programs and allow for necessary adjustments.

- **Impact Assessment Tools**: Develop and utilize impact assessment tools to measure the success of social cohesion initiatives. Key metrics might include community engagement levels, social capital, and reductions in conflict and social tensions.
- **Feedback Mechanisms**: Establish feedback mechanisms that allow community members to share their experiences and suggestions. Regularly gathering and analyzing feedback will enable programs to adapt to changing needs and improve outcomes.
- **Transparent Reporting**: Maintain transparent reporting practices by regularly publishing reports on the progress and impacts of social cohesion programs. This transparency will build trust and accountability among community members and stakeholders.

Funding and Sustainability

Securing Resources for Long-Term Impact

Sustainable funding and resource management are crucial for the longevity and effectiveness of social cohesion programs.

- **Diversified Funding Sources**: Secure funding from multiple sources, including government budgets, international grants, private donations, and corporate sponsorships. This diversified funding strategy will ensure stability and resilience.
- **Public-Private Partnerships**: Establish public-private partnerships to leverage the resources and expertise of the private sector. Partnerships with businesses can provide financial support, volunteer opportunities, and collaborative initiatives.
- **Community Fundraising**: Encourage community-led fundraising efforts to support social cohesion projects. Local fundraising campaigns can generate resources and foster a sense of ownership and investment among residents.

Conclusion

Social cohesion programs are fundamental to Ukraine's reconstruction and the creation of a resilient and inclusive society. By developing comprehensive frameworks, empowering communities, supporting vulnerable groups, leveraging international partnerships, ensuring continuous monitoring, and securing sustainable funding, Ukraine can foster unity and rebuild the social fabric of its cities. These efforts will not only heal the wounds of conflict but also pave the way for a vibrant and cohesive future, where all citizens feel valued and connected to their communities.

Section 15.3: Citizen Feedback and Participation

The Power of Inclusive Engagement

Citizen feedback and participation are fundamental pillars in the sustainable and resilient reconstruction of Ukraine. Inclusive engagement ensures that municipal rebuilding efforts truly reflect the aspirations, needs, and concerns of the people. This section details a comprehensive approach to establishing robust feedback mechanisms and enhancing citizen participation throughout the reconstruction process, harnessing modern technology, fostering trust, and facilitating effective communication between the government and the public.

Creating Platforms for Continuous Feedback

Harnessing Technology for Real-Time Interaction

Digital platforms are essential tools for collecting and managing citizen feedback efficiently.

- **Online Feedback Portals**: Develop user-friendly online portals where citizens can submit comments, suggestions, and complaints related to reconstruction activities. These platforms will be equipped with functionalities that allow for easy navigation, multilingual support, and anonymity to encourage honest input from all demographics.

- **Mobile Applications**: Implement mobile applications that provide real-time updates on reconstruction projects and allow citizens to report issues or provide suggestions directly through their smartphones. Features such as geotagging, multimedia submissions, and push notifications will enhance the functionality and user engagement of these applications.

- **Social Media Integration**: Leverage social media platforms to gather community feedback and foster open dialogue. Regularly post updates on project progress, solicit input through polls and surveys, and respond to citizen inquiries promptly to ensure transparency and build trust .

Establishing Citizen Advisory Councils

Empowering Communities through Structured Representation

Citizen advisory councils will serve as vital links between the government and the community, ensuring grassroots involvement in decision-making processes.

- **Formation of Councils**: Create citizen advisory councils at local, regional, and national levels, comprising a diverse cross-section of the community, including representatives from various age groups, genders, socio-economic backgrounds, and ethnicities. These councils will provide regular feedback, advise on policy decisions, and help prioritize reconstruction projects.

- **Regular Meetings and Consultations**: Schedule regular meetings between advisory councils and government officials to discuss project updates, address concerns, and integrate citizen feedback into planning and execution phases. Structured agendas and transparent minutes will ensure these meetings are productive and inclusive .
- **Capacity Building Workshops**: Organize workshops to build the capacity of citizen council members, focusing on topics such as urban planning, sustainable development, and governance. Providing these educational opportunities will empower council members to contribute more effectively and knowledgeably .

Implementing Participatory Budgeting

Direct Citizen Involvement in Financial Decisions

Participatory budgeting initiatives will empower citizens by giving them a direct say in how reconstruction funds are allocated.

- **Budget Proposal Platforms**: Develop digital platforms where citizens can submit budget proposals for community-based projects and vote on funding priorities. This democratic process will ensure that financial resources are directed toward the most impactful and relevant initiatives as determined by the community.
- **Community Budget Assemblies**: Host community budget assemblies where citizens can present their proposals, discuss priorities, and make collective decisions on budget allocations. These assemblies will foster a sense of ownership and communal responsibility for the outcomes of funded projects.
- **Transparent Reporting**: Maintain transparency by regularly publishing detailed reports on how funds are allocated and spent, including project outcomes and financial audits. This practice will build trust and accountability between the government and the public .

Enhancing Two-Way Communication

Facilitating Open and Constructive Dialogue

Effective two-way communication channels are essential for fostering mutual understanding and responsiveness.

- **Public Information Campaigns**: Launch comprehensive public information campaigns to keep citizens informed about reconstruction plans, progress, and results. Utilize various media channels, including TV, radio, print, and digital platforms, to reach a wide audience.
- **Interactive Town Halls and Forums**: Organize regular town hall meetings and public forums where citizens can engage directly with officials,

ask questions, and provide feedback. Interactive elements such as Q&A sessions, live polls, and moderated discussions will enhance participation and ensure diverse voices are heard.

- **Feedback Loops**: Implement feedback loops that not only collect input but also demonstrate how citizen feedback is integrated into decision-making processes. Providing updates on how suggestions are used and the impact of community input will enhance transparency and trust .

Building a Culture of Participation

Fostering Long-Term Civic Engagement

Promoting and nurturing a culture of participation is key to sustaining long-term community involvement in governance and development.

- **Civic Education Programs**: Develop educational programs for schools and community centers that emphasize the importance of civic engagement and participatory governance. These programs will instill values of citizenship and responsibility from an early age.
- **Celebrating Citizen Contributions**: Recognize and celebrate the contributions of citizens through awards, public acknowledgments, and media features. Highlighting successful community-driven projects and commending active participants will encourage ongoing involvement.
- **Partnerships with NGOs and Civil Society**: Collaborate with non-governmental organizations and civil society groups to promote and facilitate citizen participation. These partnerships will bring additional resources, expertise, and networks to support engagement initiatives .

Monitoring and Improvement

Ensuring Effectiveness and Adaptation

Continuous monitoring and iterative improvement are essential to the success of citizen feedback and participation mechanisms.

- **Impact Assessment Tools**: Utilize impact assessment tools to measure the effectiveness of feedback and participation mechanisms. Metrics such as engagement levels, satisfaction rates, and the tangible impact of citizen input will guide improvements.
- **Adaptive Management Practices**: Apply adaptive management practices by regularly reviewing feedback data and making necessary adjustments to engagement strategies. Flexibility and responsiveness will ensure that participation mechanisms remain relevant and effective.
- **Independent Evaluations**: Conduct independent evaluations of participatory processes to ensure objectivity and accountability. These evalu-

ations will provide valuable insights and recommendations for enhancing engagement initiatives .

Conclusion

Citizen feedback and participation are vital components of Ukraine's reconstruction strategy, ensuring that rebuilding efforts are transparent, inclusive, and responsive to community needs. By creating robust platforms for feedback, establishing advisory councils, implementing participatory budgeting, enhancing two-way communication, fostering a culture of participation, and ensuring continuous improvement, Ukraine can build a resilient and empowered society. These efforts will not only enhance the effectiveness of reconstruction projects but also strengthen the bond between citizens and their government, paving the way for a prosperous and democratic future .

Chapter 16: Sustainability and Climate Resilience

Section 16.1: Renewable Energy Integration

Harnessing Clean Energy for a Resilient Future

In the monumental task of reconstructing Ukraine, integrating renewable energy sources is pivotal to ensuring a resilient, sustainable, and self-reliant nation. The strategic deployment of renewable energy not only mitigates the adverse impacts of climate change but also fosters energy independence, economic growth, and environmental stewardship. This section presents a comprehensive plan for integrating renewable energy into Ukraine's post-war recovery, leveraging cutting-edge technologies, fostering community engagement, and ensuring sustainability for future generations.

Strategic Assessment and Planning

Laying the Groundwork for Renewable Integration

A detailed assessment and strategic planning phase are crucial to identify the most effective and efficient renewable energy solutions for Ukraine.

Comprehensive Energy Needs Assessment

Conduct a nationwide assessment to evaluate energy needs and potential renewable resources. This involves:

- **Resource Mapping**: Utilize satellite imagery, geographic information systems (GIS), and ground surveys to map renewable resources such as solar, wind, hydro, and biomass across Ukraine.

- **Infrastructure Evaluation**: Assess the existing energy infrastructure, identifying areas that require upgrades or expansions to accommodate renewable energy integration.
- **Community Consultations**: Engage with local communities to understand their energy needs, preferences, and potential contributions to renewable energy projects. This inclusive approach ensures that the energy transition aligns with local priorities.

Development of a Renewable Energy Roadmap

Create a comprehensive renewable energy roadmap that outlines short-term, medium-term, and long-term goals for energy transformation:

- **Short-term (0-2 years)**: Focus on rapid deployment of modular solar and wind energy systems to provide immediate relief to critical infrastructure such as hospitals, schools, and emergency services.
- **Medium-term (2-5 years)**: Expand renewable energy infrastructure to residential, commercial, and industrial sectors. Develop microgrids and decentralized energy systems for urban and rural areas.
- **Long-term (5-20 years)**: Aim for a complete transition to a renewable energy-powered grid, incorporating advanced technologies such as offshore wind farms, large-scale solar parks, and next-generation bioenergy systems.

Innovative Renewable Energy Solutions

Leveraging Advanced Technologies

Deploying cutting-edge renewable energy technologies will maximize efficiency, reduce costs, and accelerate the transition to clean energy.

Solar Energy

Solar power offers immense potential for Ukraine due to its abundant sunlight:

- **Solar Photovoltaic (PV) Systems**: Install PV panels on rooftops, open spaces, and brownfield sites. Use smart inverters and energy storage systems to enhance efficiency and reliability.
- **Solar Thermal Systems**: Implement solar thermal systems for water heating and industrial applications. These systems reduce reliance on fossil fuels and enhance energy efficiency.

Wind Energy

Harnessing wind energy can significantly contribute to Ukraine's renewable energy portfolio:

- **Onshore Wind Farms**: Develop onshore wind farms in regions with high wind potential. Invest in advanced wind turbines with improved efficiency and durability.
- **Offshore Wind Farms**: Explore offshore wind energy in coastal areas. Offshore wind farms provide higher energy yields and are less obtrusive to urban landscapes.

Hydro and Biomass Energy

Diversifying energy sources ensures a stable and resilient energy supply:

- **Small Hydro Projects**: Develop small hydro projects in rivers and streams to provide localized energy solutions. These projects have minimal environmental impact and can be integrated into community-based energy systems.
- **Biomass Energy**: Utilize agricultural and forestry residues for biomass energy production. Implement anaerobic digestion and gasification technologies to convert organic waste into renewable energy.

Community Engagement and Empowerment

Mobilizing Communities for Clean Energy

Engaging local communities is vital for the success and sustainability of renewable energy projects:

Community-Owned Energy Projects

Foster community ownership and participation in renewable energy projects to build local capacity and ensure equitable benefits:

- **Cooperative Energy Models**: Establish energy cooperatives where community members can invest in and benefit from local renewable energy projects. Cooperatives create a sense of ownership and provide economic incentives for participation.
- **Training and Education Programs**: Develop training programs to educate residents on renewable energy technologies, maintenance, and management. Empowering locals with the necessary skills ensures the sustainability of energy projects and fosters job creation.

Transparent and Inclusive Processes

Ensure transparency and inclusivity in decision-making processes to build trust and support:

- **Public Consultations**: Conduct public consultations and workshops to involve citizens in the planning and implementation of renewable energy projects. Soliciting feedback and addressing concerns fosters a collaborative atmosphere.

- **Information Campaigns**: Launch information campaigns to raise awareness about the benefits of renewable energy and the importance of sustainability. Use multimedia platforms to reach a broad audience and dispel myths about renewable energy.

Financing and Investment Strategies

Securing Resources for Renewable Projects

Adequate financing is essential for the successful implementation of renewable energy initiatives:

Public-Private Partnerships

Leverage public-private partnerships (PPPs) to mobilize financial resources and technical expertise:

- **Investment Incentives**: Provide tax breaks, subsidies, and grants to attract private investment in renewable energy projects. Ensure that incentives are aligned with long-term sustainability goals.
- **Risk Mitigation Mechanisms**: Develop risk mitigation mechanisms such as insurance and guarantees to de-risk investments in renewable energy. These mechanisms enhance investor confidence and facilitate capital inflows.

International Cooperation

Engage with international donors and financial institutions to access funding and support:

- **Multilateral Funding Agencies**: Collaborate with entities such as the World Bank, European Union, and Global Environment Facility (GEF) to secure grants and low-interest loans for renewable energy projects.
- **Green Bonds**: Issue green bonds to raise capital specifically for environmental and renewable energy projects. Green bonds attract socially responsible investors and provide a steady stream of funding.

Monitoring and Evaluation

Ensuring Accountability and Continuous Improvement

Robust monitoring and evaluation frameworks are crucial for the success of renewable energy projects:

Key Performance Indicators (KPIs)

Develop KPIs to measure the performance and impact of renewable energy projects:

- **Energy Output**: Track the amount of renewable energy generated and its contribution to the overall energy mix.
- **Carbon Emissions Reduction**: Monitor reductions in greenhouse gas emissions resulting from the implementation of renewable energy projects.
- **Economic Benefits**: Measure economic benefits such as job creation, local investment, and cost savings for consumers.

Continuous Improvement Processes

Implement continuous improvement processes to enhance project outcomes:

- **Regular Audits**: Conduct regular audits to ensure compliance with environmental and technical standards. Audits provide accountability and identify areas for improvement.
- **Stakeholder Feedback**: Collect and incorporate feedback from stakeholders, including community members, investors, and technical experts. Feedback loops facilitate adaptive management and continuous project enhancement.

Conclusion

Integrating renewable energy into Ukraine's post-war reconstruction is not only a necessity for sustainability but also a strategic imperative for building a resilient, energy-independent nation. By leveraging innovative technologies, engaging communities, securing diversified funding, and ensuring rigorous monitoring, Ukraine can transform its energy landscape and lead the way toward a sustainable future. The commitment to renewable energy integration will pave the way for economic growth, environmental preservation, and a brighter, more resilient future for all Ukrainians.

Section 16.2: Green Building Standards

Elevating Sustainable Construction for Future Urban Resilience

In the ambitious journey to rebuild Ukraine, establishing green building standards is paramount to promoting sustainable, energy-efficient, and resilient urban development. Green buildings not only reduce environmental impact but also enhance the health, well-being, and economic prosperity of communities. This section outlines a comprehensive strategy to integrate stringent green building standards into Ukraine's reconstruction efforts, leveraging cutting-edge technologies, international best practices, and community engagement for creating buildings that stand the test of time and nature.

Developing Comprehensive Green Building Standards

Framework and Policy Development

Creating a robust framework for green building standards involves a multidisciplinary approach that includes policy development, stakeholder engagement, and enforcement mechanisms.

- **National Green Building Council**: Establish a National Green Building Council (NGBC) responsible for setting and overseeing green building standards. This council will include experts from government, academia, industry, and civil society to ensure comprehensive and balanced regulations.
- **Green Building Codes and Standards**: Develop and implement green building codes and standards that mandate energy efficiency, water conservation, and the use of sustainable materials in construction. These standards will align with international benchmarks such as LEED (Leadership in Energy and Environmental Design) and BREEAM (Building Research Establishment Environmental Assessment Method).
- **Regulatory Mechanisms**: Enforce compliance with green building standards through stringent regulatory mechanisms, including regular inspections, certifications, and penalties for non-compliance. Provide incentives such as tax breaks and grants to encourage adherence to green building practices.

Promoting Sustainable Construction Practices

Materials and Technologies

Adopting sustainable construction practices is fundamental to achieving green building objectives.

- **Eco-Friendly Materials**: Prioritize the use of eco-friendly and locally sourced materials such as recycled steel, bamboo, and reclaimed wood. Implement guidelines for reducing the carbon footprint of construction materials through lifecycle assessments.
- **Energy-Efficient Technologies**: Incorporate energy-efficient technologies such as high-performance insulation, energy-efficient windows, and advanced HVAC systems to reduce energy consumption in buildings. Use smart building technologies to optimize energy use and reduce wastage.
- **Water Conservation Systems**: Install water conservation systems including rainwater harvesting, greywater recycling, and low-flow fixtures to reduce water usage and promote sustainability in urban environments.

Designing for Climate Resilience

Adaptive and Resilient Architecture

Integrating climate resilience into building design ensures that structures can withstand and adapt to changing environmental conditions.

- **Climate-Responsive Design**: Ensure buildings are designed to respond to local climatic conditions. This includes considerations for passive solar heating, natural ventilation, and shading systems to enhance energy efficiency and occupant comfort.
- **Flood and Drought Resilience**: Design buildings with elevated foundations and permeable pavements to mitigate flood risks. Incorporate drought-resistant landscaping and xeriscaping to reduce water dependency in green spaces.
- **Heat Mitigation Strategies**: Employ strategies such as green roofs, cool roofs, and reflective materials to reduce urban heat island effects and improve the overall thermal comfort of urban areas.

Fostering Community and Industry Engagement

Collaborative Efforts for Sustainable Building

Active engagement with communities and the construction industry is vital for the successful implementation of green building standards.

- **Industry Workshops and Training**: Conduct workshops and training programs for architects, engineers, and builders to educate them on green building practices and technologies. Promote continuous learning and professional development to keep the industry updated on the latest advancements.
- **Public Awareness Campaigns**: Launch public awareness campaigns to educate citizens on the benefits of green buildings. Use multimedia channels, community events, and educational programs to foster a culture of sustainability and encourage community participation in green initiatives.
- **Green Building Certification Programs**: Develop certification programs that recognize and reward excellence in green building practices. Highlighting certified projects will set a benchmark for quality and inspire widespread adoption of green standards.

Leveraging International Best Practices

Global Standards and Collaboration

Drawing from international best practices will ensure that Ukraine's green building standards are world-class and effective.

- **International Collaboration**: Partner with international organizations such as the World Green Building Council, C40 Cities, and the International Energy Agency to gain insights, technical assistance, and funding for green building projects.
- **Adoption of Global Benchmarks**: Adopt global benchmarks like LEED and BREEAM for setting high standards in green building

certification and ensure alignment with the latest sustainable building practices.
- **Knowledge Exchange Programs**: Implement exchange programs that allow Ukrainian professionals to learn from successful green building initiatives in other countries. These programs will facilitate knowledge transfer and inspire innovative solutions tailored to Ukraine's context .

Financing and Incentives for Green Buildings

Securing Resources and Encouraging Adoption

Adequate financing and incentivization are crucial for promoting the widespread adoption of green building practices.

- **Green Bonds and Climate Funds**: Issue green bonds and secure climate funds to finance large-scale green building projects. These financial instruments will attract investors committed to sustainability and provide the necessary capital for ambitious projects .
- **Subsidies and Tax Incentives**: Offer subsidies, tax breaks, and grants to developers and homeowners who implement green building practices. Financial incentives will lower the initial costs and accelerate the adoption of sustainable construction methods .
- **Public-Private Partnerships**: Form public-private partnerships to leverage private sector expertise and investment in green building projects. These collaborations will enhance innovation, efficiency, and resource mobilization .

Monitoring and Evaluation

Ensuring Compliance and Continuous Improvement

Robust monitoring and evaluation systems are essential for ensuring that green building standards are met and continuously improved.

- **Performance Metrics and KPIs**: Develop key performance indicators (KPIs) to measure the performance of green buildings in terms of energy efficiency, water conservation, and environmental impact. Regularly review these metrics to ensure compliance and identify areas for improvement .
- **Third-Party Audits**: Conduct regular third-party audits of green buildings to ensure adherence to standards and certifications. Independent assessments will provide transparency and credibility to the green building certification process .
- **Feedback Mechanisms**: Establish feedback mechanisms to gather input from occupants, developers, and stakeholders on the performance of green buildings. Use this feedback to refine standards and enhance the quality and sustainability of green buildings .

Conclusion

Establishing and enforcing green building standards in Ukraine's reconstruction is a transformative step towards a sustainable and resilient future. By developing comprehensive standards, promoting sustainable practices, fostering community and industry engagement, leveraging international best practices, securing financing, and ensuring rigorous monitoring, Ukraine can lead the way in sustainable urban development. These efforts will not only restore and rejuvenate the built environment but also create healthier, more vibrant communities that are prepared to face the challenges of the future.

Section 16.3: Climate Adaptation Measures

Adapting to a Changing Climate for Sustainable Reconstruction

In the face of escalating climate challenges, integrating climate adaptation measures into Ukraine's reconstruction efforts is imperative. Climate adaptation not only ensures the resilience of rebuilt infrastructure but also safeguards the well-being and economic stability of communities. This section outlines a comprehensive strategy for implementing robust climate adaptation measures, leveraging technology, international best practices, and community involvement to build a future-ready Ukraine.

Comprehensive Climate Risk Assessment

Identifying Vulnerabilities and Planning Accordingly

Effective climate adaptation begins with a thorough understanding of climate risks and vulnerabilities.

- **Climate Risk Mapping**: Conduct detailed climate risk mapping using satellite imagery, remote sensing, and geographical information systems (GIS) to identify areas prone to flooding, landslides, heatwaves, and other climate-related risks.
- **Vulnerability Assessments**: Perform community-level vulnerability assessments to understand the specific needs and risks faced by different populations, including marginalized groups and those living in high-risk areas.
- **Scenario Planning**: Utilize advanced climate models and scenario planning tools to project future climate conditions and their potential impact on infrastructure and communities. This data-driven approach ensures that adaptation strategies are robust and forward-looking.

Implementing Flood Management Strategies

Protecting Communities from Increasing Flood Risks

With the rising frequency and intensity of flood events, implementing comprehensive flood management strategies is critical.

- **Flood Barriers and Retention Areas**: Construct flood barriers, levees, and retention basins to protect urban and rural areas from flooding. These structures will control water flow and minimize flood damage to critical infrastructure and residential areas.
- **Natural Water Management**: Restore wetlands, rivers, and floodplains to enhance their natural ability to absorb and manage floodwaters. Nature-based solutions such as these provide sustainable and cost-effective flood protection while enhancing biodiversity.
- **Urban Drainage Systems**: Upgrade urban drainage systems with green infrastructure elements such as permeable pavements, rain gardens, and bioswales. These systems will reduce surface runoff, promote groundwater recharge, and mitigate urban flooding.

Addressing Extreme Heat Events

Mitigating the Impact of Heatwaves in Urban Areas

As climate change exacerbates heatwaves, it is essential to implement measures that reduce heat stress and improve urban livability.

- **Urban Greening**: Increase urban greenery through the planting of trees, creation of parks, and implementation of green roofs and walls. Vegetation provides shade, reduces urban heat island effects, and improves air quality.
- **Cool Roofs and Pavements**: Utilize reflective materials for roofs and pavements to lower surface temperatures and reduce heat absorption. Cool roofs and pavements can significantly mitigate the impact of heatwaves in densely built environments.
- **Cooling Centers and Public Awareness**: Establish cooling centers in public buildings such as libraries, community centers, and schools to provide respite during extreme heat events. Launch public awareness campaigns to inform citizens about the dangers of heatwaves and strategies for staying cool and safe.

Enhancing Water Security

Ensuring Sustainable Water Supply Amidst Climate Variability

Climate adaptation strategies must address the increasing variability in water availability due to changing precipitation patterns.

- **Rainwater Harvesting**: Implement rainwater harvesting systems in residential, commercial, and public buildings to capture and store rainwater for non-potable uses. This practice reduces dependence on traditional water sources and enhances drought resilience.
- **Efficient Irrigation Systems**: Promote the use of efficient irrigation systems such as drip and sprinkler irrigation in agriculture and urban landscaping. These systems optimize water use and minimize wastage.

- **Water Recycling and Reuse**: Develop infrastructure for the recycling and reuse of greywater and wastewater. Treated water can be used for irrigation, industrial processes, and other non-potable purposes, ensuring a sustainable water supply.

Building Climate-Resilient Infrastructure

Designing Infrastructure to Withstand Climate Impacts

Incorporating climate resilience into the design and construction of infrastructure is essential for long-term sustainability.

- **Climate-Resilient Building Codes**: Develop and enforce building codes that require new construction and retrofits to incorporate climate resilience measures, such as elevated foundations, wind-resistant designs, and the use of durable materials.
- **Resilient Transportation Networks**: Design transportation infrastructure to withstand extreme weather events. This includes elevating roadways and rail lines in flood-prone areas, reinforcing bridges, and implementing erosion control measures along coastal and riverine routes.
- **Energy Resilience**: Ensure that energy infrastructure is resilient to climate impacts by incorporating redundancy, decentralization, and diversification of energy sources. This approach will enhance energy security and reduce vulnerability to climate-related disruptions.

Fostering Community Engagement and Education

Empowering Communities through Awareness and Participation

Community engagement and education are critical components of effective climate adaptation.

- **Community-Based Adaptation Plans**: Involve local communities in the development and implementation of climate adaptation plans. This participatory approach ensures that strategies are culturally appropriate and address local needs and priorities.
- **Educational Programs**: Develop educational programs and materials to increase awareness about climate change and adaptation strategies. Schools, community centers, and online platforms can serve as hubs for disseminating this information.
- **Capacity Building Workshops**: Conduct workshops and training sessions to build the capacity of local governments, community leaders, and residents in climate adaptation practices. Empowered communities will be better equipped to implement and maintain adaptation measures.

Leveraging Technology and Innovation

Harnessing Technological Advancements for Climate Resilience

Innovative technologies play a key role in enhancing climate adaptation efforts.

- **Smart Climate Monitoring Systems**: Deploy IoT-enabled sensors and smart climate monitoring systems to collect real-time data on environmental conditions such as temperature, humidity, and precipitation. This data can inform adaptive management strategies and early warning systems.
- **Geospatial Analysis Tools**: Use geospatial analysis tools and remote sensing technologies to monitor and model climate impacts, guiding the development of targeted adaptation measures and informing policy decisions.
- **Blockchain for Resource Management**: Implement blockchain technology to enhance the transparency and efficiency of resource management in climate adaptation projects. Blockchain can track the allocation and use of funds, materials, and other resources, ensuring accountability and reducing the risk of mismanagement.

International Cooperation and Best Practices

Building on Global Knowledge and Support

International cooperation and the adoption of best practices enhance the effectiveness of climate adaptation strategies.

- **Global Partnerships**: Engage in partnerships with international organizations, governments, and non-governmental organizations to access technical expertise, funding, and best practices in climate adaptation.
- **Knowledge Exchange Programs**: Participate in knowledge exchange programs to learn from successful climate adaptation initiatives worldwide. These programs can provide valuable insights and innovative approaches tailored to Ukraine's specific challenges.
- **Climate Finance Mechanisms**: Tap into international climate finance mechanisms such as the Green Climate Fund, Adaptation Fund, and bilateral climate aid programs to secure funding for large-scale climate adaptation projects.

Monitoring and Evaluation

Ensuring Continuous Improvement and Adaptability

Robust monitoring and evaluation frameworks are essential for the success and adaptability of climate adaptation measures.

- **Performance Metrics and Indicators**: Develop key performance indicators (KPIs) to measure the effectiveness and impact of climate adaptation strategies. Regularly review these metrics to assess progress and identify areas for improvement.
- **Adaptive Management**: Implement adaptive management practices that allow for the continuous adjustment and refinement of adaptation measures based on monitoring results and emerging climate data.

- **Stakeholder Feedback Mechanisms**: Establish mechanisms for collecting and incorporating feedback from stakeholders, including local communities, policymakers, and technical experts. This inclusive approach ensures that adaptation strategies remain relevant and effective.

Conclusion

Integrating climate adaptation measures is crucial for the sustainable reconstruction of Ukraine. By conducting comprehensive risk assessments, implementing robust flood and heat management strategies, enhancing water security, designing climate-resilient infrastructure, engaging communities, leveraging technology, and fostering international cooperation, Ukraine can build a resilient future that withstands the challenges posed by a changing climate. These efforts will not only protect vulnerable populations and critical infrastructure but also position Ukraine as a leader in climate resilience and sustainable development.

Chapter 17: Innovative Educational Ecosystems

Section 17.1: AR and VR Learning Environments

Transforming Education with Augmented and Virtual Reality

As Ukraine rebuilds from the ravages of war, there lies a unique opportunity to leapfrog traditional educational paradigms and embrace cutting-edge technologies that redefine learning. Augmented Reality (AR) and Virtual Reality (VR) offer groundbreaking ways to create immersive, interactive, and engaging educational environments. This section outlines a comprehensive plan to integrate AR and VR into Ukraine's educational system, ensuring that students, educators, and communities benefit from the most advanced learning tools available.

Vision for AR and VR in Education

Revolutionizing Learning Experiences

The integration of AR and VR into education aims to transform how students interact with information, allowing them to explore and engage with content in unparalleled ways.

- **Immersive Learning**: AR and VR facilitate deeply immersive learning experiences where students can virtually explore historical sites, complex scientific phenomena, and other educational content beyond the confines of traditional textbooks.
- **Enhanced Engagement**: Interactive environments created using AR and VR increase student engagement by making learning experiences more dynamic and captivating.
- **Personalized Education**: These technologies enable personalized learning paths, allowing students to progress at their own pace and according

to their unique learning needs.

Implementation Strategy

Structured Phases for Effective Integration

Implementing AR and VR in education will follow a phased approach to ensure smooth integration, scalability, and sustainability.

Phase 1: Pilot Projects and Feasibility Studies

- **Pilot Programs**: Launch pilot programs in select schools to test AR and VR technologies in various educational settings. Focus on diverse subjects such as history, biology, and engineering to gauge the versatility and impact of these tools.
- **Feasibility Studies**: Conduct feasibility studies to assess the technical requirements, costs, and potential challenges associated with large-scale implementation. Utilize feedback from pilot programs to refine strategies and address any barriers to adoption.

Phase 2: Infrastructure Development and Capacity Building

- **Technology Infrastructure**: Develop the necessary technological infrastructure, including high-speed internet, VR headsets, AR-enabled devices, and supporting software. Ensure that schools across urban and rural areas have equitable access to these technologies.
- **Teacher Training Programs**: Implement comprehensive training programs for educators to familiarize them with AR and VR technologies. These programs will cover technical aspects, pedagogical integration, and strategies for maximizing the educational benefits of immersive learning environments.

Phase 3: Curriculum Integration and Expansion

- **Curriculum Overhaul**: Integrate AR and VR content into the national curriculum, ensuring that immersive learning modules are aligned with educational standards and learning objectives.
- **Resource Development**: Develop and curate high-quality AR and VR educational resources in collaboration with content creators, educational institutions, and technology companies.
- **Scalable Models**: Create scalable models for AR and VR integration that can be adapted to different educational contexts, from primary schools to universities and vocational training centers.

Community and Stakeholder Engagement

Fostering Collaborative Efforts

Engaging stakeholders and the broader community is crucial for the successful implementation of AR and VR in education.

- **Partnerships with Technology Providers**: Establish partnerships with leading technology providers to facilitate access to the latest AR and VR tools and resources. These collaborations will also provide opportunities for joint research and innovation.
- **Parent and Community Involvement**: Involve parents and community members in the process to build support and understanding of the benefits of AR and VR in education. Host informational sessions, demonstrations, and hands-on workshops to showcase the potential of these technologies.
- **Student Ambassadors**: Create student ambassador programs where tech-savvy students can assist peers and teachers in navigating AR and VR tools. This peer-to-peer support system will enhance the adoption and effective use of new technologies.

Monitoring and Evaluation

Ensuring Continuous Improvement

Robust monitoring and evaluation frameworks are essential for measuring the impact and effectiveness of AR and VR integration.

- **Performance Metrics**: Develop key performance indicators (KPIs) to measure student engagement, retention, and academic performance as a result of using AR and VR tools. Regularly review these metrics to assess progress and identify areas for improvement.
- **Feedback Loops**: Establish feedback mechanisms for students, teachers, and parents to share their experiences and suggestions. Use this feedback to make data-driven adjustments to the implementation strategy and resource development.
- **Independent Evaluations**: Conduct independent evaluations by educational experts and researchers to ensure objectivity and comprehensive analysis of the program's impact. Publish findings and share best practices with other educational institutions and policymakers.

Case Studies and Success Stories

Learning from Global Pioneers

Drawing from successful AR and VR implementations worldwide will provide valuable insights and inspiration for Ukraine's educational transformation.

- **International Collaborations**: Engage with international educational institutions and organizations experienced in AR and VR integration. Study their models, successes, and challenges to inform Ukraine's approach.

- **Showcase Success Stories**: Highlight success stories from pilot programs and early adopters within Ukraine. Use these stories to demonstrate the tangible benefits of AR and VR in education and build momentum for wider adoption.

Conclusion

Integrating AR and VR into Ukraine's educational ecosystem represents a bold and forward-thinking step towards revolutionizing learning. By leveraging immersive technologies, Ukraine can create dynamic, engaging, and personalized educational experiences that prepare students for the future. Through structured implementation, collaborative community efforts, and continuous evaluation, Ukraine will set a new standard for educational excellence and innovation. This transformative approach will not only enhance academic outcomes but also empower students and educators to thrive in a rapidly changing world.

Section 17.2: AI-Powered Personalized Education

Revolutionizing Learning Through Artificial Intelligence

The integration of Artificial Intelligence (AI) into educational environments represents a transformative leap in how education is delivered and experienced. In Ukraine's journey to rebuild and modernize its education system post-conflict, AI-powered personalized education offers a means to tailor learning experiences to individual needs, fostering a more effective and inclusive educational ecosystem. This section outlines a comprehensive strategy for implementing AI-powered personalized education, leveraging advanced algorithms, and fostering a partnership between technology and teaching to ensure that all students have access to the highest quality education.

Vision for AI-Powered Personalized Education

Customized Learning for Every Student

The primary goal of AI-powered personalized education is to provide individualized learning experiences that adapt to each student's unique needs, abilities, and learning styles.

- **Adaptive Learning Systems**: Implement AI-driven adaptive learning systems that continuously assess students' performance and tailor instructional content accordingly. These systems can provide immediate feedback and adjust difficulty levels to match student progress, ensuring an optimized learning path for each student.
- **Personalized Learning Plans**: Develop personalized learning plans using AI algorithms to identify students' strengths, weaknesses, and learning preferences. These plans will guide students through customized educational journeys, maximizing their potential and engagement.

Implementation Strategy

Phased Integration and Capacity Building

A phased approach ensures a smooth transition to AI-powered personalized education, allowing for adjustments and scalability.

Phase 1: Foundation and Pilot Programs

- **Pilot Programs**: Introduce pilot programs in selected schools to test and refine AI-powered personalized education tools. These pilots will focus on a variety of subjects to evaluate the effectiveness and versatility of the AI systems.
- **Infrastructure Development**: Establish the necessary IT infrastructure, including high-speed internet, cloud-based platforms, and AI-enabled devices. Ensure equitable access to technology across urban and rural schools.
- **Data Collection and Privacy**: Implement robust data collection protocols while ensuring stringent data privacy measures. Secure consent and ethical use of student data to build trust and compliance with international data protection standards.

Phase 2: Professional Development and Expansion

- **Teacher Training Programs**: Conduct extensive training programs to equip educators with the knowledge and skills to effectively integrate AI tools into their teaching practices. Teacher training will cover AI basics, using AI-powered systems, and interpreting AI-generated insights.
- **Curriculum Integration**: Embed AI-driven personalized learning modules into the national curriculum, ensuring alignment with educational standards and objectives. Collaborate with curriculum developers and AI experts to create comprehensive and engaging content.

Phase 3: Scaling and Continuous Improvement

- **Nationwide Rollout**: Expand AI-powered personalized education to all schools nationwide, ensuring consistent quality and access. Develop scalable models that accommodate diverse educational settings and resource availability.
- **Feedback and Iteration**: Establish feedback loops involving students, teachers, and parents to continuously refine AI systems. Use insights from these feedback mechanisms to improve AI algorithms and educational content.

Enhancing Educator Roles

Augmenting Teaching with AI

AI-powered education is designed to support and enhance the role of educators, not replace them.

- **Teacher Empowerment**: Provide teachers with AI-generated insights into student performance, enabling them to make informed decisions about their teaching strategies. AI tools can highlight areas where students need additional support or enrichment, allowing teachers to focus their efforts where they are most needed.
- **Collaborative Learning Environments**: Foster collaborative learning environments where AI facilitates personalized education, while teachers and students engage in interactive, project-based learning. This approach encourages critical thinking, creativity, and teamwork.

Student-Centric Learning Ecosystems

Creating Inclusive and Engaging Learning Experiences

AI-powered personalized education aims to create student-centric learning ecosystems that cater to diverse learning needs.

- **Inclusive Education**: Use AI to identify and support students with learning disabilities and special educational needs. Personalized learning paths and adaptive technologies ensure that every student has the opportunity to succeed.
- **Engagement and Motivation**: Implement gamified learning modules and AI-driven engagement tools to keep students motivated. By making learning fun and interactive, AI helps maintain high levels of student interest and investment in their education.

International Collaboration and Partnerships

Leveraging Global Expertise and Resources

Collaboration with international partners will provide valuable expertise and resources for implementing AI-powered personalized education.

- **Partnerships with Tech Companies**: Collaborate with leading technology companies to access the latest AI tools and platforms. Joint ventures and partnerships can accelerate the development and deployment of AI-powered educational systems.
- **Knowledge Exchange Programs**: Engage in knowledge exchange programs with educational institutions worldwide that have successfully implemented AI in education. These programs will share best practices, lessons learned, and innovative approaches.

Monitoring and Evaluation

Ensuring Effectiveness and Adaptability

Continuous monitoring and evaluation are crucial to the success of AI-powered personalized education.

- **Performance Metrics**: Develop key performance indicators (KPIs) to assess the impact of AI on student learning outcomes, engagement levels, and teacher effectiveness. Regularly review these metrics to track progress and identify areas for improvement.
- **Adaptive Management**: Implement adaptive management practices that allow for real-time adjustments based on monitoring data. This approach ensures that AI tools remain responsive to the evolving needs of students and educators.
- **Independent Evaluations**: Conduct independent evaluations by educational researchers and AI experts to ensure objectivity and comprehensive analysis. Share evaluation results to foster transparency and continuous improvement.

Building Public Trust and Addressing Ethical Concerns

Navigating Privacy and Ethical Considerations

Addressing ethical concerns and building public trust are essential for the successful implementation of AI in education.

- **Data Privacy and Security**: Ensure that all data collected by AI systems is securely stored and protected. Develop transparent data usage policies and obtain informed consent from students and parents.
- **Ethical AI Use**: Establish ethical guidelines for the use of AI in education, addressing issues such as bias, fairness, and accountability. Create oversight bodies to monitor compliance with these guidelines and address any ethical concerns that arise.

Case Studies and Success Stories

Learning from Global Leaders in AI Education

Drawing inspiration from successful implementations worldwide will provide valuable insights for Ukraine.

- **Finland's AI in Education**: Study Finland's model of integrating AI into classrooms, focusing on their approach to teacher training, curriculum development, and student engagement.
- **Singapore's Smart Nation Initiative**: Examine Singapore's Smart Nation initiative, which leverages AI and data analytics to transform education and other sectors. Learn from their strategies for scaling AI solutions and ensuring accessibility.

Conclusion

The integration of AI-powered personalized education in Ukraine represents a significant opportunity to revolutionize learning experiences and ensure that every student reaches their full potential. By adopting a phased implementation strategy, enhancing educator roles, fostering student-centric ecosystems, leveraging international partnerships, and ensuring rigorous monitoring and ethical practices, Ukraine can build a world-class education system that is resilient, inclusive, and future-ready. These efforts will not only benefit current and future generations of students but also position Ukraine as a leader in educational innovation and excellence.

Section 17.3: Virtual Reality Historical Reconstructions

Bringing History to Life: Immersive Educational Experiences

In the dynamic landscape of post-war reconstruction, Ukraine has the extraordinary opportunity to merge education with cutting-edge technology. Virtual Reality Historical Reconstructions (VRHR) stand at the forefront of this transformative approach. By leveraging the immersive capabilities of VR, we can bring Ukraine's rich history to life, providing students and the general public with engaging, interactive, and impactful historical narratives that deepen understanding and appreciation of the country's cultural heritage. This section presents a comprehensive strategy for developing and implementing VRHR projects, ensuring they become an integral part of Ukraine's educational and cultural revival.

Vision for Virtual Reality Historical Reconstructions

Immersive Engagement with History

The primary goal of VRHR projects is to create immersive environments where users can explore historical events, sites, and figures as if they were living through them in real time.

- **Realistic Reenactments**: Utilize high-fidelity VR technology to recreate historical events with realistic details, allowing users to experience moments of history in 3D environments.
- **Interactive Storytelling**: Offer interactive elements where users can engage with historical figures, artifacts, and pivotal moments, making the learning experience active and participatory.
- **Educational Toolkits**: Develop comprehensive educational toolkits that accompany VR experiences, including lesson plans, discussion questions, and supplementary materials to enhance learning outcomes.

Implementation Strategy

Phased Development for Comprehensive Integration

A structured, phased approach will ensure the effective and sustainable integration of VRHR into Ukraine's educational and cultural frameworks.

Phase 1: Research and Development

- **Historical Accuracy**: Collaborate with historians, archaeologists, and cultural experts to ensure that VR reconstructions are accurate and reflective of true historical contexts.
- **Technology Partnerships**: Form partnerships with leading VR technology companies and content creators to develop high-quality VR experiences.
- **Pilot Projects**: Launch pilot VRHR projects in select museums, schools, and cultural institutions to gather feedback and assess impact.

Phase 2: Content Creation and Capacity Building

- **Content Libraries**: Develop extensive content libraries covering various historical periods, events, and figures significant to Ukraine's history.
- **Training Programs**: Train educators, museum staff, and cultural workers in using VRHR tools and integrating them into their programs. Provide ongoing support and professional development opportunities.
- **Infrastructure Development**: Ensure that institutions have the necessary infrastructure, including VR headsets, high-speed internet, and technical support, to facilitate seamless VRHR experiences.

Phase 3: National Rollout and Community Engagement

- **Widespread Implementation**: Roll out VRHR projects across educational institutions, museums, and cultural centers nationwide, ensuring broad access and usability.
- **Community Workshops**: Conduct workshops and community events to introduce VRHR technology to the public, encouraging community-wide engagement and appreciation of historical narratives.
- **Feedback Mechanisms**: Establish robust feedback mechanisms to continuously collect user experiences and improve VRHR content and delivery practices.

Fostering Educational Excellence

Enhancing Learning through Immersive Technology

VRHR offers unparalleled opportunities to enrich educational practices and outcomes.

- **Enhanced Cognitive Retention**: Studies show that experiential learning through VR significantly improves cognitive retention by engaging multiple senses and creating lasting impressions.

- **Inclusive Education**: VRHR can be tailored to accommodate diverse learning needs and styles, making history accessible to students with different abilities, including those with disabilities.
- **Critical Thinking and Analysis**: Interactive VR experiences promote critical thinking by allowing students to explore various historical scenarios, analyze events from different perspectives, and engage in problem-solving activities.

Preserving Cultural Heritage

Digital Preservation of History

In addition to educational benefits, VRHR plays a crucial role in the preservation and promotion of cultural heritage.

- **Digital Archives**: Create digital archives of significant historical sites and events, ensuring that even if physical locations are damaged or destroyed, their essence is preserved and accessible.
- **Global Access**: VRHR projects can be made available online, allowing a global audience to explore and learn about Ukraine's rich history, fostering international understanding and appreciation.
- **Cultural Ambassadors**: Use VRHR as a tool to train cultural ambassadors who can lead virtual tours and educational sessions, promoting Ukrainian culture worldwide.

International Collaboration and Best Practices

Learning from Global Leaders

Building on international experiences and best practices will enhance the quality and impact of VRHR projects.

- **Global Partnerships**: Collaborate with international museums, universities, and tech companies experienced in VRHR projects. Joint efforts can provide new insights, technical support, and funding opportunities.
- **Case Studies and Success Models**: Study successful VRHR implementations, such as the British Museum's VR tours or the Anne Frank House VR experience, applying relevant lessons to Ukraine's context.
- **Cultural Exchanges**: Foster cultural exchanges where Ukrainian VRHR platforms can be showcased internationally and vice versa, promoting cultural diplomacy and mutual learning.

Monitoring and Evaluation

Ensuring Sustainable Impact

Continuous monitoring and evaluation are key to the success and sustainability of VRHR projects.

- **Performance Metrics**: Develop key performance indicators (KPIs) to measure engagement levels, educational impact, user satisfaction, and cultural reach of VRHR projects.
- **User Feedback**: Integrate user feedback into regular project reviews, ensuring that VRHR experiences are constantly improved based on real-world usage data.
- **Independent Reviews**: Conduct independent reviews and assessments by educational and cultural experts to validate the effectiveness and historical accuracy of VRHR content.

Conclusion

Virtual Reality Historical Reconstructions represent a transformative pathway for Ukraine to rebuild and promote its rich historical and cultural heritage. By implementing a structured strategy that includes research, development, extensive content creation, capacity building, and community engagement, Ukraine can create immersive educational environments that resonate deeply with both national and international audiences. These innovative approaches will not only enhance learning and cognitive retention but also ensure the preservation and global dissemination of Ukraine's rich historical legacy, positioning the nation as a leader in educational and cultural innovation on the world stage.

Chapter 18: Healthcare Transformation

Section 18.1: Autonomous Mobile Clinics

A New Horizon in Ukrainian Healthcare: Autonomous Mobile Clinics

As Ukraine steps into a future shaped by resilience and innovation, the transformation of its healthcare landscape stands as a beacon of hope. Autonomous Mobile Clinics (AMCs) represent a cutting-edge solution to bridge the healthcare accessibility gap, especially in rural and underserved areas devastated by conflict. These technological marvels are not merely vehicles; they are lifelines that carry advanced medical care into the heart of communities, ensuring no one is left behind.

Revolutionizing Access to Healthcare

The deployment of Autonomous Mobile Clinics is a strategic initiative to ensure that comprehensive healthcare reaches every corner of the nation, particularly remote and conflict-affected regions. These clinics are equipped with autonomous navigation systems, advanced diagnostics, and telemedicine capabilities, redefining the delivery of healthcare services.

Meeting the Urgent Needs In the wake of war, countless medical facilities have been rendered inoperative, leaving a significant portion of the population without access to essential health services. Autonomous Mobile Clinics are designed to immediately address this gap by providing:

- **Rapid Deployment:** With autonomous navigation, these clinics can traverse difficult terrains and reach inaccessible areas swiftly, ensuring timely medical intervention.
- **Scalability and Flexibility:** The modular design of AMCs allows for the incorporation of new medical technologies as they evolve, making them adaptable to the ever-changing healthcare needs of the population.

Leveraging Advanced Medical Technology

Autonomous Mobile Clinics are more than mobile units; they are advanced medical hubs that bring high-quality care directly to the people. Each clinic is outfitted with cutting-edge technology to provide a wide range of medical services:

- **Telemedicine Integration:** Enables real-time consultations with specialists based in urban centers or international locations, thus providing remote areas with access to high-level medical expertise.
- **Artificial Intelligence:** Utilizes AI algorithms to enhance diagnostic accuracy and speed, facilitating early detection and treatment of conditions.

Humanitarian and Economic Impacts

The introduction of Autonomous Mobile Clinics is poised to deliver substantial humanitarian and economic benefits, creating a ripple effect that extends beyond immediate healthcare needs.

Humanitarian Benefits

- **Improved Public Health:** By ensuring that vulnerable populations have consistent access to healthcare, AMCs help reduce morbidity and mortality rates, improving the overall health of the nation.
- **Enhanced Social Stability:** Reliable access to healthcare fosters social stability by addressing health disparities and ensuring that all citizens can lead healthier, more productive lives.

Economic Efficiency

- **Reduced Burden on Urban Facilities:** By providing essential services locally, AMCs diminish the strain on urban hospitals, allowing these facilities to focus on more complex cases.
- **Cost-Effective Healthcare:** Autonomous clinics reduce the need for costly patient transportation and lower overall healthcare expenses, freeing up resources for other reconstruction efforts.

Promoting Public Health Education and Community Trust

Beyond immediate medical care, Autonomous Mobile Clinics can serve as pivotal centers for public health education, promoting preventive care and building community trust in the healthcare system.

- **Health Campaigns:** Regular visits by AMCs can initiate public health campaigns, vaccination drives, and health screenings, tailored to the specific needs of the communities they serve.
- **Building Trust:** By consistently providing reliable healthcare, AMCs strengthen the relationship between the healthcare system and the community, encouraging greater participation in health programs.

Conclusion: A Pathway to a Healthier Future

The implementation of Autonomous Mobile Clinics marks a revolutionary step in Ukraine's healthcare transformation. These clinics embody innovation, resilience, and a commitment to reaching every citizen, regardless of location. Through technology, strategic deployment, and a focus on comprehensive care, Autonomous Mobile Clinics are poised to transform Ukraine's healthcare landscape, setting a new standard for accessibility and quality.

Embracing this future ensures that Ukraine not only recovers from the ravages of war but also rebuilds stronger, with a healthcare system that is inclusive, advanced, and prepared for the challenges ahead. Autonomous Mobile Clinics are not just a solution; they are a testament to Ukraine's enduring spirit and a commitment to a brighter, healthier future for all.

Section 18.2: Nanomedicine and Personalized Treatments

Embracing the Future of Medicine in Post-War Ukraine

In the quest to rebuild and modernize Ukraine's healthcare system, nanomedicine and personalized treatments stand out as groundbreaking innovations poised to revolutionize patient care. By integrating these advanced medical solutions, Ukraine can ensure that its healthcare provision is not only restored but also enhanced to meet global standards of excellence.

The Promise of Nanomedicine

Revolutionizing Treatment at the Nanoscale

Nanomedicine leverages molecular-scale engineering to develop highly precise therapeutic and diagnostic tools. This emerging field holds immense potential for transforming healthcare in Ukraine by offering targeted treatments, reducing side effects, and improving patient outcomes.

- **Targeted Drug Delivery:** Nanomedicine allows for the development of nanoparticles designed to deliver drugs directly to diseased cells, thus

minimizing damage to healthy tissues and reducing side effects. This precision increases the efficacy of treatments, particularly in combating cancer and infectious diseases.
- **Advanced Diagnostics**: Nanotechnology enhances diagnostic imaging and biomarker detection, enabling early and accurate diagnosis of diseases. Techniques such as quantum dots and nanosensors provide high-resolution images and detailed biological information at the molecular level.

Developing Nanomedicine Infrastructure

Building Centers of Excellence

The successful implementation of nanomedicine in Ukraine requires the establishment of dedicated facilities, access to advanced technologies, and strong collaboration with international experts.

- **Nanomedicine Research and Production Centers**: Establish state-of-the-art research and production centers specializing in nanomedicine. These centers will focus on developing new nanotherapeutics, conducting clinical trials, and scaling up production for widespread use.
- **Collaboration with Global Experts**: Forge partnerships with leading nanomedicine institutions worldwide to gain access to cutting-edge research and development insights. Collaborative efforts will accelerate the assimilation of advanced nanotechnological methods and foster innovation.

Personalized Medicine: Tailoring Treatment to Individuals

Precision Healthcare Innovation

Personalized medicine involves tailoring medical treatments to individual genetic profiles and specific health conditions, ensuring more effective and personalized healthcare delivery.

- **Genomic Medicine**: Utilize genomic sequencing to identify genetic variants linked to diseases and responses to treatments. Personalized medicine allows for the creation of customized treatment plans that target the unique genetic makeup of each patient.
- **Biomarker Identification**: Identify and use biomarkers to predict disease risk, progression, and response to therapies. Biomarkers enable clinicians to monitor patients closely and adjust treatment plans in real-time for optimized health outcomes.

Implementing Personalized Treatment Programs

Infrastructure and Education

A robust framework for personalized treatment necessitates significant infrastructural and educational investments.

- **Genomic Centers**: Establish genomic centers equipped with state-of-the-art sequencing technologies and bioinformatics capabilities. These centers will conduct comprehensive genomic analyses and support personalized treatment plans.
- **Healthcare Professional Training**: Implement specialized training programs for healthcare professionals in genomics, bioinformatics, and personalized medicine. Continual professional development ensures that practitioners remain updated on the latest advancements and best practices.

Public Health and Ethical Considerations

Ensuring Equitable Access and Ethical Conduct

The widespread adoption of nanomedicine and personalized treatments must address public health equity and ethical issues to ensure inclusivity and fairness.

- **Accessibility**: Develop strategies to ensure that advanced treatments are accessible to all segments of the population, including marginalized and rural communities. Public health programs should focus on reducing disparities in healthcare access and outcomes.
- **Ethical Frameworks**: Establish robust ethical guidelines for the use of genetic information and nanotechnology in healthcare. Implement transparent consent processes, data protection measures, and independent ethical reviews to safeguard patient rights and privacy.

Integration with Existing Healthcare Systems

Seamlessly Enhancing Current Practices

Integrating nanomedicine and personalized treatments with existing healthcare systems is essential for a cohesive and effective healthcare delivery.

- **Hybrid Treatment Models**: Develop treatment models that combine traditional medical practices with nanomedicine and personalized approaches. This integrated approach ensures comprehensive care and optimizes patient outcomes.
- **Technology Adoption Roadmap**: Create a clear roadmap for the adoption and implementation of these advanced treatments within existing healthcare frameworks. This roadmap will outline phases for introduction, scaling, and full integration into routine medical practice.

Financing and International Support

Securing Sustainable Funding

Securing adequate funding and leveraging international support are critical for the successful advancement of nanomedicine and personalized treatments.

- **Public-Private Partnerships**: Foster partnerships between the government, private sector, and international donors to secure funding for

research, infrastructure development, and implementation of advanced healthcare programs.
- **International Grants and Aid**: Explore international grants and aid opportunities from institutions such as the European Union, World Health Organization, and other global health initiatives focusing on technological and medical innovation 17:13†source .

Community Engagement and Education

Empowering the Public with Knowledge

Educating the public about the benefits and implications of nanomedicine and personalized treatments is vital for fostering acceptance and encouraging informed participation in healthcare innovations.

- **Public Awareness Campaigns**: Launch comprehensive awareness campaigns to educate the public on the potential of nanomedicine and personalized treatments. Use various media platforms to disseminate information and highlight success stories.
- **Patient Education Programs**: Develop patient education programs to provide individuals with the knowledge needed to understand their treatment options and participate actively in their healthcare decisions.

Conclusion: A Future-Forward Healthcare System

The integration of nanomedicine and personalized treatments into Ukraine's healthcare system represents a pioneering step towards creating a future-forward, resilient, and inclusive healthcare ecosystem. By harnessing the precision and potential of these advanced medical technologies, Ukraine can not only rebuild but also elevate its healthcare standards to unprecedented levels, ensuring high-quality care for all its citizens.

Nanomedicine and personalized treatments stand as beacons of hope and innovation, heralding a new era in which healthcare is tailored to the individual and delivered with unprecedented efficacy. As Ukraine embraces these advancements, it sets a visionary example for post-war reconstruction and serves as an inspiration for healthcare innovation worldwide.

Section 18.3: Bioprinting Centers for Organ Engineering

The Pinnacle of Medical Innovation: A Lifeline for Ukraine

As Ukraine embarks on the herculean task of rebuilding its healthcare system, bioprinting centers for organ engineering emerge as a paramount innovation that could radically transform medical care. Bioprinting, a cutting-edge field at the intersection of technology and biology, offers the potential to create custom-engineered tissues and organs, addressing critical shortages and enhancing patient outcomes. This section explores the strategic planning, development, and integration of bioprinting centers into Ukraine's healthcare infrastructure, positioning the nation at the forefront of medical innovation.

Vision for Bioprinting in Healthcare

Revolutionizing Medical Treatments

The integration of bioprinting technology into healthcare aims to provide revolutionary treatments, reduce dependence on organ donations, and improve patient survival rates through customized medical solutions.

- **Custom-Engineered Organs**: Bioprinting allows for the creation of organs and tissues tailored to individual patients' genetic profiles, significantly reducing the risk of rejection and improving compatibility.
- **Enhanced Recovery and Rehabilitation**: Engineered tissues can be used to repair and regenerate damaged organs, enhancing recovery and reducing the need for long-term treatments.

Strategic Implementation and Development

Structured Phases for Effective Integration

A phased approach ensures systematic and scalable integration of bioprinting centers into Ukraine's healthcare system.

Phase 1: Research and Collaboration

- **Feasibility Studies**: Conduct comprehensive feasibility studies to evaluate the technical, economic, and ethical aspects of bioprinting. Collaborate with academic institutions, research organizations, and international experts to leverage global knowledge and best practices.
- **Pilot Projects**: Launch pilot bioprinting projects focused on specific tissues, such as skin, cartilage, or simple organ structures. These pilots will help refine techniques, establish protocols, and build expertise within the healthcare system.

Phase 2: Infrastructure Development

- **Establishing Bioprinting Centers**: Develop state-of-the-art bioprinting centers equipped with advanced 3D printers, cleanroom facilities, and bioinformatics platforms. Ensure that these centers are strategically located within major hospitals and research hubs to facilitate easy access and integration.
- **Equipment and Technology**: Invest in cutting-edge bioprinting technology and materials, including bioinks and scaffolding materials that support cell growth and organ development. Collaborate with tech companies to secure the latest innovations in bioprinting equipment.

Phase 3: Medical Integration and Scaling

- **Clinical Integration**: Integrate bioprinting techniques into clinical practice, focusing on applications such as tissue repair, organ regeneration, and custom implants. Develop protocols for the use of printed tissues in surgical procedures and therapeutic applications.
- **Scaling Up Production**: Expand the capacity of bioprinting centers to meet increasing demand. Establish production lines for commonly required tissues and organs, ensuring a steady supply for clinical use.

Advancements in Biomedical Research

Fostering Innovation and Discovery

Bioprinting centers will serve as epicenters for groundbreaking biomedical research, driving innovation and advancing medical knowledge.

- **Cutting-Edge Research**: Conduct research on new bioprinting techniques, materials, and applications. Explore the potential of creating more complex organs, such as kidneys, hearts, and livers.
- **Collaborative Platforms**: Create collaborative platforms that bring together researchers, clinicians, and technology experts. Foster interdisciplinary research initiatives that push the boundaries of what bioprinting can achieve.

Training and Capacity Building

Empowering Healthcare Professionals

Building a workforce skilled in bioprinting technology is essential for the successful implementation and sustainability of bioprinting centers.

- **Specialized Training Programs**: Develop specialized training programs for healthcare professionals, including surgeons, technicians, and research scientists. These programs will cover bioprinting fundamentals, advanced techniques, and clinical applications.
- **Continuous Professional Development**: Offer ongoing professional development opportunities to ensure that staff remain updated on the latest advancements in bioprinting and regenerative medicine.

Ethical and Regulatory Considerations

Ensuring Responsible Innovation

The integration of bioprinting technology must be guided by robust ethical and regulatory frameworks to ensure responsible use and public trust.

- **Ethical Guidelines**: Establish ethical guidelines for the research, development, and application of bioprinting technology. Address issues such

as informed consent, genetic privacy, and the long-term implications of bioprinted organs.
- **Regulatory Oversight**: Implement strong regulatory oversight to monitor bioprinting practices, ensure compliance with safety standards, and protect patient rights. Develop clear protocols for the approval and use of bioprinted tissues in clinical settings.

Public Awareness and Community Engagement

Building Public Trust and Support

Educating the public about bioprinting and its benefits is crucial for fostering acceptance and support.

- **Public Information Campaigns**: Launch campaigns to raise awareness about the potential and benefits of bioprinting technology. Use multimedia platforms to share success stories, explain procedures, and highlight the transformative impact on healthcare.
- **Community Involvement**: Involve community representatives in discussions about bioprinting initiatives. Gather feedback and address concerns to ensure that public perspectives are considered in the development and implementation processes.

International Collaboration and Funding

Securing Global Partnerships

International collaboration and funding are vital for advancing bioprinting technology and ensuring its successful integration into healthcare.

- **Global Partnerships**: Engage with international bioprinting research institutions, technology companies, and medical organizations to share knowledge, resources, and expertise. Collaborative research projects and joint ventures will drive innovation and expansion.
- **Funding and Grants**: Secure funding and grants from international health organizations, philanthropic institutions, and government bodies. Ensure transparent management and allocation of funds to build trust and attract further investment.

Monitoring and Evaluation

Ensuring Success and Sustainability

Continuous monitoring and evaluation are essential to assess the impact of bioprinting technology and ensure its sustainability.

- **Performance Metrics**: Develop key performance indicators (KPIs) to evaluate the success of bioprinting centers, including patient outcomes, technology efficacy, and research advancements.

- **Regular Audits**: Conduct regular audits and reviews to ensure compliance with ethical and regulatory standards. Use audit findings to improve practices and address any identified issues.
- **Stakeholder Feedback**: Establish feedback mechanisms for healthcare professionals, patients, and the public to share their experiences and suggestions. Use this feedback to refine and enhance bioprinting services and operations.

Conclusion: A Trailblazing Future in Healthcare

The establishment of bioprinting centers for organ engineering represents a pioneering leap in Ukraine's healthcare reconstruction efforts. By embracing this transformative technology, Ukraine can not only address critical healthcare challenges but also position itself as a global leader in medical innovation. Through strategic planning, robust infrastructure development, interdisciplinary collaboration, and ethical oversight, bioprinting centers will herald a new era of precise, personalized, and advanced medical care, ensuring a healthier, more resilient future for all Ukrainians.

Chapter 19: Governance and Adaptive Structures

Section 19.1: AI-Assisted Policy-Making Platforms

Transforming Governance with Artificial Intelligence

In the crucial rebuilding phase following the conflict, Ukraine has the unique opportunity to reinvent its governance infrastructure using cutting-edge technology. Artificial Intelligence (AI) offers a transformative path for policy-making, enabling a responsive, transparent, and efficient governance system. This section details the strategic implementation of AI-assisted policy-making platforms, emphasizing their potential to revolutionize decision-making processes and enhance public trust.

Vision for AI-Assisted Governance

Revolutionizing Policy-Making

Ukraine's adoption of AI-assisted policy-making platforms aims to streamline governance, enhance data-driven decision-making, and improve the efficiency and transparency of government operations.

- **Data-Driven Decisions**: AI can analyze vast amounts of data in real-time, providing valuable insights to inform policy decisions, predict outcomes, and foster evidence-based governance.
- **Enhanced Transparency**: AI platforms can ensure that decision-making processes are transparent, with accessible data and clear

documentation of how decisions are made.
- **Operational Efficiency**: Automating routine tasks and data processing frees up governmental resources to focus on strategic planning and high-impact initiatives.

Implementation Strategy

Phased Integration of AI in Governance

A structured, phased approach is critical for the effective integration of AI-assisted policy-making platforms.

Phase 1: Foundation and Pilot Programs

- **Needs Assessment**: Conduct a comprehensive assessment to identify the specific needs and areas within the government where AI can have the most significant impact.
- **Pilot Projects**: Launch pilot programs in select governmental departments to test and refine AI platforms. Focus areas can include economic planning, healthcare policy, and urban development.
- **Data Infrastructure**: Develop the necessary data infrastructure, including data collection, storage systems, and security protocols to support AI integration.

Phase 2: Capacity Building and Expansion

- **Training and Education**: Implement training programs for government officials and employees to ensure they are proficient in using AI tools. Continuous professional development will keep officials informed about the latest advancements.
- **Scalable Solutions**: Expand AI integration across various departments based on the success and learnings from pilot projects. Develop scalable models that can be tailored to different governmental functions.

Phase 3: Full Integration and Optimization

- **Comprehensive Rollout**: Implement AI-assisted policy-making platforms across all government sectors, ensuring a uniform, integrated approach.
- **Continuous Monitoring and Optimization**: Regularly evaluate the effectiveness of AI systems and optimize them based on feedback and performance metrics. Adaptation and continuous improvement will be key to long-term success.

Technological Architecture

Building Robust AI Systems

The success of AI-assisted governance relies on robust technological infrastructure and advanced AI systems.

- **AI Algorithms and Models**: Develop sophisticated AI algorithms capable of analyzing diverse data sets, predicting trends, and providing actionable insights.
- **Data Security and Privacy**: Ensure that all data processed by AI systems are securely stored and adhere to privacy regulations. Implement robust encryption methods and data protection protocols .
- **User-Friendly Interfaces**: Create intuitive, user-friendly interfaces for AI platforms to ensure that government officials can easily access and interpret AI-generated insights.

Enhancing Decision-Making Processes

Leveraging AI for Strategic Advantage

AI can significantly enhance the decision-making processes in various domains of governance.

- **Economic Planning**: AI can analyze economic trends, forecast economic outcomes, and provide recommendations for financial planning and budgeting .
- **Healthcare Policy**: Use AI to predict healthcare needs, optimize resource allocation, and plan for future healthcare infrastructure. AI-driven health data analytics can support more effective public health interventions 20:13†source .
- **Urban Development**: AI can assist in urban planning by analyzing demographic trends, infrastructure needs, and environmental impacts to create sustainable, resilient urban environments 17:13†source .

Transparency and Accountability

Building Public Trust through Open Governance

AI-assisted policy-making platforms can significantly enhance transparency and accountability in government.

- **Public Data Access**: Provide public access to AI-generated data and decision-making processes through online portals. This transparency ensures that citizens are informed and can participate in governance .
- **Accountability Mechanisms**: Develop mechanisms for auditing and reviewing AI-generated decisions to ensure that they align with ethical standards and public interest.

Case Studies and Success Models

Learning from Global Leaders

Studying successful implementations of AI in governance worldwide provides valuable insights.

- **Singapore's Smart Nation Initiative**: Singapore has successfully integrated AI in various aspects of governance, from urban planning to public health. Ukraine can learn from Singapore's model to develop its AI infrastructure.
- **Estonia's e-Governance**: Estonia's e-governance platform leverages AI for efficient public service delivery and decision-making. Ukraine can adapt Estonia's best practices to its context of post-war reconstruction.

Ethical Considerations and Regulatory Frameworks

Ensuring Ethical and Fair Use of AI

Ethical considerations and a robust regulatory framework are critical for the responsible use of AI in governance.

- **Ethical AI Use**: Develop ethical guidelines for the use of AI in policy-making, addressing issues such as bias, fairness, and accountability. Ensure that AI systems are designed to promote equality and justice .
- **Regulatory Oversight**: Establish regulatory bodies to oversee the implementation and operation of AI systems in governance. Regular audits and reviews ensure compliance with ethical standards and public trust.

Monitoring and Evaluation

Continuous Improvement and Adaptation

Regular monitoring and evaluation are essential to the success and sustainability of AI-assisted governance.

- **Performance Metrics**: Develop key performance indicators (KPIs) to measure the impact of AI on governance efficiency, transparency, and public satisfaction.
- **Feedback Loops**: Create feedback loops to gather input from government officials and the public. Use this feedback to make necessary adjustments and improve AI systems.
- **Independent Evaluations**: Conduct independent evaluations to assess the effectiveness and fairness of AI-assisted policy-making platforms. Share findings to promote transparency and continuous improvement.

Conclusion

The integration of AI-assisted policy-making platforms marks a transformative step in Ukraine's journey towards effective, transparent, and innovative governance. By leveraging AI technology, Ukraine can revolutionize its decision-making processes, ensuring that policies are data-driven, transparent, and aligned with the needs and aspirations of its citizens. This forward-thinking approach not only accelerates Ukraine's post-war recovery but also sets the groundwork for a resilient, future-ready governance system that exemplifies the potential of technology in public administration.

Section 19.2: Blockchain-Based Voting Systems

Revitalizing Democracy Through Technology

The reconstruction of Ukraine presents a profound moment of renewal, where adopting innovative technologies like blockchain can fortify democratic processes and engender a more transparent, secure, and participatory electoral system. Blockchain-based voting systems offer an unparalleled opportunity to safeguard electoral integrity, enhance voter confidence, and promote inclusivity in the democratic process.

The Potential of Blockchain in Voting

Ensuring Trust and Security

Blockchain technology, with its decentralized, immutable ledger, addresses many vulnerabilities and inefficiencies inherent in traditional voting systems.

- **Enhanced Security**: Blockchain's cryptographic principles ensure that each vote is securely recorded and immutable, making tampering virtually impossible.
- **Transparency**: Every transaction (vote) on the blockchain is transparent to all stakeholders, enabling comprehensive auditing and verification without compromising voter anonymity.
- **Decentralization**: A decentralized ledger eliminates the risk of a single point of failure or manipulation, providing powerful safeguards against fraud and ensuring each vote counts.

Implementation Strategy

Structured Deployment for Effective Integration

Implementing blockchain-based voting systems in Ukraine involves a phased approach to ensure robust, secure, and user-friendly solutions are in place.

Phase 1: Pilot Projects and Feasibility Studies

- **Initial Pilots**: Launch pilot projects in select jurisdictions to evaluate the practical application of blockchain in voting. Focus on small-scale elections, such as local council or municipal votes, to test and refine the technology and processes.
- **Feasibility Studies**: Conduct detailed feasibility studies to identify challenges, requirements, and potential impact. Collaborate with blockchain technology experts, cybersecurity specialists, and electoral bodies to gather insights and develop best practices.

Phase 2: Infrastructure Development and Capacity Building

- **Blockchain Infrastructure**: Develop the necessary blockchain infrastructure, including node deployment, consensus mechanisms, and smart contract development tailored for electoral purposes.
- **Training Programs**: Implement extensive training programs for election officials, IT staff, and electoral overseers on blockchain technology and its application in voting. Equip them with the skills needed to manage and operate blockchain voting systems effectively.

Phase 3: Nationwide Implementation and Scaling

- **Comprehensive Rollout**: Expand blockchain-based voting systems nationwide, ensuring all electoral processes from local to national levels are integrated. Develop a phased rollout plan to systematically scale up from regional to country-wide elections.
- **Continuous Optimization**: Regularly monitor, review, and optimize the system based on feedback, technological advancements, and emerging challenges. Maintain a proactive approach to cybersecurity and technical support.

Enhancing Electoral Integrity

Building Public Trust Through Transparency

Blockchain voting systems can significantly enhance public trust by ensuring that all electoral processes are transparent and verifiable.

- **Public Access Portals**: Develop public portals where citizens can view, in real-time, the number of votes cast, tallies, and other relevant data, thus promoting transparency and public trust in the electoral process.
- **Audit Trails**: Enable comprehensive audit trails where third-party oversight bodies can trace and verify every vote from casting to counting, ensuring electoral integrity and accountability.

Inclusivity and Accessibility

Promoting Broad Participation

Blockchain-based voting systems can address barriers to voter participation, ensuring greater inclusivity.

- **Remote Voting Capabilities**: Allow citizens, including those in remote areas and expatriates, to cast their votes securely from anywhere, thus enhancing voter turnout and participation.
- **User-Friendly Interfaces**: Design intuitive and accessible voting interfaces compatible with various devices, ensuring ease of use for all voters regardless of technical proficiency.

International Collaboration and Best Practices

Leveraging Global Expertise

Drawing from international experiences and best practices can enrich the implementation of blockchain-based voting systems.

- **Global Partnerships**: Collaborate with countries and organizations that have successfully implemented blockchain voting, such as Estonia's pioneering efforts in e-governance and blockchain voting.
- **Knowledge Exchanges**: Participate in knowledge exchange programs and workshops to learn from global experts in blockchain technology, cybersecurity, and electoral management.

Monitoring and Evaluation

Ensuring Continuous Improvement

A robust monitoring and evaluation framework is essential to assess the effectiveness and integrity of blockchain-based voting systems.

- **Performance Metrics**: Develop key performance indicators (KPIs) to measure the system's security, transparency, voter turnout, and user satisfaction.
- **Regular Audits**: Conduct regular audits and security assessments to ensure the system's integrity, identify vulnerabilities, and implement improvements.
- **Stakeholder Feedback**: Establish feedback mechanisms for voters, electoral officials, and independent observers to continuously refine and enhance the system.

Overcoming Challenges

Addressing Potential Barriers

Implementing blockchain-based voting systems involves overcoming various technical, logistical, and social challenges.

- **Cybersecurity**: Ensure robust cybersecurity measures are in place to protect against hacking and other cyber threats. Continuously update and improve security protocols to address emerging risks.
- **Technical Literacy**: Address technical literacy by providing comprehensive voter education campaigns to ensure all citizens are familiar with the new technology and voting process.
- **Regulatory Compliance**: Develop and ensure compliance with robust legal and regulatory frameworks that align with democratic principles and international standards to govern the use of blockchain technology in elections.

Conclusion

Blockchain-based voting systems represent a transformative innovation in Ukraine's journey to rebuild and strengthen its democracy. By ensuring enhanced security, transparency, and inclusivity, blockchain technology can significantly fortify the integrity of the electoral process, fostering public trust and engagement. Through strategic, phased implementation, continuous monitoring, and international collaboration, Ukraine can set a benchmark in democratic innovations, showcasing the profound potential of technology in governance.

The adoption of blockchain-based voting systems is not merely a technological advancement; it is a bold step towards a resilient, transparent, and inclusive democracy that reflects Ukraine's commitment to integrity, citizen participation, and progressive governance.

Section 19.3: Gamified Citizen Engagement Platforms

Transforming Civic Engagement through Gamification

As Ukraine embarks on the journey of post-war reconstruction, revitalizing civic engagement is pivotal. Citizens must have a voice in shaping the future of their cities. Gamified citizen engagement platforms leverage the power of gamification to foster active participation, transparency, and community cohesion in urban planning and governance processes.

The Essence of Gamification in Civic Participation

Making Engagement Fun and Effective

By incorporating game design elements into civic platforms, gamification can transform the often mundane tasks of public participation into engaging and motivating activities. Here is how it can invigorate civic life:

- **Increased Participation**: Gamification makes participation more appealing, encouraging broader citizen involvement.
- **Transparency and Trust**: Gamified platforms provide transparent mechanisms for tracking input and feedback, fostering trust between citizens and authorities.
- **Skill Development**: Citizens develop various skills through interactive problem-solving and collaborative tasks.

Strategic Implementation of Gamified Platforms

Phases of Integration

A structured, phased approach will ensure the successful integration of gamified citizen engagement platforms into Ukraine's urban planning and governance framework.

Phase 1: Concept Development and Pilot Projects

- **Stakeholder Workshops**: Conduct workshops with community members, urban planners, and technology experts to define objectives and desired outcomes of the gamified platforms.
- **Pilot Initiatives**: Launch pilot projects in select municipalities to test and refine game mechanics and engagement strategies. Use these pilots to gather data and feedback to inform broader implementation.

Phase 2: Platform Development and Rollout

- **Platform Design**: Develop robust and user-friendly platforms utilizing best practices in UX/UI, ensuring inclusivity and accessibility for all citizens.
- **Gamification Elements**: Integrate key gamification elements such as points, leaderboards, challenges, and rewards to motivate and sustain user engagement.
- **Community Training**: Offer training programs to familiarize citizens with the platform and its capabilities. This will ensure active and informed participation from a broad demographic.

Phase 3: Broad Implementation and Optimization

- **Nationwide Rollout**: Expand gamified platforms nationwide, incorporating lessons learned from pilot projects. Ensure the platform is adaptable to local contexts and needs.
- **Continuous Improvement**: Regularly update the platform based on user feedback, technological advancements, and emerging civic needs.

Enhancing Urban Planning through Gamification

Practical Applications in Urban Development

Gamified citizen engagement platforms can play a crucial role in various urban planning processes:

- **Participatory Budgeting**: Citizens can use the platform to propose, debate, and vote on budget allocations for public projects, ensuring that funds are used where they are most needed and desired.
- **Urban Design Competitions**: Host competitions where citizens propose and vote on designs for public spaces, fostering creativity and community pride.
- **Feedback Loops**: Create dynamic feedback mechanisms that allow citizens to provide real-time input on ongoing projects and policies.

Building Community Trust and Social Cohesion

Fostering a Culture of Participation

Gamified platforms go beyond mere participation—they build community trust and social cohesion:

- **Transparency in Decision-Making**: Clear tracking of proposals, votes, and decisions fosters trust and ensures that citizen input is valued.
- **Collaborative Problem-Solving**: Platforms can unite citizens around common challenges, promoting collaborative solutions and community bonds.
- **Recognition and Rewards**: Acknowledge active participants through virtual badges, public leaderboards, and tangible rewards, reinforcing positive engagement behaviors.

International Collaboration and Best Practices

Learning and Adapting from Global Examples

Global examples offer valuable insights into the successful deployment of gamified engagement platforms:

- **Case Study: Reykjavik, Iceland**: The city's "Better Reykjavik" platform allows residents to propose and vote on local initiatives, leading to tangible improvements in public services and infrastructure.
- **Case Study: Madrid, Spain**: The "Decide Madrid" platform engages citizens in participatory budgeting, enabling them to allocate a portion of the city's budget to projects they prioritize.

Ethical Considerations and Data Security

Ensuring Responsible Usage

Ethical considerations and data security are critical for the success and integrity of gamified citizen engagement platforms:

- **Data Privacy**: Implement robust data privacy measures to protect user information, ensuring compliance with international data protection standards.
- **Equity and Accessibility**: Ensure that the platforms are accessible to all citizens, including marginalized communities and individuals with disabilities, preventing digital exclusion.
- **Ethical Use of Gamification**: Design gamification elements to encourage positive behavior and avoid manipulative practices. Ethical guidelines should govern the design and implementation.

Monitoring and Evaluation

Measuring Impact and Improving Strategies

Continuous monitoring and evaluation are vital to assess the effectiveness of gamified platforms and their impact on civic engagement:

- **Key Performance Indicators (KPIs)**: Develop KPIs to measure participation rates, user satisfaction, and the real-world impact of citizen proposals.
- **User Feedback Mechanisms**: Regularly solicit feedback from users to identify areas for improvement and adjust strategies accordingly.
- **Performance Reviews**: Conduct independent performance reviews to ensure the platform meets its objectives and upholds ethical standards.

Conclusion

Gamified citizen engagement platforms represent a groundbreaking approach to revitalizing civic participation in Ukraine's post-war reconstruction. By making citizen involvement fun, rewarding, and impactful, these platforms can foster a more engaged, transparent, and cohesive community. Through strategic implementation, international collaboration, ethical oversight, and continuous improvement, Ukraine can set a global example in utilizing gamification to transform governance and urban planning, ensuring that every citizen has a voice in building a resilient and thriving future.

Chapter 20: Resilient Food Systems

Section 20.1: Rooftop and Vertical Hydroponic Farms

Transforming Urban Agriculture for Resilience

In the heart of every resilient city lies a robust food system, agile enough to withstand disruptions and sustainable enough to support its inhabitants in perpetuity. As Ukraine rebuilds, integrating rooftop and vertical hydroponic farms into urban environments will play a pivotal role in securing food sovereignty, enhancing urban resilience, and fostering sustainable development.

Embracing Technological Innovations

Ukraine's journey towards resilience and sustainability must be powered by the adoption of cutting-edge agricultural technologies that maximize output while minimizing environmental impact.

Hydroponics Defined: Hydroponics, a method of growing plants without soil, uses mineral nutrient solutions in aqueous solvents. This system allows for precise control over nutrient uptake, leading to higher yields and resource efficiency.

Rooftop Farms: Rooftop farms capitalize on unused urban spaces, transforming idle rooftops into productive green zones. These farms leverage hydroponic systems to produce fresh vegetables and herbs, contributing to local food supply chains.

Vertical Farms: Vertical farms employ stackable layers in controlled environments, utilizing LED lighting and climate control systems to create optimal growing conditions year-round. This method significantly increases growing capacity within a limited footprint.

Advantages: - **Space Efficiency:** Hydroponic systems can be implemented in urban settings where traditional farming is impractical. - **Resource Conservation:** These systems use up to 90% less water than conventional farming methods. - **Reduced Carbon Footprint:** Local food production minimizes the need for transportation, thereby reducing greenhouse gas emissions.

Implementation Strategy

To successfully integrate rooftop and vertical hydroponic farms into urban reconstruction, a structured, multi-phase approach is essential.

Phase 1: Pilot Projects and Feasibility Studies Initial Deployment: Commence with pilot projects in select urban areas to test the feasibility and refine the mechanisms of hydroponic farming. Focus on rooftops of hospitals, schools, and government buildings, ensuring diverse environmental and operational conditions.

Feasibility Studies: Conduct feasibility studies to identify optimal locations, assess potential yield, and evaluate economic viability. Collaborate with agricultural experts, urban planners, and local communities to gather comprehensive insights and tailor solutions to specific urban areas.

Phase 2: Infrastructure Development and Capacity Building Construction and Setup: Develop the physical and technological infrastructure necessary for hydroponic farms, including water distribution systems, nutrient supply chains, and climate control technologies. Ensure installations are robustly built to withstand urban weather conditions and designed to maximize operational efficiency.

Training Programs: Implement extensive training programs for urban farmers, providing knowledge on hydroponic techniques, crop management, and system maintenance. Partner with educational institutions to develop curricula and provide certification for urban agriculture professionals.

Phase 3: Nationwide Implementation and Optimization Scaling Up: Expand hydroponic farming systems across major cities, integrating them into the urban fabric. Focus on scalability and adaptability, ensuring that systems can be replicated in varying urban environments across Ukraine.

Continuous Improvement: Establish monitoring and evaluation mechanisms to assess performance, gather user feedback, and identify areas for improvement. Continuously upgrade systems with advancements in hydroponic technology and environmental control.

Integrating Community Engagement and Education

Community Involvement: Engage local communities in the planning and implementation phases to ensure that hydroponic farms meet local needs and preferences. Develop community gardens and involve residents in the cultivation process, fostering a sense of ownership and responsibility towards sustainable urban agriculture.

Educational Initiatives: Promote urban farming through educational programs in schools and community centers. Highlight the benefits of hydroponic farming, including its environmental impact and role in enhancing urban resilience, to inspire future generations of urban farmers.

Securing Funding and International Collaboration

Funding Mechanisms: Leverage international aid, grants, and private investments to finance hydroponic projects. Coordinate with global organizations committed to sustainable development to secure funds and technical expertise.

Global Partnerships: Form partnerships with international entities experienced in urban agriculture, such as vertical farming industry leaders and global agricultural research institutions. Participate in knowledge exchange programs to learn from successful implementations worldwide and bring best practices to Ukraine.

Monitoring and Evaluation

Performance Metrics: Develop key performance indicators (KPIs) to measure the success of hydroponic farms, such as crop yield, resource consumption, and economic impact. Utilize data analytics to monitor system performance and optimize operations.

Independent Reviews: Conduct independent evaluations by agricultural experts and urban planners to ensure that hydroponic systems meet their objectives and deliver on promised benefits. Share findings with stakeholders to maintain transparency and drive continuous improvement.

Conclusion: A Sustainable Urban Future

By integrating rooftop and vertical hydroponic farms into urban reconstruction plans, Ukraine can build a resilient and sustainable food system, turning urban spaces into green, productive areas that support local food networks and enhance urban resilience. This forward-thinking approach will not only address immediate food security challenges but also pave the way for a sustainable, vibrant future where cities and nature coexist harmoniously.

Harnessing innovation, community engagement, and international cooperation, Ukraine sets a powerful precedent for sustainable urban agriculture, demonstrating the resilience and adaptability of its cities in the face of adversity.

Section 20.2: Underground Mushroom Farms

Cultivating Resilience Beneath the City

As Ukraine forges a path towards sustainable urban reconstruction, leveraging innovative agricultural methods is crucial in establishing food security and resilience. Underground mushroom farms embody a unique and highly efficient means of utilizing urban spaces, particularly in post-war cities where surface-level real estate may be scarce or damaged. This section explores the strategic incorporation of underground mushroom farms into urban food systems, detailing their benefits, implementation strategies, and potential for fostering sustainable urban development.

The Potential of Underground Agriculture

Maximizing Space and Efficiency

Underground mushroom farming utilizes subterranean spaces—ranging from basements to repurposed bunkers or tunnels—transforming them into productive agricultural sites. This approach offers several advantages:

- **Space Optimization**: Converts otherwise unused underground areas into productive farms.
- **Environmental Control**: Underground environments provide natural insulation and stable conditions, ideal for controlled agriculture.
- **Year-Round Production**: Allows for consistent, year-round cultivation unaffected by surface weather conditions.

Implementing Underground Mushroom Farms

Strategic Framework for Development

A structured, phased approach ensures the successful integration of underground mushroom farms into Ukraine's urban agricultural framework.

Phase 1: Assessment and Pilot Projects Preliminary Studies and Initial Setups

- **Site Assessment**: Conduct detailed surveys to identify suitable underground locations, such as basements, defunct tunnels, and bunkers. Evaluate these sites for stability, accessibility, and potential for agricultural conversion.
- **Pilot Projects**: Launch pilot operations in select cities to test and refine underground farming techniques. Focus on diverse urban environments to gather comprehensive data on conditions and adaptability.

Phase 2: Infrastructure Development and Capacity Building Building and Equipping the Farms

- **Construction and Retrofits**: Develop the necessary infrastructure to convert identified underground spaces into mushroom farms. This includes installing climate control systems, lighting, ventilation, and irrigation.
- **Training Programs**: Establish training programs for potential urban farmers, covering the basics of mycology, underground farming techniques, and system maintenance. Partner with agricultural universities and research institutions to ensure high-quality education.

Phase 3: Expansion and Optimization Scaling Up and Enhancing Systems

- **Replication and Scaling**: Expand the successful pilot projects across major urban centers. Implement standardized protocols to streamline processes and ensure uniformity in production.
- **Continuous Improvement**: Regularly monitor farm performance and gather feedback. Leverage advancements in agricultural technology to optimize conditions and maximize yields.

Key Benefits of Underground Mushroom Farms

Boosting Urban Resilience and Sustainability

Underground mushroom farms contribute significantly to urban resilience and sustainability:

- **Food Security**: Provide a stable supply of nutritious, locally grown mushrooms to urban populations, reducing dependency on external food supplies.
- **Economic Opportunities**: Create job opportunities and stimulate local economies by fostering new businesses in urban agriculture.
- **Environmental Benefits**: Minimize the environmental footprint by utilizing existing underground spaces and requiring relatively low resource inputs for climate control.

Community Engagement and Educational Outreach

Fostering Public Involvement and Awareness

Active community engagement and public education are pivotal in the success of underground farming initiatives:

- **Community Outreach**: Involve local communities in the planning and operation of underground farms. Host workshops and tours to educate residents about the benefits and processes of underground mushroom cultivation.
- **School Programs**: Develop educational programs in collaboration with schools to teach students about sustainable agriculture and the science of mycology. Incorporate hands-on activities and projects to inspire the next generation of urban farmers.

Funding and International Collaboration

Securing Resources and Expertise

Sustainable funding and leveraging international expertise are critical to the success of underground mushroom farming:

- **Funding Mechanisms**: Secure financial support from international donors, green investment funds, and private sector investors. Explore innovative funding models such as crowdsourcing and social impact bonds.
- **Global Partnerships**: Form alliances with international agricultural research centers and urban farming experts. Engage in knowledge exchange programs to adopt best practices and cutting-edge technologies.

Monitoring and Evaluation

Ensuring Continuous Improvement

Robust monitoring and evaluation frameworks are essential to assess the performance and impact of underground mushroom farms:

- **Performance Indicators**: Develop key performance indicators (KPIs) to measure yield, resource efficiency, economic impact, and community benefits.
- **Regular Audits**: Conduct regular audits and evaluations to ensure compliance with best practices and to identify areas for improvement. Use data analytics to inform decision-making and optimize operations.
- **Feedback Mechanisms**: Establish channels for gathering feedback from farm operators, community members, and stakeholders. Incorporate this feedback into continuous improvement processes.

Conclusion: Cultivating Resilience Below the Surface

Underground mushroom farms represent a transformative approach to urban agriculture, contributing to food security, economic vitality, and sustainability in post-war Ukrainian cities. By strategically utilizing subterranean spaces, Ukraine can rebuild its urban food systems with a focus on innovation, resilience, and community engagement. This forward-thinking approach not only addresses immediate food production challenges but also sets the stage for long-term urban resilience and sustainability.

As Ukraine rebuilds, underground mushroom farms will stand as a testament to the nation's ingenuity and commitment to creating a resilient, prosperous, and sustainable future. By harnessing the full potential of subterranean agriculture, Ukraine can ensure that its cities are well-nourished and its communities are empowered for generations to come.

Section 20.3: Aquaponic Systems in Public Spaces

Transforming Urban Environments into Productive Ecosystems

As Ukraine rebuilds its cities with an eye toward resilience and sustainability, integrating aquaponic systems into public spaces represents a visionary approach to urban food production, environmental stewardship, and community engagement. These innovative systems, combining aquaculture and hydroponics, offer a powerful solution to multiple urban challenges while creating vibrant, productive public spaces that nourish both body and spirit.

The Revolutionary Potential of Urban Aquaponics

Sustainable Food Production at the Heart of Cities

Aquaponic systems in public spaces are not merely an innovation in urban agriculture; they are a paradigm shift in how we conceptualize the role of cities in food production and ecological stewardship.

- **Exponential Productivity**: Aquaponic systems can produce up to 6-8 times more food per unit area compared to traditional agriculture, making them ideal for space-constrained urban environments.
- **Water Conservation**: These closed-loop systems use up to 90% less water than conventional farming methods, addressing critical water scarcity issues in urban areas.
- **Year-Round Production**: Climate-controlled aquaponic facilities ensure continuous food production regardless of external weather conditions, enhancing food security and stability.

Strategic Implementation

From Vision to Reality

Implementing aquaponic systems in public spaces requires a strategic, phased approach to ensure successful integration and maximum impact.

Phase 1: Pilot Projects and Community Engagement

- **Showcase Installations**: Begin with high-visibility pilot projects in central public spaces, such as city squares or popular parks. These installations will serve as living demonstrations of the technology's potential, educating the public and building support.
- **Community Workshops**: Conduct hands-on workshops to involve local residents in the setup and maintenance of these systems, fostering a sense of ownership and commitment to urban agriculture.

Phase 2: Scaling and Diversification

- **Neighborhood Integration**: Expand the program to incorporate aquaponic systems into neighborhood parks, community centers, and school grounds, creating a distributed network of food production hubs.
- **Diverse Crop Selection**: Cultivate a wide variety of fish species and plant crops, tailored to local preferences and nutritional needs, showcasing the versatility of aquaponic systems.

Phase 3: Urban Integration and Innovation

- **Architectural Integration**: Collaborate with architects and urban planners to seamlessly incorporate aquaponic systems into new and existing buildings, including vertical installations on facades and rooftops.
- **Smart City Integration**: Connect aquaponic systems to smart city networks, using IoT sensors and AI to optimize production, monitor water quality, and manage resource use efficiently.

Multifaceted Benefits

A Catalyst for Urban Transformation

The integration of aquaponic systems in public spaces offers a myriad of benefits that extend far beyond food production:

- **Educational Opportunities**: These living laboratories provide unparalleled hands-on learning experiences in biology, ecology, and sustainable technologies for students of all ages.
- **Community Building**: Shared aquaponic spaces foster community interaction, cooperation, and a collective sense of purpose, strengthening social bonds in post-conflict urban areas.
- **Mental Health and Well-being**: Green, productive spaces in urban environments have been shown to reduce stress, improve mental health, and enhance overall quality of life for city dwellers.
- **Economic Revitalization**: Local food production creates jobs, stimulates the local economy, and can serve as a foundation for eco-tourism and green technology industries.

Overcoming Challenges

Innovative Solutions for Implementation

While the benefits are clear, implementing aquaponic systems in public spaces comes with challenges that require innovative solutions:

- **Energy Efficiency**: Utilize renewable energy sources such as solar panels and wind turbines to power pumps and lighting, ensuring sustainable operation.
- **Winter Resilience**: Implement geothermal heating systems and innovative greenhouse designs to maintain production even in harsh Ukrainian winters.

- **Public Safety**: Design systems with safety in mind, incorporating features like secure enclosures and water safety measures to ensure public well-being.

A Vision of Urban Resilience

Integrating aquaponic systems into public spaces is more than an urban agriculture initiative; it's a bold statement about the future of cities. As Ukraine rebuilds, it has the opportunity to lead the world in creating urban environments that are not just sustainable, but regenerative – spaces that produce food, clean the air, educate citizens, and build communities.

By embracing this innovative approach, Ukrainian cities can become living examples of resilience, sustainability, and innovation. These productive public spaces will stand as a testament to Ukraine's commitment to a future where urban environments nurture both people and planet, setting a new global standard for sustainable urban development in the 21st century.

In conclusion, the integration of aquaponic systems in public spaces represents a visionary step towards creating cities that are not just livable, but truly alive – pulsing with productivity, learning, and community spirit. As Ukraine rebuilds, it has the unprecedented opportunity to redefine urban living for the better, creating a model of sustainable development that will inspire the world.

Chapter 21: Innovative Governance Systems

Section 21.1: AI-Ethics Boards for Smart City Implementation

Introduction

As Ukraine advances its urban reconstruction efforts, the integration of artificial intelligence (AI) and smart city technologies presents unprecedented opportunities for efficiency, sustainability, and improved quality of life. However, these advancements also bring complex ethical challenges that must be addressed proactively. This section outlines the crucial role of AI-Ethics Boards in ensuring that the implementation of smart city technologies aligns with ethical principles, respects human rights, and serves the best interests of all citizens.

The Imperative of Ethical AI in Urban Reconstruction

Balancing Innovation and Ethics

The rapid integration of AI in urban systems necessitates a robust ethical framework to guide development and implementation:

- **Data Privacy and Security**: As smart cities collect vast amounts of data, protecting citizens' privacy and ensuring data security become

paramount concerns.
- **Algorithmic Bias**: AI systems must be designed and monitored to prevent discrimination and ensure equitable service delivery across all demographic groups.
- **Transparency and Accountability**: The decision-making processes of AI systems in urban management must be transparent and accountable to maintain public trust.

Structure and Composition of AI-Ethics Boards

Diverse Expertise for Comprehensive Oversight

AI-Ethics Boards should be composed of a diverse group of experts to ensure a holistic approach to ethical considerations:

- **Interdisciplinary Membership**: Include experts in AI technology, ethics, law, urban planning, sociology, and public policy to cover all aspects of smart city implementation.
- **Community Representation**: Ensure representation from various community groups, including marginalized populations, to address diverse perspectives and needs.
- **Independence**: Maintain the board's independence from political and commercial interests to ensure unbiased decision-making.

Key Responsibilities of AI-Ethics Boards

Guiding Ethical Smart City Development

The AI-Ethics Board will play a crucial role in shaping the ethical landscape of smart city initiatives:

1. **Policy Development**:
    - Draft comprehensive ethical guidelines for AI use in urban systems.
    - Collaborate with policymakers to integrate ethical considerations into smart city regulations.
2. **Review and Approval Process**:
    - Evaluate proposed AI implementations for ethical compliance before deployment.
    - Conduct regular audits of existing systems to ensure ongoing adherence to ethical standards.
3. **Risk Assessment and Mitigation**:
    - Identify potential ethical risks in AI applications and develop mitigation strategies.
    - Establish protocols for addressing ethical breaches or unintended consequences.
4. **Public Engagement and Education**:
    - Organize public forums to gather citizen input on AI and smart city initiatives.

- Develop educational programs to increase public understanding of AI ethics in urban contexts.
5. **Continuous Monitoring and Adaptation:**
    - Stay abreast of technological advancements and emerging ethical challenges.
    - Regularly update ethical guidelines to address new developments in AI and smart city technologies.

Implementation Strategy

Phased Approach to Ethical Governance

Establishing effective AI-Ethics Boards requires a strategic, phased implementation:

Phase 1: Foundation and Framework

- Establish the legal basis for AI-Ethics Boards within the urban governance structure.
- Recruit board members and develop initial ethical guidelines.
- Conduct comprehensive training for board members on AI technologies and ethical frameworks.

Phase 2: Integration and Pilot Programs

- Integrate the AI-Ethics Board into the decision-making processes for smart city initiatives.
- Launch pilot programs to test the effectiveness of ethical guidelines in real-world applications.
- Refine protocols based on feedback and outcomes from pilot programs.

Phase 3: Full-Scale Implementation and Public Engagement

- Expand the board's oversight to all smart city projects across Ukraine.
- Implement public engagement initiatives to foster transparency and trust.
- Establish mechanisms for continuous feedback and improvement of ethical governance.

Case Study: Ethical AI in Kyiv's Traffic Management System

To illustrate the role of AI-Ethics Boards, consider the implementation of an AI-driven traffic management system in Kyiv:

1. **Ethical Review**: The board evaluates the system for potential biases in route optimization and ensures equitable service across all neighborhoods.
2. **Privacy Protection**: Guidelines are established for anonymizing and securing traffic data to protect individual privacy.

3. **Transparency Measures**: The board mandates clear communication to the public about how the AI system makes decisions and affects traffic flow.
4. **Accountability Framework**: A mechanism is created for citizens to appeal decisions made by the AI system, ensuring human oversight and intervention when necessary.

Conclusion: Ethical Innovation for Resilient Cities

The establishment of AI-Ethics Boards for smart city implementation represents a forward-thinking approach to urban reconstruction in Ukraine. By prioritizing ethical considerations alongside technological advancement, Ukraine can create smart cities that are not only efficient and sustainable but also just and equitable.

This ethical framework will serve as a model for responsible innovation, enhancing public trust and ensuring that the benefits of smart city technologies are realized without compromising the values and rights of citizens. As Ukraine rebuilds and reimagines its urban landscapes, the AI-Ethics Boards will play a crucial role in shaping cities that are technologically advanced, ethically sound, and truly serve the needs of all inhabitants.

By implementing these ethical governance structures, Ukraine positions itself at the forefront of responsible smart city development, setting a global standard for the ethical use of AI in urban reconstruction and management.

Section 21.2: Decentralized Autonomous Organizations (DAOs) for Urban Governance

Revolutionizing Urban Decision-Making

In the wake of Ukraine's ambitious reconstruction efforts, the integration of Decentralized Autonomous Organizations (DAOs) into urban governance presents a groundbreaking opportunity to redefine citizen participation, enhance transparency, and accelerate community-driven development. This innovative approach aligns seamlessly with Ukraine's vision for resilient, technologically advanced, and democratically empowered cities.

The Transformative Power of DAOs in Urban Contexts

Reimagining Civic Engagement and Governance

DAOs offer a paradigm shift in how urban communities organize, make decisions, and allocate resources:

- **Direct Democracy at Scale**: DAOs enable large-scale direct participation in urban decision-making, allowing citizens to have a real-time voice in the policies and projects that shape their cities.

- **Transparent Governance**: By leveraging blockchain technology, DAOs provide unprecedented transparency in budget allocation, voting processes, and project implementation.
- **Efficient Resource Allocation**: Smart contracts automate many administrative processes, reducing bureaucracy and enabling more efficient deployment of resources for urban development.

Implementing DAOs in Ukrainian Cities

Strategic Integration for Empowered Communities

The implementation of DAOs in urban governance requires a carefully planned, phased approach:

Phase 1: Foundation and Education

- **Pilot Neighborhoods**: Select diverse neighborhoods across Ukrainian cities to pilot DAO governance structures.
- **Community Education**: Launch comprehensive educational programs to familiarize residents with blockchain technology, DAO principles, and digital participation tools.
- **Infrastructure Development**: Establish the necessary technological infrastructure, including secure digital identity systems and user-friendly interfaces for DAO participation.

Phase 2: Governance Integration

- **Municipal Integration**: Integrate DAO structures into existing municipal governance frameworks, starting with specific domains such as local park management or community center programming.
- **Participatory Budgeting**: Implement DAO-driven participatory budgeting processes, allowing citizens to directly propose, vote on, and monitor community projects.
- **Smart Contract Development**: Create and deploy smart contracts tailored to urban governance needs, such as automated fund disbursement for approved projects.

Phase 3: Expansion and Interoperability

- **Inter-City Collaboration**: Develop protocols for inter-city DAO collaboration, enabling resource sharing and knowledge exchange across Ukrainian municipalities.
- **National Integration**: Explore integration of city-level DAOs with national reconstruction efforts, creating a multi-tiered, decentralized governance ecosystem.
- **Global Partnerships**: Establish partnerships with international smart city initiatives, positioning Ukrainian cities as global leaders in decentralized urban governance.

Key Features of Urban DAOs

Empowering Citizens, Enhancing Cities

1. **Tokenized Civic Participation**:
   - Issue city-specific governance tokens to residents, enabling proportional voting power in urban decision-making.
   - Implement reputation systems that reward active and constructive participation in city governance.
2. **Automated Urban Services**:
   - Deploy smart contracts to automate routine urban services, from waste management scheduling to public transportation optimization.
   - Implement IoT-enabled sensors that trigger DAO-managed responses to urban issues, such as road repairs or air quality interventions.
3. **Decentralized Urban Planning**:
   - Create open-source, community-driven urban planning platforms where citizens can propose, model, and vote on development projects.
   - Utilize AI and data analytics within the DAO framework to simulate and assess the impact of proposed urban changes.
4. **Transparent Fund Management**:
   - Implement real-time, blockchain-based tracking of municipal funds, from tax collection to project expenditures.
   - Enable micro-funding initiatives where citizens can directly contribute to and monitor specific urban improvement projects.

Case Study: Kharkiv's DAO-Driven Green Space Revitalization

To illustrate the potential of DAOs in urban reconstruction, consider the implementation of a DAO for green space revitalization in Kharkiv:

1. **Community Proposal**: Local residents use the DAO platform to propose and vote on plans for converting a vacant lot into a community garden and recreational space.
2. **Decentralized Funding**: The project is funded through a combination of allocated municipal funds and community-driven cryptocurrency contributions, all managed transparently through smart contracts.
3. **Automated Execution**: Once approved, smart contracts automatically disperse funds to pre-approved suppliers and contractors as project milestones are met and verified.
4. **Ongoing Management**: The DAO continues to govern the space post-completion, with community members voting on maintenance schedules, event programming, and future enhancements.

Overcoming Challenges

Navigating the Path to Decentralized Urban Governance

While DAOs offer immense potential, their implementation in urban governance faces several challenges:

- **Digital Divide**: Ensure equitable access to DAO participation through public digital literacy programs and the provision of community access points for internet and technology.
- **Legal Framework**: Work with national and local legislators to create a supportive legal environment for DAO operations in urban governance.
- **Security and Stability**: Implement robust security measures to protect against potential vulnerabilities in smart contracts and ensure the stability of DAO platforms.

Conclusion: DAOs as Catalysts for Urban Renaissance

The integration of Decentralized Autonomous Organizations into Ukraine's urban governance structures represents a bold step towards creating truly smart, responsive, and citizen-centric cities. By empowering residents with direct decision-making capabilities, ensuring unprecedented transparency, and leveraging the efficiency of blockchain technology, DAOs have the potential to accelerate Ukraine's urban reconstruction while setting new global standards for democratic urban governance.

As Ukraine rebuilds its cities, the implementation of DAOs offers a unique opportunity to not just reconstruct physical infrastructure, but to reimagine the very fabric of urban society. This innovative approach promises to create resilient, engaged communities that are actively involved in shaping their urban environments, fostering a sense of ownership and pride that will be crucial for the long-term success and sustainability of Ukraine's urban centers.

By embracing DAOs, Ukrainian cities can become living laboratories for the future of urban governance, attracting global attention, investment, and expertise. This forward-thinking approach will position Ukraine at the forefront of urban innovation, turning the challenges of reconstruction into opportunities for revolutionary progress in how cities are governed, developed, and experienced by their citizens.

Section 21.3: Dynamic Regulatory Frameworks

Adapting Governance to the Pace of Innovation

In the context of Ukraine's ambitious urban reconstruction, the implementation of Dynamic Regulatory Frameworks represents a crucial innovation in governance. These frameworks are designed to evolve in real-time, keeping pace with technological advancements, changing urban needs, and emerging challenges. By adopting this approach, Ukraine can create a regulatory environment that fosters innovation, ensures public safety, and adapts swiftly to the realities of modern urban life.

The Imperative for Adaptive Regulation

Bridging the Gap Between Innovation and Governance

Traditional regulatory approaches often struggle to keep up with the rapid pace of technological and social change in urban environments. Dynamic Regulatory Frameworks address this challenge by:

- **Reducing Time Lag**: Minimizing the delay between the emergence of new technologies or urban challenges and the implementation of appropriate regulations.
- **Encouraging Innovation**: Creating a regulatory environment that supports and guides innovation rather than stifling it with outdated or overly rigid rules.
- **Enhancing Resilience**: Enabling cities to quickly adapt regulations in response to crises, emergencies, or unforeseen circumstances.

Key Components of Dynamic Regulatory Frameworks

Building Blocks of Adaptive Urban Governance

1. **AI-Powered Regulatory Analysis**:
    - Implement AI systems to continuously analyze urban data, identifying regulatory gaps and opportunities for optimization.
    - Use machine learning algorithms to predict potential impacts of new technologies or urban trends, informing proactive regulatory adjustments.
2. **Sunset Clauses and Automatic Review Mechanisms**:
    - Incorporate sunset clauses in all new regulations, ensuring they are automatically reviewed and updated at regular intervals.
    - Implement systems for continuous evaluation of regulatory effectiveness, with automatic triggers for review based on predefined metrics.
3. **Regulatory Sandboxes**:
    - Create safe spaces for testing innovative urban solutions under relaxed regulatory conditions, allowing for real-world evaluation before full-scale implementation.
    - Develop frameworks for quickly scaling successful sandbox initiatives into citywide policies.
4. **Stakeholder Feedback Loops**:
    - Establish real-time feedback mechanisms for citizens, businesses, and experts to report on the impacts of current regulations and suggest improvements.
    - Utilize blockchain-based voting systems to allow rapid, secure community input on proposed regulatory changes.
5. **Modular Regulatory Design**:
    - Develop regulations as interconnected modules that can be quickly updated or replaced without overhauling entire regulatory frameworks.

- Create standardized interfaces between regulatory modules to ensure coherence and minimize conflicts when individual components are updated.

Implementation Strategy

Phased Approach to Regulatory Innovation

The successful implementation of Dynamic Regulatory Frameworks requires a strategic, phased approach:

Phase 1: Foundation and Pilot Programs

- **Legal Groundwork**: Work with national and local legislators to create the legal basis for dynamic regulatory systems.
- **Pilot Sectors**: Identify key urban sectors (e.g., transportation, energy, housing) for initial implementation of dynamic regulations.
- **Technology Infrastructure**: Develop the necessary technological infrastructure, including AI systems and data analytics platforms.

Phase 2: Expansion and Integration

- **Cross-Sector Implementation**: Expand dynamic regulatory frameworks across all major urban sectors.
- **Interoperability**: Ensure seamless integration between different regulatory modules and with existing governance structures.
- **Capacity Building**: Train government officials, urban planners, and legal experts in managing and utilizing dynamic regulatory systems.

Phase 3: Full-Scale Adoption and Continuous Improvement

- **Citywide Implementation**: Roll out dynamic regulatory frameworks across all Ukrainian cities involved in reconstruction efforts.
- **International Collaboration**: Engage in knowledge exchange with other cities and countries implementing similar systems.
- **Continuous Optimization**: Regularly assess and refine the dynamic regulatory system itself, ensuring it remains effective and adaptive.

Case Study: Kyiv's Dynamic Regulations for Urban Mobility

To illustrate the potential of Dynamic Regulatory Frameworks, consider their application to urban mobility in Kyiv:

1. **Real-Time Adaptation**: AI systems continuously analyze traffic patterns, air quality data, and citizen feedback to suggest regulatory adjustments for vehicle usage and public transportation.

2. **Rapid Response**: When a new mobility technology (e.g., electric scooters) enters the market, the framework quickly generates provisional regulations based on data from other cities, adjusting in real-time as local usage data becomes available.
3. **Modular Updates**: Regulations for different aspects of urban mobility (e.g., parking, ride-sharing, bike lanes) are designed as interconnected modules, allowing for targeted updates without disrupting the entire transportation regulatory ecosystem.
4. **Community Engagement**: Citizens use a blockchain-based platform to vote on proposed mobility regulations, with the system automatically implementing changes that reach a predefined consensus threshold.

Overcoming Challenges

Navigating the Complexities of Adaptive Regulation

Implementing Dynamic Regulatory Frameworks comes with several challenges that must be addressed:

- **Balancing Flexibility and Stability**: Ensure that the adaptability of regulations doesn't lead to uncertainty or instability in urban governance.
- **Ethical Considerations**: Develop robust ethical guidelines for AI-driven regulatory systems, addressing issues of bias, transparency, and accountability.
- **Digital Literacy**: Implement programs to ensure all citizens can effectively participate in and benefit from dynamic regulatory processes.

Conclusion: Paving the Way for Responsive Urban Governance

The adoption of Dynamic Regulatory Frameworks represents a paradigm shift in urban governance, one that is particularly well-suited to the challenges and opportunities presented by Ukraine's urban reconstruction efforts. By creating regulatory systems that can evolve as quickly as the cities they govern, Ukraine can foster an environment of innovation, resilience, and responsiveness.

These frameworks will enable Ukrainian cities to navigate the complexities of rapid technological change, shifting social dynamics, and emerging urban challenges with unprecedented agility. They offer a powerful tool for balancing the need for stable governance with the imperative for rapid adaptation in a world of accelerating change.

Moreover, by pioneering the implementation of Dynamic Regulatory Frameworks, Ukraine positions itself as a global leader in innovative urban governance. This approach will not only support the immediate goals of reconstruction but will also create a lasting legacy of adaptive, citizen-centric urban management that can serve as a model for cities around the world.

As Ukraine rebuilds and reimagines its urban landscapes, Dynamic Regulatory Frameworks will play a crucial role in ensuring that its cities are not just rebuilt, but are reborn as dynamic, resilient, and future-ready urban centers. This innovative approach to regulation will be a key factor in transforming the challenges of post-war reconstruction into opportunities for revolutionary progress in urban governance and quality of life.

Chapter 22: Monitoring, Evaluation, and Adaptation

Section 22.1: IoT Sensor Networks for Progress Monitoring

Harnessing the Power of Data for Intelligent Reconstruction

In the ambitious task of rebuilding Ukraine's urban landscape, the deployment of Internet of Things (IoT) sensor networks represents a transformative approach to progress monitoring. These advanced systems offer unprecedented capabilities in real-time data collection, analysis, and decision-making support, ensuring that reconstruction efforts are efficient, transparent, and adaptable to changing needs and conditions.

The Revolutionary Potential of IoT in Urban Reconstruction

Creating Smart, Responsive Cities from the Ground Up

IoT sensor networks provide a comprehensive, real-time view of the urban environment, offering numerous advantages:

- **Continuous Monitoring**: 24/7 data collection on various aspects of urban infrastructure and environmental conditions.
- **Predictive Maintenance**: Early detection of potential issues, allowing for proactive interventions and cost savings.
- **Resource Optimization**: Real-time data on resource usage enables efficient allocation and management of energy, water, and other critical resources.
- **Transparency and Accountability**: Open access to data fosters trust between citizens and governing bodies, ensuring transparency in reconstruction efforts.

Comprehensive IoT Sensor Network Architecture

Building a Digital Nervous System for Cities

The implementation of IoT sensor networks requires a well-planned, layered approach:

1. **Sensor Layer**:
    - Deploy a diverse array of sensors across urban environments, including:
        - Environmental sensors (air quality, noise, temperature)

- Infrastructure sensors (structural integrity, traffic flow, utility usage)
- Safety and security sensors (flood detection, seismic activity)

2. **Network Layer**:
    - Implement robust, secure communication networks to transmit sensor data:
        - 5G and future 6G networks for high-bandwidth, low-latency data transmission
        - LoRaWAN for long-range, low-power sensor communications
        - Mesh networks for resilient, self-healing connectivity
3. **Data Processing Layer**:
    - Establish edge computing nodes for real-time data processing and analysis
    - Utilize cloud computing for complex analytics and long-term data storage
4. **Application Layer**:
    - Develop user-friendly dashboards and applications for data visualization and interaction
    - Create APIs for third-party developers to build innovative solutions using the sensor data

Strategic Implementation Plan

Phased Deployment for Comprehensive Coverage

Implementing IoT sensor networks across Ukrainian cities requires a strategic, phased approach:

Phase 1: Foundation and Pilot Projects

- **Critical Infrastructure Monitoring**: Begin with sensors on key bridges, major roads, and vital utility networks.
- **Environmental Baseline**: Establish a network of environmental sensors to monitor air quality, noise levels, and climate conditions.
- **Pilot Neighborhoods**: Select diverse neighborhoods for comprehensive sensor deployment, serving as testbeds for wider implementation.

Phase 2: Expansion and Integration

- **Citywide Deployment**: Expand sensor networks to cover entire urban areas, focusing on both public spaces and infrastructure.
- **Integration with Existing Systems**: Connect IoT networks with existing urban management systems, creating a unified urban data platform.
- **Smart Building Initiative**: Encourage integration of IoT sensors in new construction and major renovation projects.

Phase 3: Advanced Applications and Citizen Engagement

- **Predictive Urban Management**: Implement AI-driven predictive models for urban planning and resource management.
- **Citizen Science Programs**: Launch initiatives for citizens to contribute to data collection using personal devices and community-operated sensors.
- **Open Data Portals**: Develop user-friendly platforms for public access to non-sensitive urban data, fostering transparency and innovation.

Key Applications in Urban Reconstruction

Transforming Data into Action

1. **Infrastructure Health Monitoring**:
   - Real-time structural health monitoring of bridges, buildings, and critical infrastructure.
   - Predictive maintenance alerts to prevent failures and optimize repair schedules.
2. **Environmental Quality Management**:
   - Continuous monitoring of air quality, noise levels, and water quality.
   - Dynamic responses to environmental issues, such as traffic rerouting during high pollution events.
3. **Smart Energy and Resource Management**:
   - Real-time monitoring of energy consumption in public buildings and infrastructure.
   - Intelligent street lighting systems that adjust based on natural light and pedestrian activity.
4. **Urban Mobility Optimization**:
   - Traffic flow sensors for real-time traffic management and signal optimization.
   - Parking space sensors to guide drivers to available spots, reducing congestion.
5. **Disaster Early Warning Systems**:
   - Flood detection sensors in flood-prone areas for early warning and rapid response.
   - Seismic sensors for earthquake detection and immediate alert dissemination.

Case Study: Kharkiv's Smart Water Management

To illustrate the potential of IoT sensor networks, consider their application in water management in Kharkiv:

1. **Leak Detection**: A network of acoustic sensors along water mains detects and locates leaks with high precision, reducing water loss and repair times.
2. **Quality Monitoring**: Real-time water quality sensors throughout the distribution system ensure safe drinking water and enable rapid response to contamination events.
3. **Consumption Optimization**: Smart water meters provide granular

data on usage patterns, enabling targeted conservation efforts and fair pricing structures.
4. **Flood Prevention**: River level sensors and weather stations work together to predict and mitigate potential flooding events.

Overcoming Challenges

Navigating the Complexities of Ubiquitous Sensing

Implementing comprehensive IoT sensor networks comes with several challenges:

- **Data Privacy and Security**: Implement robust encryption and anonymization protocols to protect sensitive data. Develop clear policies on data collection, use, and retention.
- **Interoperability**: Ensure sensors and systems from different manufacturers can communicate seamlessly. Adopt open standards and protocols to facilitate integration.
- **Power Management**: Utilize renewable energy sources and low-power sensor technologies to create sustainable, long-lasting sensor networks.
- **Public Acceptance**: Engage in transparent communication about the benefits and safeguards of IoT sensor networks to build public trust and acceptance.

Conclusion: A Data-Driven Future for Ukrainian Cities

The implementation of IoT sensor networks for progress monitoring represents a cornerstone in Ukraine's vision for smart, resilient, and transparent urban reconstruction. By creating a digital nervous system for cities, Ukraine can ensure that its rebuilding efforts are not just efficient and effective, but also adaptive to the evolving needs of its urban populations.

These sensor networks will provide an unprecedented level of insight into the functioning of urban systems, enabling data-driven decision-making, predictive maintenance, and rapid response to emerging challenges. Moreover, by making much of this data publicly accessible, Ukraine can foster a new era of civic engagement, where citizens are active participants in the ongoing development and management of their cities.

As Ukraine rebuilds, IoT sensor networks will serve as the foundation for truly smart cities – urban environments that are not just technologically advanced, but also more livable, sustainable, and responsive to the needs of their inhabitants. This forward-thinking approach positions Ukraine as a global leader in smart urban reconstruction, setting a new standard for how cities can leverage technology to create better, more resilient urban futures.

Section 22.2: AI-Driven Impact Assessment Tools
Revolutionizing Urban Planning and Evaluation

As Ukraine embarks on its ambitious journey of urban reconstruction, the integration of Artificial Intelligence (AI) in impact assessment represents a paradigm shift in how we evaluate and refine urban development strategies. AI-driven impact assessment tools offer unprecedented capabilities in analyzing complex data sets, predicting outcomes, and providing actionable insights for decision-makers. This innovative approach ensures that reconstruction efforts are not only efficient and effective but also sustainable and beneficial to all citizens.

The Power of AI in Urban Impact Assessment
Transforming Data into Foresight

AI-driven impact assessment tools bring several revolutionary advantages to urban planning and reconstruction:

- **Predictive Analysis**: Ability to forecast potential outcomes of urban interventions before implementation.
- **Multi-dimensional Evaluation**: Simultaneous assessment of social, economic, environmental, and cultural impacts of urban projects.
- **Real-time Adaptation**: Continuous monitoring and analysis allow for rapid adjustments to urban strategies as conditions change.
- **Bias Reduction**: AI algorithms, when properly designed, can help minimize human biases in decision-making processes.

Key Components of AI-Driven Impact Assessment Systems
Building a Comprehensive Evaluation Framework

1. **Data Integration Platform**:
   - Aggregate data from various sources including IoT sensors, satellite imagery, social media, economic indicators, and historical records.
   - Implement data cleaning and normalization processes to ensure consistency and reliability.
2. **AI Analysis Engine**:
   - Utilize machine learning algorithms, including deep learning and natural language processing, to analyze complex urban data sets.
   - Develop predictive models that can simulate various urban development scenarios.
3. **Visualization Interface**:
   - Create intuitive dashboards and 3D visualizations to present complex data in an easily understandable format.
   - Implement virtual and augmented reality tools for immersive exploration of potential urban designs.
4. **Feedback Mechanism**:

- Integrate citizen feedback through mobile apps and web platforms to continuously refine AI models.
- Implement blockchain technology to ensure transparency and immutability of feedback data.

Implementation Strategy

Phased Approach to AI Integration

The successful implementation of AI-driven impact assessment tools requires a strategic, phased approach:

Phase 1: Foundation and Pilot Projects

- **Data Infrastructure**: Establish robust data collection and storage systems, ensuring interoperability and security.
- **AI Model Development**: Develop initial AI models focused on key reconstruction priorities such as housing, infrastructure, and economic revitalization.
- **Pilot Assessments**: Conduct pilot impact assessments in select cities, comparing AI-driven insights with traditional methods.

Phase 2: Expansion and Refinement

- **Comprehensive Model Integration**: Expand AI models to cover all aspects of urban development, including social, environmental, and cultural factors.
- **Cross-City Learning**: Implement machine learning algorithms that can transfer knowledge between different urban contexts across Ukraine.
- **Stakeholder Training**: Provide extensive training to urban planners, policymakers, and community leaders on interpreting and utilizing AI-generated insights.

Phase 3: Advanced Applications and Citizen Engagement

- **Predictive Urban Planning**: Develop AI systems capable of generating and evaluating multiple urban development scenarios.
- **Real-time Impact Monitoring**: Implement continuous assessment capabilities, allowing for immediate detection of unintended consequences.
- **Participatory AI**: Create platforms for citizens to interact with AI models, contributing local knowledge and preferences to refine assessments.

Key Applications in Urban Reconstruction

AI-Powered Decision Support

1. **Sustainable Infrastructure Planning**:

- Assess long-term environmental impacts of proposed infrastructure projects.
- Optimize placement of renewable energy installations for maximum efficiency and minimal disruption.

2. **Social Equity Analysis**:
   - Evaluate the distributional effects of urban policies and projects across different demographic groups.
   - Identify and mitigate potential gentrification risks in redeveloping areas.
3. **Economic Impact Forecasting**:
   - Predict the economic outcomes of various urban development strategies.
   - Assess the potential for job creation and economic growth in different sectors.
4. **Health and Well-being Optimization**:
   - Analyze the health impacts of urban design choices, from air quality to access to green spaces.
   - Optimize the placement of healthcare facilities for maximum accessibility.
5. **Cultural Heritage Preservation**:
   - Assess the impact of reconstruction efforts on historical and cultural landmarks.
   - Generate preservation strategies that balance modernization with cultural significance.

Case Study: Lviv's AI-Driven Urban Core Revitalization

To illustrate the potential of AI-driven impact assessment tools, consider their application in the revitalization of Lviv's historic city center:

1. **Multi-scenario Analysis**: The AI system generates multiple revitalization scenarios, assessing each for its impact on tourism, local economy, residents' quality of life, and cultural preservation.
2. **Predictive Heritage Conservation**: AI models predict the long-term effects of various preservation techniques on historical buildings, optimizing restoration efforts.
3. **Dynamic Traffic Management**: The system continually assesses the impact of pedestrianization efforts on traffic flow, local businesses, and air quality, suggesting real-time adjustments.
4. **Social Cohesion Metrics**: AI algorithms analyze social media data and local surveys to gauge community sentiment and social cohesion as the project progresses.

Overcoming Challenges

Navigating the Complexities of AI-Driven Assessment

Implementing AI-driven impact assessment tools comes with several challenges that must be addressed:

- **Data Quality and Availability**: Ensure comprehensive and accurate data collection across all urban sectors. Develop strategies for filling data gaps and validating data quality.
- **Algorithmic Transparency**: Implement explainable AI techniques to ensure that decision-making processes are transparent and accountable.
- **Ethical Considerations**: Develop clear ethical guidelines for AI use in urban planning, addressing issues of privacy, consent, and potential biases.
- **Balancing AI and Human Insight**: Create frameworks that effectively combine AI-generated insights with human expertise and local knowledge.

Conclusion: Shaping a Smart, Sustainable Future for Ukrainian Cities

The integration of AI-driven impact assessment tools into Ukraine's urban reconstruction efforts represents a groundbreaking approach to creating smart, sustainable, and resilient cities. By harnessing the power of AI to analyze complex urban systems, predict outcomes, and generate actionable insights, Ukraine can ensure that its rebuilding efforts are not just efficient, but truly transformative.

These tools will enable urban planners and policymakers to make informed decisions based on comprehensive, data-driven assessments of potential impacts across multiple dimensions. From optimizing infrastructure placement to ensuring social equity and preserving cultural heritage, AI-driven assessments will play a crucial role in shaping the future of Ukrainian cities.

Moreover, by involving citizens in the AI-driven planning process, Ukraine can foster a new era of participatory urban development, where technology enhances rather than replaces human judgment and local knowledge. This approach not only leads to better urban outcomes but also builds trust and engagement between citizens and their urban environments.

As Ukraine rebuilds, AI-driven impact assessment tools will serve as a cornerstone of its commitment to innovation, sustainability, and citizen-centric urban development. This forward-thinking approach positions Ukraine as a global leader in smart urban reconstruction, setting a new standard for how cities can leverage advanced technologies to create better, more resilient urban futures for all their inhabitants.

Section 22.3: Citizen Feedback Platforms and Continuous Improvement

Empowering Citizens in the Reconstruction Process

In the ambitious journey of rebuilding Ukraine's urban landscapes, the role of citizen engagement cannot be overstated. Citizen Feedback Platforms represent a crucial nexus between the populace and the reconstruction efforts, ensuring that the voices of those most affected by urban changes are heard, valued, and integrated into the decision-making process. This section outlines the implementation of advanced citizen feedback systems that not only collect input but drive continuous improvement in urban reconstruction and governance.

The Transformative Power of Citizen Engagement

Creating Responsive and Resilient Cities

Citizen Feedback Platforms offer numerous advantages in the context of urban reconstruction:

- **Real-time Insights**: Gathering immediate feedback on reconstruction projects and urban initiatives as they unfold.
- **Inclusive Decision-making**: Ensuring diverse perspectives are considered in urban planning and policy formulation.
- **Enhanced Accountability**: Creating transparent channels for citizens to monitor and evaluate reconstruction efforts.
- **Community Ownership**: Fostering a sense of ownership and pride in the rebuilding process among residents.

Key Components of Advanced Citizen Feedback Platforms

Building a Comprehensive Engagement Ecosystem

1. **Multi-channel Feedback Collection**:
    - Mobile applications for easy, on-the-go feedback submission.
    - Web platforms for detailed project information and in-depth feedback.
    - Integration with social media for broader reach and real-time sentiment analysis.
    - IoT-enabled physical feedback stations in public spaces for inclusive participation.
2. **AI-Powered Analysis Engine**:
    - Natural Language Processing (NLP) to analyze textual feedback and identify key themes and sentiments.
    - Machine Learning algorithms to categorize and prioritize feedback based on urgency and impact.
    - Predictive analytics to forecast potential issues based on feedback trends.
3. **Visualization and Reporting Tools**:
    - Interactive dashboards for citizens to view aggregated feedback and its impact.
    - Real-time reporting tools for decision-makers to monitor public sentiment and project performance.
    - Augmented Reality (AR) interfaces for citizens to visualize proposed changes and provide contextual feedback.

4. **Feedback Loop Closure Mechanism**:
   - Automated systems to inform citizens of how their feedback has been addressed.
   - Blockchain-based tracking of feedback implementation to ensure transparency and accountability.

Implementation Strategy

Phased Approach to Citizen Engagement

Implementing comprehensive Citizen Feedback Platforms requires a strategic, phased approach:

Phase 1: Foundation and Pilot Programs

- **Platform Development**: Create user-friendly mobile and web platforms for feedback submission and tracking.
- **Community Outreach**: Launch awareness campaigns to educate citizens about the importance of their participation.
- **Pilot Projects**: Implement feedback systems in select neighborhoods, focusing on high-priority reconstruction projects.

Phase 2: Expansion and Integration

- **Citywide Rollout**: Expand the feedback platform to cover all major urban areas and reconstruction initiatives.
- **Data Integration**: Connect feedback platforms with other urban data systems (e.g., IoT sensors, municipal databases) for comprehensive analysis.
- **Capacity Building**: Train municipal staff and community leaders in utilizing feedback data for decision-making.

Phase 3: Advanced Features and Continuous Evolution

- **AI-Driven Insights**: Implement advanced AI algorithms for deeper analysis of feedback patterns and predictive modeling.
- **Gamification Elements**: Introduce gamification features to encourage sustained citizen engagement.
- **Cross-City Collaboration**: Develop systems for sharing insights and best practices across different Ukrainian cities.

Key Applications in Urban Reconstruction

Harnessing Collective Intelligence

1. **Project Prioritization**:
   - Enable citizens to vote on and prioritize reconstruction projects in their neighborhoods.

- Use feedback data to inform resource allocation decisions across different urban initiatives.

2. **Design Refinement**:
   - Gather citizen input on proposed designs for public spaces, buildings, and infrastructure.
   - Utilize AR tools to allow citizens to visualize and comment on proposed changes in real-time.

3. **Service Quality Improvement**:
   - Collect continuous feedback on the quality of public services during the reconstruction phase.
   - Implement rapid response systems to address urgent issues identified through citizen feedback.

4. **Community Cohesion Monitoring**:
   - Assess the impact of reconstruction efforts on community relationships and social dynamics.
   - Identify and address potential conflicts or social tensions early in the rebuilding process.

5. **Environmental Impact Assessment**:
   - Engage citizens in monitoring and reporting environmental changes during reconstruction.
   - Use crowdsourced data to complement scientific environmental assessments.

Case Study: Odesa's Participatory Waterfront Redevelopment

To illustrate the potential of Citizen Feedback Platforms, consider their application in the redevelopment of Odesa's historic waterfront:

1. **Vision Co-creation**: Citizens use the platform to submit and vote on ideas for the waterfront's future, ranging from recreational facilities to cultural spaces.
2. **Real-time Design Feedback**: As architects develop plans, citizens provide feedback through AR visualizations, influencing design iterations.
3. **Construction Phase Monitoring**: During reconstruction, residents use the app to report issues like noise pollution or safety concerns, enabling quick mitigation.
4. **Post-completion Evaluation**: After project completion, continuous feedback helps fine-tune the space's management and informs future urban projects.

Overcoming Challenges

Navigating the Complexities of Mass Participation

Implementing effective Citizen Feedback Platforms comes with several challenges:

- **Digital Divide**: Ensure equitable access to feedback platforms through public kiosks, community centers, and digital literacy programs.
- **Feedback Fatigue**: Design engaging, user-friendly interfaces and implement reward systems to maintain long-term participation.
- **Data Privacy**: Implement robust data protection measures and transparent policies on how citizen data is used and stored.
- **Balancing Voices**: Develop systems to ensure that feedback from marginalized or underrepresented groups is adequately considered.

Conclusion: Co-Creating the Future of Ukrainian Cities

The implementation of advanced Citizen Feedback Platforms in Ukraine's urban reconstruction efforts represents a commitment to democratic, responsive, and adaptive urban development. By creating robust channels for citizen input and closing the feedback loop through transparent action, Ukraine can ensure that its rebuilt cities truly reflect the needs, aspirations, and values of their inhabitants.

These platforms will transform the relationship between citizens and their urban environments, fostering a sense of ownership and shared responsibility for the city's future. The continuous flow of feedback and ideas will drive innovation, improve the quality of urban services, and enhance the overall livability of Ukrainian cities.

Moreover, by engaging citizens as active participants in the reconstruction process, Ukraine can build social capital and community resilience, crucial factors in the long-term success of urban areas. This participatory approach will not only lead to better urban outcomes but also strengthen the fabric of civil society, promoting democratic values and civic engagement.

As Ukraine rebuilds, Citizen Feedback Platforms will serve as a cornerstone of its commitment to transparent, inclusive, and responsive urban governance. This forward-thinking approach positions Ukraine as a global leader in participatory urban reconstruction, setting a new standard for how cities can leverage collective intelligence to create vibrant, resilient, and truly citizen-centric urban environments.

By embracing the power of citizen feedback and continuous improvement, Ukraine is not just rebuilding cities – it's reimagining the very nature of urban life, creating spaces that are adaptive, inclusive, and primed for a future of ongoing positive transformation.

Printed in Great Britain
by Amazon